FIFTY YEARS IN TEXAS

Mockingbird Books
201 2nd Street
Boerne, Texas 78006
www.mockingbirdbooks.com

Original edition © 1883 by J. J. Linn
This edition © 2016 by Mockingbird Books
All rights reserved.

ISBN 978-1932801293

Yours Truly
John J. Linn

Fifty Years in Texas
THE BIRTH OF THE REPUBLIC

JOHN J. LINN

Mockingbird Books
Boerne, Texas

Editor's Note

John J. Linn's reminiscences are well known to Texas history scholars, but less familiar to general readers. The book is one of the first-person reflections on early Texas that has the hallmarks of both authenticity and personal interpretation. Written in 1883 by an octogenarian who had been an early trader, merchant, and soldier based in and around Victoria,[1] the text begins with Austin's colony and chronicles the state's vicissitudes through the revolution, statehood and the Civil War.

There is seldom any doubt about where Linn stands, whether the subject is Sam Houston, the Confederacy, or the many remarkable characters that populate his narrative. Linn views the past through lenses of his own coloring, but he relates the facts fairly, as he remembers them.

The book is as much a documentary compilation as reminiscence. Linn freely draws extracts from historical documents, speeches, letters, and newspapers. At times there is a feel of thumbing through his scrapbook of history, but the approach provides a beneficial authenticity and exposes the reader to the original words that shaped Texas.

When Linn expresses himself, he alternates between plainspoken narrative and a flowery and lofty oratory that was popular in his

---

[1] The book was put into words by Linn's close friend, historian Victor Marion Rose, but the opinions are too strong, the tales too personal, and the language too idiosyncratic not to have come from Linn himself.

time. He speaks highly of the great orators of early Texas, and believes that important subjects must be described with important words.

If the reader pays attention and tracks names and events carefully, Linn's book offers a great deal of valuable on-the-spot detail. The less meticulous reader will pass over the details and simply enjoy the astounding romp that was early Texas.

Dedication

To my old comrades, living and dead, whose fortitude rose superior to the trials of privation and want, and whose fidelity to the eternal principles of truth and justice was only surpassed by their heroism on the field, these reminiscences of a half-century in Texas are affectionately inscribed by their friend and comrade,

The Author
Victoria, Texas, 1883

Introductory

After so many "histories of Texas" have been presented to the reading public it would seem to be a work of supererogation to add another to the already-long list. This the author does not design. His work does not aspire to the dignified appellation of "history," although his reminiscences, in that they are true, are strictly historical. He was induced primarily to take up the pen by reason of the omissions of those who have preceded him in this field. While he would not impugn the truth of any of his predecessors, he nevertheless feels certain, as do those who know from personal observation whereof he writes, that the whole truth has never been fully told.

It is, then, rather his province to elucidate what has heretofore been omitted than to attempt any presentation of a concise narrative of Texas history.

It is believed that many such facts, herein for the first time introduced to type, will prove interesting to the general reader and edifying to the student of Texas history. The author would claim no peculiar merit on this score, simply because he enjoyed sources of information denied to others.

But being the custodian of facts absolutely essential to a correct history of our State, he feels, in view of his advanced age and the uncertainties of life, that duty imperatively demands that he shall place on enduring record his contribution to the future history of Texas.

To this labor of love he comes in the evening of life, and presents his retrospective view to the golden-hued morning of the rising generation, with the fond hope that the sturdy virtues of their ancestors, who reclaimed empire from the wilds of nature, may always be unto them as the palladium of their hopes. In their Caesars, Scipios, and Vespasians the youth of Rome could boast no prouder exemplars than the annals of Texas present.

Of that immortal band which, though mustering fewer hundreds than the "Napoleon of the West" had marshaled thousands, achieved the independence of Texas but few now remain.

The recollections of that struggle, forty-five years after "the twin sisters" proclaimed the natal day of Texas upon the field of San Jacinto, seem invested with the air of romance. Seven hundred determined men attack and rout one thousand four hundred! A few frontiersmen drive in the outposts of an empire, eliminate the boundary line of States, and change the map of the world!

The Texan Revolution, and the wonderful results that marked its various stages to a final and complete success, must for all time remain an anomaly in the history of mankind.

Though Leonidas encountered greater odds at the mountain pass which his heroic defence has rendered classic, yet "Thermopylae had her messenger of defeat, but the Alamo had none!"

But those who laid the humble foundation are not destined to witness the magnificent fabric of a fully developed Texas. They planted that others might reap. Remember those stalwart men, ye who feel a just pride in the greatness of your empire State!

It were well if their simple and frugal lives, their rugged manhood and industry, and their patriotic devotion to country should excite in your bosoms a spirit of generous emulation!

To the memory of his friends and comrades who have passed "over the river to rest under the shade of the trees" the author drops this pebble on the cairn to their remembrance. May future offerings at this patriotic shrine mount the marble column high in air as an incentive to Texan pride and glory—*Texas one! undivided!! and indivisible for all time!!!* is the wish of

The Author

Chapter 1

The author of these reminiscences was born in the county of Antrim, Ireland, on the 19th day of June, A.D. 1798—a period of social and political earthquakes that burst forth in response to the terrible explosion historically known as the "French Revolution." His ancestors incurred the displeasure of Cromwell, and were summarily dispossessed of their landed estates and forced to pay an alien landlord rent for the occupation of a few of their patrimonial acres. His father, John Linn, of course identified himself with the patriotic movement and acted as a member of the "United Irish" brotherhood.

Despairing of success for the patriots, and detesting the tyrannous misrule of the English, he, with his wife and one child, the author of these reminiscences, took passage on a ship bound for New York, which port they reached after a voyage of two months. Several years were spent in that city, and fourteen subsequent years in Dutchess County of that State, when the family again returned to New York City. Here the author enjoyed the friendship of the father of the illustrious Charles O'Conor, Thomas Addis Emmet, and other less eminent, though equally dear, refugees from British tyranny. In the year 1822 the author removed to New Orleans, where he remained in the employ of a mercantile house for a time, and afterwards engaged in business on his own account until the year 1829. These seven years were pregnant with events to the land that was soon to become his home. Mexico had declared her independence of Spain; Iturbide's ephemeral empire had given way to the republic; Santa Anna was hailed as one of the liberators of his country; the Fredonian "tempest in a teapot" had subsided; Stephen F. Austin had securely planted his colony on the Brazos River, and

Americans had gained a footing on Texan soil which they were destined never more to relinquish.

How I was induced to come to Texas.

During the month of July 1829, I made the acquaintance of a sea captain, John Pierce, who owned a small schooner and had visited Texas several times. In one of his trips to Texas he met with a Mexican trader named Wright, to whom he agreed to deliver a certain number of bales of tobacco in Corpus Christi Bay. Wright promised to provide fifty mules, upon the backs of which it was intended to transport the tobacco to the Rio Grande. Wright represented that he could sell the cargo at very advantageous profits, and it was stipulated that they would divide the net results equally.

Captain Pierce arrived with the cargo at the designated time and place. Through a misunderstanding Wright did not arrive, and Captain Pierce, disappointed at his failure, suggested that I should assume the part of the delinquent contractor, which, after careful deliberation, I consented to do.

We set out upon our commercial enterprise in the month of August.

We entered Corpus Christi Bay during the latter days of August 1829. We remained at this point one week without encountering any of the human family, save Indians. Finally we met two Mexicans from Camargo who knew Wright, who, they informed us, was in that town, but that he declined to carry out his contract. I set out, in company of one of the Mexicans, for the Rio Grande to procure mules. At the rancho of a friend of my fellow voyager I succeeded in obtaining twenty "pack" mules; returned to the bay and loaded them with forty bales of tobacco, Pierce agreeing to await my return for the remainder of the cargo. Encountering some difficulty in disposing of this lot at Camargo, I engaged an American who was well acquainted with the people to assist me. After the loss of much time I engaged another man, a citizen of Camargo and a man of some means, to go to Corpus Christi Bay and convey over the remainder of the tobacco. He brought a portion of it and aided me materially in making sales. I soon learned, by diligent study, to speak the language of the country. Having finally disposed of the whole cargo of tobacco, and after visiting friends in Matamoras, I embarked for New Orleans. Before leaving Matamoras I made arrangements with a friend, Don Bruno Garcia, to purchase another stock of tobacco and an assortment of dry goods that would be suitable for the trade, and promised to advise him as to the time I would require his mules. After some delay in New Orleans, occasioned by the necessity for closing my former business and the purchase of a suitable vessel, I left.

I arrived at the mouth of the Rio Grande in due course, and entered after experiencing a few thumps on the bar.

The captain ran the vessel up the river about fifteen miles, where we encountered some customhouse officials, among whom was Colonel Garey, whose name appears among the participants of the campaign of 1836. Another was the somewhat subsequently celebrated Colonel John D. Bradburn. I assisted Captain Noyes, who commanded the schooner, in making out his "manifest" in Spanish, which he gave to the proper official. Colonel Garey was a temporary inspector at the time. He informed me that he was in the regular army and not permanently connected with the revenue service.

Bradburn was a "looker-on," as he informed me, but was expecting an appointment every day.

After leaving the vessel I proceeded to Camargo, and from thence to Corpus Christi.

Upon arriving at this latter place I was confronted by some twenty officers and soldiers. My vessel had arrived from the Rio Grande River and was lying at anchor in the Corpus Christi Bay, some six or eight miles below.

I found that I could do nothing with my cargo at Corpus Christi, and consequently ordered the captain to hoist sail and steer for Matagorda Bay, intending to meet him at or near the mouth of the Garcitas Creek.

Acting upon the advice of Mr. John McHenry, I sent the mules back to Camargo, and left via Goliad for Victoria. At the latter place I received the intelligence of the safe arrival of my vessel. This episode changed the whole plan of my life, and finally made me a permanent citizen of Texas. I succeeded in getting my goods to Victoria, after passing the customhouse officials of Goliad without any trouble.

In travelling from Corpus Christi to Victoria I was delighted with the appearance of the country. It was in the last days of April, and the landscape was rendered charming by the profusion of many-colored wild flowers that greeted the eye on all sides.

I opened my goods in Victoria, and, the assortment comprising articles most needed, I succeeded in gaining a very profitable business.

After a month or so I despatched the vessel back to New Orleans for fresh supplies. During this year General Teran sent two hundred soldiers to establish a military post on the Lavaca River. This addition to our scant population gave a decided impetus to trade. I engaged to supply the troops with all articles suitable to their wants.

During the summer of 1830 I purchased a drove of horses and mules, which my brother Charles drove to Louisiana and sold. He returned in the fall with a new stock of goods.

I purchased a lot fronting the public square in Victoria, and caused the framework of a house to be erected, of cypress timber, of which a quantity was then to be had in the bottom south of the town. This house was completed 1831, and I have continued to reside in it up to the present date (1883). My parents arrived in Victoria in the spring, 1831, in conformity to previous arrangements.

On my second trip to Texas I had purchased a fine schooner, called *The Opposition*. She was coppered and put up in the best possible manner. I landed my cargo in Lavaca Bay and carted the effects to Victoria. Shortly afterwards I sent the vessel back to New Orleans for other goods that I had contracted for, and she returned in good time. I then despatched her a third time with seventeen thousand dollars in money and also some goods not suitable for the trade. She left the landing at Pass Cavallo in July 1830, with the following persons on board: John

Pierce, captain; _____ Nelson, mate; Jacob Baker, seaman; Joe Cook, Edward Linn, and an invalid (name now forgotten) who was in the last stages of consumption. The winds being light and variable, the schooner made but little headway. When about six or seven days out, those on board heard a rushing wind which was rapidly approaching the vessel. The captain ordered the sails to be lowered, but before it could be done the squall struck the schooner and "keeled" her over. She began to take in water, and filled so rapidly that they barely had time to unlash the small boat. The schooner went down, leaving them in the small boat on the high sea. The captain, remembering his observation, knew pretty correctly his position. A coat was improvised as a sail, and the prow of the little cedar craft was turned for the Louisiana coast. Their sufferings were extreme for water. The invalid died the first night, perfectly conscious of his approaching end; he directed the captain to throw his body overboard, which was done. The only consolation the miserable men had was the fact that the little boat sped through the water with astonishing velocity.

On the afternoon of the next day they made the mouth of Mermenteau Bayou and succeeded in effecting a landing. Some were too weak to stand.

They commenced digging for water with shells, and finally succeeded in obtaining a supply which, though brackish, refreshed them considerably. Eventually they discovered a man fishing, to whom they made known their forlorn condition. He immediately supplied them with fresh water and cooked a large redfish, which they greedily devoured as soon as done. This Good Samaritan then conducted them up the bayou to his house, where all their necessities were supplied; and the next day he accompanied them to the next settlement, where they were hospitably entertained, and after some days reached New Orleans. The loss of my vessel, money, and other effects was quite a loss to my business; but I did not learn of the disaster until some time in the following October, so scant were our means of information from the outside world. In the meantime I had almost entirely disposed of my goods; and by the timely assistance of a friend in New Orleans, who forwarded me some new goods that I had previously ordered, I was enabled to continue my business.

During one of my journeys to the Rio Grande I was accompanied by a Mexican. Stopping one night about fifty miles from the Rio Grande, we pitched our camp in close proximity to that of a shepherd. Feeling fatigued, I retired early to bed and was soon wrapped in refreshing slumbers. I awoke with the early dawn; but the old shepherd was already calling his family up for their customary morning devotions.

I heard them recite their prayers and sing a hymn; and being moved by curiosity—if, indeed, I was not actuated by a deeper interest—I crossed the intervening space that separated us, and confronted them. The patriarchal head of this family was fully sixty years of age, his wife about fifty, and the children two boys of about fifteen and twelve, and a daughter of ten. After some conversation the venerable head of the family informed me that he had been a shepherd all his life, being then the possessor of three thousand sheep, about one dozen shepherd dogs, and three or four horses upon which to transport his tent and baggage from camp to camp.

What an instructive lesson was thus presented by this poor man in the primeval wilds of Nature! With the earliest dawn his first duties were rendered to his God. Here, then, were some of the fruits that had germinated from the sacred seed sown by the consecrated messengers of the Church in early Texas.

This little episode made a lasting impression on my mind. How like the patriarchs this man appeared! What a glorious commentary upon the blessed work of the Church!

Chapter 2

In the month of June 1832, William B. Travis and P. C. Jack, together with other Texans, were arrested and imprisoned by Colonel Bradburn, who had drifted east and was now commandant of the post of Anahuac. Bradburn was a tyrant in office and of a domineering nature in private relations. Jack and Travis enjoyed the respect, confidence, and love of the colonists in general. Consequently the citizens determined to make an effort to secure their release; and, in conformity to this desire, a number waited on the commandant and in respectful terms asked the liberation of their compatriots.

Bradburn, with a duplicity as false as his own nature, promised compliance with the petition, but adjourned its execution with cunningly devised and plausible reasons therefor. Time in which to prepare his defences was all that the treacherous officer desired, and he immediately set about the task.

The exasperated citizens were soon confronted by mounted cannon and serried ranks of soldiery. But their resolution to release their friends from the clutches of this renegade American rather grew firmer as the difficulties which environed the situation increased. Realizing the impotency of an attack upon the fort without ordnance, they demanded of the commanding officer at Velasco cannon. He, as a matter of course, refused to comply with the unreasonable demand. The citizens, however, rallied in force and took possession of the guns. Captain John Austin, the alcalde of the second department of Austin's colony and commander of the citizen soldiery on this occasion, in reply to an official letter of Colonel Mexia, who came with a fleet of five vessels and four hundred men to the mouth of the Brazos in order to ascertain the cause of the trouble and to arrest and punish the offenders, thus briefly summarizes this chapter in the history of Texas:

"We are farmers, and not soldiers; therefore desire that the military commandants shall not interfere with us at all. Since 1830 we have been pretty much governed by the military subalterns of the general government. We have not insulted the flag of our adopted country, as we had been surprised from our first movements; but, on the contrary, we have sustained its true dignity, and attacked those who had outraged it by using it as a pretext for their encroachments upon the constitution and sovereignty of the state of Coahuila and Texas, and as a cover for their baseness and personal crimes. The commandant at Anahuac, Colonel Juan Davis Bradburn—an investigation of the conduct of that officer will inform you fully of the details of many despotic acts. He was sustained by the commandant at Nacogdoches, Colonel Piedras, and by the commandant at Port Velasco, Lieutenant Colonel Ugartechea, and consequently we were compelled to oppose them all; therefore we attacked Fort Velasco on the 26th of last month with one hundred and twenty farmers hastily collected, without discipline, and badly armed, and after an obstinate and bloody engagement it surrendered on the terms expressed in the enclosed copy of the capitulation, every article of which has been strictly complied with on our part, besides furnishing the provisions needed for the troops."

This was a bold act on the part of the people of Brazoria and vicinity, and the consequences resulting from it proved to be of the utmost importance ultimately to the colonists. The fort of Velasco was constructed in a circular form, covering about one half acre. It was situated on the east bank of the Brazos River, and near its mouth. I saw the Mexican soldiers as they passed through Victoria on the retreat to Matamoras. Many of them had received gunshot wounds in the wrist, which were inflicted by the Americans while they were loading the cannon, which was mounted on a parapet above the walls of the fort. Colonel Ugartechea discovered after daylight that every one of his men that appeared exposed above the fort was instantly shot dead. He therefore ordered his gunners to cease firing, and in a short time made an overture of capitulation, which was accepted.

There were in Victoria and on the Lavaca River above two hundred soldiers, who had been sent thither by the orders of General Teran in 1831. He had intended building a fort on the Lavaca; the definite position had not been decided upon, but the manufacture of brick had been commenced at a place called "El Banco Colorado," or "The Red Bank," on the west bank of the Lavaca and about three miles west of Texana. The works were under the control of Don Manuel Choval, a gentleman of birth and education, commissioned by General Teran.

The immediate commander of the troops was Captain Artiaga, also a perfect gentleman and an old officer, who had served throughout the Mexican Revolution.

After the surrender of Velasco and the intrigues of General Santa Anna had been developed, and after the death of General Teran, who committed suicide by falling upon his sword, Commissioner Choval resigned, and Captain Artiaga informed General Mexia that he wished to be relieved of the responsibilities of his position, as he did not favor the movements of Santa Anna. An order arrived directing the removal of the whole army, together with the workmen at the brick kiln, some thirty or forty in number. These latter were from various parts of Mexico, who had been convicted of offences against the laws and were known here as "the chain gang." Among them was a young villain of a wealthy family, whose parents being dead had been adopted by an uncle, who was sparing no pains or expense in his education. During a visit home from school the youth, then about fifteen years of age, demanded more money of his uncle than the latter thought proper to give him. An angry altercation ensued, and the young rascal murdered his relative. He was tried and sentenced to fifteen years of hard labor on the public works. His relatives, persons of wealth and influence, felt the disgrace keenly and petitioned Governor Latono[2] to pardon him. The governor would grant the petition only on the sole condition that one

---

[2] Ed. Note: Jose Maria de Letona

of the convict's relatives should undergo the same penalty in lieu of the convict—a kind of vicarious sacrifice, as it were. The governor declared that as the laws of God and man had been violated the penalty should not be commuted, and that either the convict or his voluntary substitute must serve out the sentence of the court. This incident was related to me by Colonel Powers,[3] who was in Saltillo at the time and well acquainted with all the parties to the circumstance.

Lieutenant Colonel Villasana arrived in a schooner in the bay to transport the troops to Matamoras, but had no funds with which to pay for provisions and other expenses. He had, however, authority to draw on the customhouse at Matamoras.

As the "Lavaca command" was indebted to me for supplies, Captain Artiaga called on me and stated that he was ordered to abandon the purposed fort; that he needed supplies, and that Villasana would draw on the Matamoras customhouse for the same. I knew their impecunious condition and the venture of accepting Villasana's check in payment, but so anxious were we all to get rid of the military that I determined to supply their necessities and run the risk of ever receiving pay, in order to contribute to the peace and prosperity of our country. All this was consummated. I supplied all their wants, and received of Villasana an order on the customhouse at Matamoras for some *eight hundred* and odd dollars. I sent the draft to a friend in Matamoras for collection. He was offered payment upon the basis of ilvestreinous discount which he did not deem at all equitable or just, and the proposed liquidation was rejected.

But I have failed to receive one cent of that sum up to the present day. After the departure of the above-mentioned troops Texas enjoyed a period of peaceful quiet, absolutely free from the presence of Mexican soldiery, until the year 1835.

In La Bahia (Goliad) there was a local military company, composed of citizens identified with the country.

---

[3] Ed. Note: James Power

In San Antonio there was one or more military companies, composed of material similar to that of the next preceding, and in 1833 a small company of Mexican soldiers was established at La Pantitlan, on the Rio Nueces.

But, alas! this was but the deceitful calm that precedes the storm.

With that political hurricane the following pages will deal in a more or less direct manner.

Not wishing to anticipate the thread of the narrative, we will recur once more to the situation of affairs immediately before and after the fall of Fort Velasco.

Colonel Ugartechea, the commandant of the fort, evinced a disposition and bearing by no means palatable to the colonists. He was a man of sagacity and foresaw the coming storm, and was possessed of a sufficient knowledge of the art of war to know that he could not uphold with a bare handful of men the supremacy of Mexico in the midst of an exasperated American colony. Consequently he despatched couriers to Victoria, and possibly to other posts, for reinforcements. Captain Artiaga, who commanded on the Lavaca River, positively refused to send his men to Velasco, saying he was not under the command of Colonel Ugartechea. Captain Artiaga sought advice from some of the leading citizens of Victoria in regard to his relation to the Velasco affair.

The citizens consulted were Sylvester de Leon, Fernando de Leon, John McHenry and the author of these reminiscences.

Artiaga stated that he was opposed to the policy being pursued by General Santa Anna; that he was not acquainted with the topography of the country, and especially was he ignorant of that in the vicinity of the Brazos, etc.

The citizens of Austin's colony were excited at the "Bradburn outrage," as the imprisonment of Travis, Jack, and others was very justly styled, and Ugartechea's position in holding out against the demands of the excited multitude was anything but encouraging.

Finally Captain Artiaga concluded that it would be dangerous for his men to march through the "Caney Swamp."

Sylvester de Leon improved the opportunity by saying that in his opinion not one of the soldiers who attempted to do so would ever reach Velasco alive; that the Texans, concealed in the dense cane, could destroy them with impunity; that the Mexicans would have their faces burned by powder from the muzzles of rifles without being able to see the men at the other end of the guns.

Ultimately Captain Artiaga very wisely concluded to allow Colonel Ugartechea to conduct his troubles alone with "*Los Tejanos*" which that doughty warrior proceeded to do, with the results heretofore adverted to.

The appearance of Colonel Mexia at the mouth of the Brazos with ships, and men to what number no one knew, seemed to give a serious phase to the appearance of the political horoscope. Mexia, after receiving the letter from Captain John Austin which was given in a preceding page, sought a personal interview with that officer. He discovered that Austin and the colonists in general were, like himself, not opposed to the policy of General Santa Anna. This bond of political affinity led him to take a conservative view of the late proceedings, and Mexia departed for Matamoras, leaving behind him his good wishes for Texas and the Texans.

It is only with the most pleasant reflections that I recur to the period in Texas history, that reposes like a cultivated garden in the wilds of nature, from the capitulation of Ugartechea to the year 1835. Texas was then a terrestrial paradise.

Health, Plenty, and Good Will teemed throughout the land. A live mastodon would not have been a greater curiosity than a tax collector. There were no courts at law in the land, for there was no litigation, and knights of the technical exegesis beat their sharp two-edged swords into pruning hooks.

Money sufficient for all purposes was in circulation. The theft of cattle was an unknown crime, and a body snatcher from the new-made grave would have received more consideration at the hands of the honest yeomanry of Texas than a cow thief. Corn cribs knew nothing of locks, and smokehouses stood close by, equally open to the world. In those good old days, by tacit agreement, a cow and calf were legal tender for ten dollars. They are worth forty dollars now, some will say; and just in this ratio have we progressed in all the material relations of life. But compare the moral obliquity of the present, rich and prosperous as it is, with the Arcadian simplicity of manners and purity of morals that characterized the period adverted to, and there will be but few who will not say that the prices paid for the elaborations of wealth, culture, and position have been exorbitant.

It is well to cultivate the physical sciences, to develop the resources of the land, to aim as high as the zenith and as far ahead as illimitable space, but never at the expense of the moral education of the young.

Personal incidents during those days

After my return to New Orleans from Matamoras in the fall of 1833, I purchased another stock of goods intended for the Mexican market. Arriving at Linnville in the spring of 1834, I concluded to send my brother, Edward Linn, in charge of the goods to Saltillo. He arrived at this city while an annual fair was being held. I soon began to see in the signs of the times evidences of prospective trouble between Texas and Mexico, and despatched a message to my brother to sell the goods at cost or to consign them to some responsible merchant, so that if trouble came he would not be the ostensible owner. He had, however, in conformity to the advice of a Dr. Hewitson,[4] who was well posted in Mexican affairs, shipped the goods to Zacatecas, where they were sold through the instrumentality of one J. A. Porter, an American resident of Zacatecas.

Edward Linn was about returning home when he was arrested by the Mexican authorities under pretence of a demand from the customhouse in Matamoras. This was false, he having the prescribed papers from the regular commandant of Goliad, and certificate of good citizenship signed by the military commandant at the same place. He

---

[4] Ed. Note: James Hewetson.

was forced to employ a lawyer to defend him, and, after much delay and expense, the court remanded the defendant to the custody of the town marshal on the pretence of awaiting new evidence. Edward Linn had perfected arrangements to accompany a convoy to Tampico; but his official companion, the marshal, stood as an insuperable barrier between him and his desires. However, at the suggestion of the lawyer the official was bribed, and his prisoner departed on his way rejoicing. His funds in hand had been consigned to Messrs. Leman & Perry, of Tampico. He held, however, a note for three thousand dollars signed by Porter, which was not yet quite due. Upon Porter's refusing to liquidate the instrument before maturity he placed it in the hands of Leman & Perry for collection. Finally he refused payment upon maturity of the note, and threatened if sued he would prove that Edward Linn was a Texan rebel.[5] And so it was that I lost three thousand dollars; but Porter did not live long to enjoy his ill-gotten gains, as he died six months afterwards.

(This Mexican adventure proved disastrous. Edward Linn arrived safely in New Orleans after the fall of the Alamo, and could return home only via the Red River and Nacogdoches. He was in New Orleans when my letter arrived bearing the news of the victory of San Jacinto. This letter was published in the newspapers of that city, and was the first announcement there received of the battle and of its terrible consequences to the president of Mexico, General Santa Anna, who was captured in an effort to escape the disastrous field.)

During my business visit to Monclova and other towns in Mexico in the year 1833 I met in Saltillo Dr. Hewitson, the partner of Colonel James Powers in the colony of Powers and Hewitson.

---

[5] Had Porter executed this threat the immediate confiscation of Edward Linn's effects would have been the consequence. Practically the result was the same as it was, as we never realized anything from the transaction. To reconcile a seeming discrepancy as to the dates, I would state that Edward Linn went to Saltillo in 1835, and that my trip to Chihuahua was in 1834. Edward was in Mexico at the commencement of hostilities between the two countries, hence the force of the threat to denounce him as a rebel.

Intelligence reached us that the cholera was raging in Tampico and Vera Cruz. Upon parting with Dr. Hewitson to return to Monclova he gave me some medicines to be used in the event that I was seized by the fell epidemic. He also gave me a prescription and directions for treating the disease. I had come off victorious from an attack of cholera the year before in the town of Mier. I was informed that the cholera had already appeared in Saltillo. I immediately proceeded to the town of Candala, en route for Texas. While here the malady appeared. Very soon the plague broke out in the village, and quite suddenly. The people were terror stricken. A meeting of the town authorities was convened for the express purpose of taking the matter into consideration. Presently a committee visited me and inquired if I was a physician. I replied in the negative. They then wished to know if I had medicines. I replied that I had a small quantity for my own use, but none for sale. Whereupon I was informed that there were five hundred dollars in the city treasury, all of which should be mine if I would consent to treat the disease. I repeated that I was not a doctor of medicine, and that I could not conscientiously consent to receive money for services that I was unable to perform. I was then importuned to act as a doctor in the name of charity. I could not withstand so earnest an appeal, and so, closing my store, I devoted my whole time to the suffering inhabitants, assisted by the good priest, who was never idle; and I am happy to know that we contributed in no small degree to the relief of the people.

My brother Charles, however, succumbed to the malady, and I was forced to lay him to rest in a strange land and far from those he loved.

When I left the town the people lined the streets to bid me adios—the most expressive of farewells, as it is a commendation to the protection of God. One youth whom I had attended exclaimed: "Don Juan, receive my best wishes, my earnest thanks and prayers. May the good God guard you and restore you once more to your family!" This, uttered in the soft, rhythmic Spanish, was certainly an expressive exclamation, and the translation wholly destroys the beauty and pathos of the sentence. But this was an unselfish manifestation of gratitude, that virtue so rare in the bosom of man, because, like the diamond among minerals, it is the most precious.

Chapter 3

The year 1834 was one of vast change in the Mexican Republic. Santa Anna's intrigues in the interest of centralization were in a measure crowned with success, the "Centralists" sweeping all opposition before them in all the states except Zacatecas, Coahuila, and Texas.

The Federal Congress declared Zacatecas to be in a state of rebellion, and instituted measures forthwith for the disarming of the state militia. The matter in issue related immediately to the authority of the state to alter the constitution of 1824, the "Liberals," or republicans, contending that the state possessed the power, while the "Centralists" denied the assumption.

Coahuila protested against the "usurpation," and Zacatecas prepared to resist the "usurper." Francisco Garcia, a good man and true republican, but with no military experience, was the governor of the latter state.

Santa Anna placed himself at the head of the array and set out for the scene of action. The governor, at the head of an equal force, met him on the field of Guadalupe, where a most sanguinary battle was fought, resulting in the disastrous defeat of the republicans.

Santa Anna reported two thousand of the enemy slain and wounded.

In Coahuila and Texas the election for governor and lieutenant governor resulted in the choice of Viesca for the former position, and of Ramon Musquies, of San Antonio, for the latter.

Upon being inaugurated at Monclova, the deputies from Saltillo withdrew and protested against the new government.

This latter movement on the part of the protesting deputies was favored by the commanding general, Cos, who was a nephew of Santa Anna. The first act of the Viesca legislature was the sale of four hundred leagues of land in Texas. This act passed in March, but was not approved by the National Congress in the April following. It is deemed that a more extended mention of this gigantic real estate transaction will not be out of place in these pages.

Under a former decree of the National Congress no lands could be disposed of by any state without the approval of the general government. Congress also claimed the privilege of becoming the purchaser, at their own option, in the event the land was wanted for any specific purpose, such as forts, military stations, etc. Governor Viesca notified the central government of the proposed sale, and was in return notified that the action was desirable. The treasury of Coahuila and Texas was empty, and none of the state officials had been paid their salaries. The sale of four hundred leagues of land was the only resource available to raise the necessary means to defray these expenses of the government. The sale of this immense body of land in the province of Texas was vehemently denounced east of the Rio Grande as an outrage by all.

On April 23, 1834, I was married, in the city of New Orleans, to Miss Margaret C. Daniel, of that city, who since that day, through all eventful times, trials, and hardships, in adversity and in prosperity, in sickness and in health, has been to me a true, noble, devoted, and loving wife. It was shortly after our marriage that my wife and I took passage on the schooner *Wild Cat* for Texas. This vessel was destined for Aransas Pass, and, as the opportunities for coming to Texas were few in those days, we accepted this one. Without anything unusual occurring on the trip we arrived at the pass, which we found stormy and bad. Notwithstanding the dangers of trying to cross this bar, the captain announced his determination to enter the bay at any hazard. As our little schooner reached the bar a rough sea broke on her and a heavy swell threw her from the channel, and she became unmanageable. The consequence was that she struck heavily on the bar in about five feet of water, where she remained fast aground. We had taken the precaution to shut and fasten the cabin door.

Another heavy sea struck her and completely washed her decks, those upon deck only saving themselves by clinging desperately to the ropes.

This "roller" lifted the vessel into shallow water, where she was permanently fixed.

The cabin doors were then opened, and the passengers within, who had imagined that we had all been swept overboard, congratulated us upon our escape, and especially Mrs. Linn in that she had not been left a young widow. Our stanch little craft withstood this warfare of the elements wonderfully well, and, though beat up on the bar by the angry waves, did not leak at all. But the water had played havoc with our culinary department, and the cook announced that it would be an impossibility to get supper. We therefore contented ourselves with bread and cheese, and passed the night quite comfortably under the circumstances. In the morning it was discovered that the schooner had taken several inches of water in the hold, and that the leak was increasing. The weather continued tempestuous.

On the following day two vessels were seen approaching the bar. One proved to be the schooner *Cardena*, loaded with merchandise for San Antonio. The other was a larger vessel and had on board colonists for Powers and Hewitson's colony. The *Cardena* headed her course for us. We signaled her to steer to the east of us, as we were on the west side of the bar; but as the atmosphere was hazy and a heavy sea running, our signals were disregarded, and the schooner struck with her broadside to the sea and wind. In about two hours the *Cardena* succumbed to the surf and gale and went to pieces. The most of her cargo was lost; but little washed ashore.

The other vessel was handled in a manner indicative of skilful seamanship, and stood "on and off" until late in the afternoon, when the captain put all sails on and stood in for the bar. She was steered too far eastward, however, and brought up on the breakers, where she thumped tremendously by reason of having her canvas all unfurled.

Each roll of the surf would take her headlong forward, her keel grating on the bar. But in about one hour she fought her way over these formidable obstacles and entered the bay, where she ran into a mud bank with several feet of water in her hold, from which position she was never rescued. Fortunately all the colonists were landed on the beach in safety.

Our captain, as agent for the insurance companies, sold the schooner and her cargo, one of the passengers becoming the purchaser. As I was insured to the full amount, I lost nothing. Subsequently I accepted a proposition from the purchaser, and took the purchase off his hands. An inspection of the cargo showed that the goods were but slightly injured. I was fortunate in being able to hail a schooner which had just discharged her cargo at Copano, and engaged her to transport my goods to Copano, at which point they were safely landed in a few days.

The cholera here broke out among the colonists in an epidemic form, and many of the unhappy people died ere transportation could be procured to convey them to their destination.

I arrived safely in Goliad with my family, and packed the goods intended for the Mexican trade in suitable packages; and as soon as the epidemic had somewhat abated I set out for Mexico.

I arrived without incident on the Rio Grande and crossed at Mier, where I met an old friend who had just returned from an extended visit into Mexico. He advised me to go to Chihuahua (pronounced Che-wa-wa). I proceeded on my journey to this destination as far as a little town called St. Margarita. My journey lay through a desert. We found water very scarce, and in one instance travelled sixty miles without being able to procure a drop with which to refresh our parched lips or to invigorate our suffering animals. I had learned before leaving Mier that the Comanche Indians were raiding on the Florido Creek beyond the desert. I despatched a courier ahead to ascertain if the Indians were on the "warpath," and, if so, instructed him to engage me an escort at St. Catharine, a village on the Florido Creek. Deeming it necessary, my courier engaged the services of an escort of fifteen well-armed men, and, returning, met us about forty miles from the Florido. We were encamped at a watering place when the escort arrived. My party had been swollen to a caravan of thirty-five men by the addition of a number of muleteers who were carrying *pelloncies*, or Mexican sugar, to Chihuahua. One of these from a hill observed the approaching escort, and sounded the alarm, "Indians." Every man who had arms prepared immediately for battle. In the bustle of preparation, summoned by the supposed emergency, I encountered a man industriously piling up stones. Upon my inquiring the cause for this strange procedure he informed me in a very matter-of-fact tone that, whereas he had no firearms, he was accumulating such ammunition as nature afforded, and that he purposed to throw rocks at the "Indios." Luckily the emergency did not arrive for this manifestation of temerity. Our escort reported the presence of Indians on the road between us and the Florido. We, however, continued our journey without molestation to St. Catharine, where I engaged carts to transport my freight to Chihuahua, as we had intelligence that the Indians were proceeding in the direction of the city of Paral, some eighty miles in the interior.

The alcalde of St. Catharine mustered twenty-five men to intercept the Indians on their return, and to attack them, if opportunity offered to do so to advantage. These improvised soldiers presented quite a novel appearance. All of them bore shields made of dried rawhide. The faces of many of these shields were decorated by curious and artistically executed devices. I remember that some of them bore dates as ancient as A.D. 1734—being a century old—having been doubtless used by the ancestors of the men who now bore them, in the constant border warfare that they were compelled to wage with the wild Bedouins of the plains for mere existence. The soldiers set out upon the campaign with the "Godspeed" of the inhabitants. They returned in three or four days, and the leader reported to the alcalde that he had seen the Indians driving off a very large drove of horses, and that, in conformity to his honor's instructions "not to attack without every advantage, as one Mexican citizen alive was worth more than one hundred dead Comanches with all their plunder, etc.," he had contented his martial inclinations by merely witnessing the barbaric pageant.

And the alcalde responded, "Well done, thou good and faithful servant!" or words to that effect.

During the time spent in St. Catharine the alcalde interrogated me very much in regard to the American people, their habits, customs, etc. He desired especially to know if they were as expert in the use of firearms as represented.

I assured him that such was the case, especially with the frontiersmen of Texas.

"At what distance could you shoot a man with the rifle?" he asked.

"Two hundred yards!" I replied in a tone of confidence. He was incredulous and invited me to make an exhibition of my skill, to which I assented.

After despatching our dinner we proceeded to the outskirts of the town, where it had been decided the trial of marksmanship should be made.

A sheet of white paper with a black "bull's-eye" was properly posted, and two hundred yards carefully measured. Just as I was preparing to shoot, a man nearby stuck over the target a new hat in front of the "bull's-eye," and for his pains I very elegantly perforated the crown with a bullet.

The alcalde was astonished at the performance, yet thoroughly satisfied as well.

While at St. Catharine I visited some of the beautiful cornfields in the vicinity, and must say that I never beheld more luxuriant growths of corn anywhere. The crops of which I now speak were the second raised on the same land that year, it now being in the latter days of November. The lands in cultivation are fertilized by an admirable system of irrigation. I also saw here some excellent fields of wheat.

I arrived in Chihuahua in due course, and, after passing my merchandise through the customhouse, opened my store, and in a few days had disposed of my entire stock to two men just from the mines.

These miners having a part of the amount due me in crude ore, an exchange was made in bars of silver. I was introduced to an old native merchant who had partially retired from business.

He conducted me through his warehouse, and I was astonished at the sight of the immense quantities of silver which he had literally "piled up." I estimated the value of the silver in this room as certainly not less than $150,000, and probably as much as $200,000.

The name of this modern Croesus was Don Juan Alveris. He had been employed in trade in that section forty-five years, and in addition to the crude silver mentioned possessed many fields of corn, wheat, and other grain, mines, and money.

He owned one copper mine that yielded ninety per cent of pure copper. In addition to all this he owned vast landed estates upon which grazed thousands of livestock.

Great quantities of silver were brought to Chihuahua to be smelted, coined, etc., which gave an impetus to trade of all kinds. The public buildings of the city are well-built and creditable structures, while the cathedral is an imposing and handsome edifice. In front of the cathedral was an excellent fountain of limpid water, which was conducted by an aqueduct constructed of masonry a distance of ten miles from a spring in the mountains. The flooring of the church was formed of boards hewn from solid logs by Indians, from trees found in the mountains, and made in panels in consequence of the shortness of the boards. On the inside of the church no expense had been spared to render it beautiful and attractive, which is generally the prevailing custom throughout Mexico. I was shown the house and the room in which Padre Hidalgo was shot; this was inside the Franciscan college, which was in ruins when I visited it.

After disposing of my goods I set out upon my return, and again travelled over the "Terra Muerta"—"Land of Death"—which is an arid, sandy desert, upon whose parched plain no vegetation appears. This desolate region extends over an area of some four or five miles in width by fifteen or twenty in length.

Travel across the "Terra Muerta" is disagreeable in the extreme; there is no water with which to slake thirst, no scenery to beguile the monotonous tedium of the journey; and the dry winds drive the blinding sand into face and eyes.

I arrived home in safety without farther incident, after an absence of several months, which, on the whole, were very pleasantly and profitably spent.

Recurring to the subject matter with which this chapter opened, I would add by way of incident that after Carbajal's[6] arrival home, immediately following the illegal disbandment of the legislature of Coahuila and Texas by order of Santa Anna, he was apprised by friends that it was the purpose of the supreme government to cause his arrest and transportation to the city of Mexico, where he was to be arraigned and tried for treason. A meeting of the citizens of Victoria was called to consider the matter, which threatened to deprive an eminent citizen of his liberty, and which, if successfully executed, would establish an evil precedent for all time.

Thirty determined men signified their willingness to meet the military who should come to make the arrest of Carbajal. The ferryman at the river was to give ample notice of the arrival of the soldiers, so that preparations could be made for their proper reception. The plan of operations determined upon, in the event of the arrival of the military, was that a squad of men should assemble at each corner of the public square in which the military would halt, as was their custom. The citizens were then to close in on the soldiers and surround them. The alcalde himself was to have charge of the operations. The citizens had not a great while to wait, for the ferryman ere long announced the presence of a body of soldiers waiting to be crossed over the river. "Forewarned was to be forearmed" in this instance, and very soon the citizens were ready for whatever turn events should take. The soldiers, as had been anticipated, rode into the public square, and the officer inquired for the

---

[6] Ed. Note: Jose Maria Jesus Carbajal.

alcalde. That functionary being in his cornfield, a messenger was despatched for him. In the interim the soldiers dismounted and unsaddled their horses.

Presently the alcalde, Señor Don Placido Benevides, arrived and inquired of the officer what was wanted. The officer replied by handing him an order from Colonel Ugartechea demanding the body of Carbajal. Placido Benevides returned the order and said to the officer that he could inform Colonel Ugartechea that neither the body of Carbajal nor the body of any other citizen of Victoria would be delivered into the hands of the military, as he was a constitutional officer, and not at all amenable to the military.

By this time the troops were completely surrounded by armed citizens. The officer, seemingly in dread of precipitating a crisis, ordered his men to saddle their horses. This they did and proceeded to the river, where they encamped for the night. The next morning the officer, who was an orderly sergeant and had seen several years' service, visited me. He remarked that he found himself in an embarrassing position the day before—as, indeed, his mission was one of which he himself could not thoroughly approve, as he was opposed to General Santa Anna politically—and he declared that if affairs were not radically changed in the administration of the government, that he would retire in disgust from the army, as he would not draw his sword against his countrymen. After some further conversation he bid me good morning, and I never saw him afterwards. This was the end of the affair.

Carbajal was married to a daughter of Don Martin de Leon, the impresario, and was a brother-in-law of Placido Benevides.

We were informed subsequently by friends that the bold and determined action of Benevides, backed by the citizens of Victoria, visibly disturbed the placidity of affairs in military circles in San Antonio.

Among other troubles of the times strolling bands of Indians occasionally contributed to the annoyances which our people had to undergo. As indicative of the boldness of our frontiersmen, I will include the following incident as related by Major James Kerr:

In the fall of 1834 Major Kerr headed a surveying party of six or seven persons, and was camped at Long Mott, ten miles below Green Lake, in Calhoun County. They were about commencing operations when one of the party discovered Indians stealthily approaching in the high sedge grass along the bank of the bay. They proved to be a squad of ten Carankua Indians who had lately been guilty of killing several citizens of the colony and perpetrating various thefts. Major Kerr's party had an ox cart in which to transport their camp equipage from place to place. This they immediately proceeded to place in position, with the tailgate bearing upon the red men. The grim mouth of an innocent camp kettle assumed the airs of a howitzer through the open tailgate, and the surveying party mustered sticks in lieu of guns, and paraded with a military air about the "dog of war."

These prompt and warlike measures abashed the untutored children of the prairie, and they slunk away like coyotes to the cover of the brush. Don Fernando de Leon rode forth and invited one of them to meet him and hold a parley. This one of the Carankuas did. He was anxious to ascertain if the men in the mott were soldiers, and if they really had a cannon. Mr. De Leon assured him that they were Texan soldiers; that they had a cannon, and that they were highly incensed against the treacherous Carankuas, who, after professing friendship, had imbued their hands in the blood of some of the colonists. In view of the radical change that had come over the spirit of their dream, the Carankuas' purposed demand was put in the form of a petition for a little tobacco. This De Leon promised them on the condition that they should immediately cross to the west side of the bay and remain there. Readily consenting to this, he gave them the coveted tobacco, when they proceeded to wade across the estuary, which was about two miles wide at this point and four feet deep. As there were no colonists occupying this immediate section, the surveying party calculated the whole as a clear gain.

Major Kerr continued his work and completed the survey, which embraced eleven leagues of land, extending from Long Mott, fronting the bay, to Matagorda Bay at the point where Indianola now stands.

The beginning of troubles

Information came in 1835 to the ears of the legislators that General Cos intended their forcible dispersion. This intelligence, of course, created the wildest alarm. The governor, accompanied by his secretary of state and suite, set out immediately for Texas, but was overhauled by the military and thrown into jail at Monterey. The Texas delegation made good their escape and arrived home in safety. Orders were sent by the central government to Wily Martin, political chief of the Brazos, to arrest certain citizens. This order Mr. Martin declined to execute. Soon another order was sent for the arrest of R. W. Williamson,[7] W. B. Travis, Samuel M. Williams, Moseley Baker, F. W. Johnson, and John H. Moore. A subsequent order directed the arrest of José M. J. Carbajal and Juan Zembrano, the latter two being Mexican citizens of San Antonio.

In Thrall's *History of Texas*, page 202, it is stated that Carbajal and Zembrano were arrested and taken to Mexico. But such was not the case, as they both were residing in Victoria at the time. Zembrano was engaged in the land office of De Leon's colony. He left his home in San Antonio because he was aware that General Cos viewed him with suspicion. He eventually removed to Louisiana. In regard to the others no attempt was made to comply with the orders of the general government, and they were not molested.

In addition to the foregoing, the following epitome of Texan history is reproduced as embracing a suitable form for easy reference. The first organized movement in Texas in opposition to the despotic measures pursued by Santa Anna was the assembling of the "General Consultation," which was composed of the following-named persons elected by the several municipalities, viz.:

---

[7] Ed. Note: Robert McAlpin Williamson, known as "Three-Legged Willie."

Municipality of Austin—William Menefee, Wily Martin, Thomas Barnett, Randall Jones, and Jesse Burnham.

Municipality of Bevil (afterwards Jasper)—John Bevil, Wyatt Hanks, Thomas Holmes, S. H. Everett, and John H. Blount.

Municipality of San Augustine—A. Huston, Jacob Garrett, William N. Sigler, A. E. C. Johnson, Henry Augustine, Alexander Horton, and A. G. Kellogg.

Municipality of Harrisburg—Lorenzo de Zavala, Clement C. Dyer, William P. Harris, M. W. Smith, J. W. Moore, and David B. Malcomb.

Municipality of Matagorda—Ira R. Lewis, R. R. Royall, Charles Wilson, and John D. Newell.

Municipality of Viesca (afterwards Milam)—J. G. W. Pierson, J. L. Hood, Samuel T. Allen, A. G. Perry, J. W. Parker, and Alexander Thompson.

Municipality of Nacogdoches—William Whitaker, Sam Houston, Daniel Parker, James W. Robinson, and N. Robbins.

Municipality of Columbia (afterwards Brazoria)—John A. Wharton, Henry Smith, Edwin Waller, and J. S. D. Byrom.

Municipality of Liberty—Henry Millard, J. B. Wood, A. B. Hardin, and George M. Patrick.

Municipality of Mina (afterwards Bastrop)—D. C. Barrett, Robert M. Williamson, and James L. Lester.

Municipality of Washington—Asa Mitchell, Elijah Collard, Jesse Grimes, Philip Coe, and Asa Hoxie.

Municipality of Gonzales—William S. Fisher, J. D. Clements, George W. Davis, Benjamin Fuqua, James Hodges, and William M. Arrington.

Municipality of Tenehaw (afterwards Shelby)—Martin Parmer.
Municipality of Jefferson—Claiborne West.
Municipality of Victoria—J. J. Linn.
Municipality of Jackson—James Kerr.

This body assembled at San Felipe, and was organized on the 3rd day of November, 1835, by the election of Branch T. Archer, president, and P. B. Dexter, secretary. It adopted a declaration against the central government of Santa Anna, and in favor of the republican principles of the federal Mexican constitution of 1824. It established a provisional government, composed of a governor, a lieutenant governor—who was ex-officio president of the council—and a general council, composed of one member from each municipality, selected by the delegation therefrom in the Consultation.

An ordinance was adopted defining the powers of the provisional government, and directing an army to be raised and organized for the defence of the country. The following officers of the provisional government were elected: Henry Smith, governor; James W. Robinson, lieutenant governor; Sam Houston, commander in chief of the army to be raised. The following commissioners to the United States were also appointed: Branch T. Archer, Stephen F. Austin, and William H. Wharton. The Consultation adjourned on the 14th of November, 1835, and the provisional government commenced its duties on the same day.

The following-named gentlemen were, at different times, members of the general council from their several municipalities:

Austin—Wily Martin, Thomas Barnett, Randall Jones.

Colorado—William Menefee and Jesse Burnham.

San Augustine—A. Horton and A. E. C. Johnson.

Nacogdoches—Daniel Parker.

Washington—Jesse Grimes, Asa Mitchell, Asa Hoxie, Philip Coe, and Elijah Collard.

Milam—A. G. Perry and Alexander Thompson.

Liberty—Henry Millard.

Shelby—Martin Parmer, James B. Tuckner.

Gonzales—J. D. Clements.

Bastrop—D. C. Barrett and Bartlett Simms.

Matagorda—R. R. Royall, Charles Wilson, I. R. Lewis.

Harrisburg—William P. Harris.

Brazoria—John A. Wharton and Edwin Waller.
Jasper—Wyatt Hanks.
Jefferson—Claiborne West and G. A. Patillo
Victoria—J. A. Padilla[8] and John J. Linn.
Refugio—James Power and John Malone.
Goliad—Ira Westover.
San Patricio—Lewis Ayers and John McMullen.
Jackson—James Kerr.
Sabine—J. S. Lane.

The following gentlemen were also officers of the provisional government: secretaries of the council, P. B. Dexter and E. M. Pease; secretaries of the governor, C. B. Stuart and Edward B. Wood; treasurer, Joshua Fletcher; auditor, J. W. Moody; comptroller, H. C. Hudson; postmaster general, John R. Jones.

The provisional government was superseded by the convention that was convened at Washington on the 1st day of March, 1836, which body was composed of the following members, viz.:

Municipality of Austin—C. B. Stuart, Thomas Barnett.
Brazoria—James Collingsworth, Edwin Waller, Asa Brigham, J. S. D. Byrom.
Bexar—Francis Ruis, J. Antonio Navarro, Jesse Bladgett, William Motley.
Colorado—William Menefee, William D. Lacy.
Gonzales—John Fisher, Mathew Caldwell.
Nacogdoches—John S. Roberts, Robert Potter, Charles Taylor, T. J. Rusk.
Refugio—James Power, Sam Houston.
Shelby—Martin Parmer, S. O. Pennington.

---

[8] J. A. Padilla was not a member-elect of the body from Victoria, and only represented Mr. John J. Linn by courtesy until his arrival. I served as a member of the General Consultation for more than two months. I was in service with the army, in the campaign against Lapantitlan, at the time of the assemblage of the Consultation. After engaging in the fight and capture of Lapantitlan I went to San Felipe and took the oath as a member of Consultation.

Sabine—James Gaines, William Clark, Jr.

Harrisburg—Lorenzo de Zavala, Andrew Briscoe.

Jasper—George W. Smythe, S. H. Everett.

Jackson—Elijah Stapp.

Jefferson—Claiborne West, William B. Scates.

Liberty—M. B. Menard, A. B. Hardin, J. B. Wood.

Bastrop—J. W. Bunton, Thomas J. Gayley, Robert M. Coleman.

Milam—Sterling C. Robinson, G. C. Childress.

Matagorda—Bailey Hardeman, S. Rhodes Fisher.

San Patricio—John Turner, John W. Bower.

Washington—Benjamin B. Goodrich, James G. Swisher, George W. Barnett, Jesse Grimes.

San Augustine—E. O. Legrand, S. W. Blount.

Red River—Robert Hamilton, Collin McKinney, A. H. Lattimer, Samuel P. Carson, Richard Ellis, William Crawford.

Goliad—David Thomas, Edward Conrad.

Richard Ellis was elected president and H. G. Kimble secretary. This convention adopted a Declaration of Independence. General Sam Houston was named commander in chief of the army; a State constitution was framed, and an ordinance adopted creating and defining the powers of a government to continue until an organization could take place under the constitution. This was called the government *ad interim*.

The principal officers of the government *ad interim* elected were as follows:

President—David G. Burnet.

Vice President—Lorenzo de Zavala.

Secretary of State—Samuel P. Carson.

Secretary of War—Thomas J. Rusk.

Secretary of the Treasury—Bailey Hardeman.

Secretary of the Navy—Robert Potter.

Attorney General—David Thomas.

During this government, which continued until October 22, 1836, there were many changes, and the following-named persons were for a time members of the cabinet, viz.: James Collingsworth and W. H. Jack were secretaries of state; M. B. Lamar, F. A. Sawyer, Alexander Somerville, and John A. Wharton, secretaries of war; Peter W. Grayson, attorney general; Barnard E. Bee, secretary of the treasury; J. E. Jones, postmaster general. The following persons were also in office under the government *ad interim*: Asa Brighton, auditor; H. C. Hudson, comptroller; Benjamin C. Franklin, judge for the district of the Brazos. When hostilities commenced in September 1835, and the volunteers assembled at Gonzales, John H. Moore was elected to command them. Subsequently, when their numbers had increased and General Austin arrived in camp, he was elected to command them, and continued in the discharge of these duties until about the first of December, when he resigned and set out for the United States as a commissioner with Archer and Wharton. Edward Burleson was then elected to the command, in which position he continued until after the surrender of General Cos at Bexar on the 10th of December, 1835. After this date the whole military force was placed under the command of General Sam Houston. General Houston discharged the duties of commander in chief until a few days after the battle of San Jacinto, when, being forced to seek surgical aid for the wound received in that battle, he turned over the command to General Rusk. The first congress was convened on the 3rd day of October, 1836, and on the 22nd of the same month a constitutional government of the Republic was organized under Houston's first administration.

A *Declaration of Principles and Purposes by the Consultation of Texas, November, 1835*

"Whereas, General Antonio Lopez de Santa Anna and other military chieftains have by force of arms overthrown the federal institutions of Mexico, and dissolved the social compact which existed between Texas and the other members of the Mexican confederacy. Now, the good people of Texas, availing themselves of their natural rights,

"Do Solemnly Declare—

"1. That they have taken up arms in defence of their rights and liberties, which are threatened by the encroachments of military despots, and in defence of the republican principles of the federal Mexican constitution of the year 1824.

"2. That Texas is no longer morally or civilly bound by the compact of union, yet, stimulated by the generosity and sympathy common to a free people, they offer their support and assistance to such members of the Mexican confederacy as will take up arms against military despotism.

"3. They do not acknowledge that the present authorities of the nominal Mexican Republic have the right to govern within the limits of Texas.

"4. They will not cease to carry on war against said authorities while their troops are within the limits of Texas.

"5. They hold it to be their right, during the disorganization of the federal system and the reign of despotism, to withdraw from the union and to establish an independent government, or to adopt such measures as they may deem best calculated to protect their rights and liberties. But they will continue faithful to the Mexican government so long as that nation is governed by the constitution and laws that were formed for the government of the political association.

"6. That Texas is responsible for the expenses of her armies now in the field.

"7. That the public faith of Texas is pledged for the payment of all debts contracted by her agents.

"8. That she will reward by donations in land all who volunteer their services in her present struggle, and receive them as citizens.

"9. These declarations we solemnly avow to the world, and call God to witness their truth and sincerity; and we invoke defeat and disgrace upon our heads should we prove guilty of duplicity.

The Declaration of Independence made by the Delegates of the People of Texas in General Convention at Washington, on March the 2nd, Anno Domini 1836

"When a government has ceased to protect the lives, liberty, and property of the people, from whom all its legitimate powers are derived, and for the advancement of whose happiness it was instituted, and, so far from being a guarantee of their inestimable and inalienable rights, becomes an instrument in the hands of evil rulers for their oppression; when the federal republican constitution of their country, which they have sworn to support, no longer has a substantial existence, and the whole nature of their government has been forcibly changed, without their consent, from a restricted federative republic, composed of sovereign states, to a consolidated, central military despotism, in which every interest is disregarded but that of the army and the priesthood—both the eternal enemies of civil liberty—the ever-ready minions of power and the usual instruments of tyrants; when, long after the spirit of the constitution has departed, moderation is at length so far from those in power that even the semblance of freedom is removed and the forms themselves of the constitution discontinued, and, so far from the petitions and remonstrances being disregarded, the agents who bear them are thrown into dungeons and mercenary armies sent forth to enforce a new government upon them at the point of the bayonet;

"When, in consequence of such acts of malfeasance and abduction on the part of the government, anarchy prevails and civil society is dissolved into its original elements, in such a crisis the first law of nature, the right of self-preservation, the inherent and inalienable right of the people to appeal to first principles and take their political affairs into their own hands in extreme cases, enjoins it as a right towards themselves and a sacred obligation to their posterity to abolish such government and create another in its stead, calculated to rescue them from impending dangers and to secure their welfare and happiness.

"Nations, as well as individuals, are amenable for their acts to the general opinion of mankind. A statement of a part of our grievances is therefore submitted to an impartial world, in justification of the hazardous but unavoidable step now taken of severing our political connection with the Mexican people and assuming an independent attitude among the nations of the earth.

"The Mexican government, by its colonization laws, invited and induced the Anglo-American population of Texas to colonize its wilderness under the pledged faith of a written constitution, and that they should continue to enjoy that constitutional liberty and republican government to which they had been habituated in the land of their birth, the United States of America.

"In this expectation they have been cruelly disappointed, inasmuch as the Mexican nation has acquiesced in the late changes made in the government by General Antonio Lopez de Santa Anna, who, having overturned the constitution of his country, now offers to us the cruel alternatives either to abandon our homes, acquired by so many privations, or submit to the most intolerable of all tyranny—the combined despotism of the sword and the priesthood. It has sacrificed our welfare to the State of Coahuila, by which our interests have been continually depressed through a jealous and partial course of legislation, carried on at a far-distant seat of government, by a hostile majority, in an unknown tongue; and this, too, notwithstanding we have petitioned in the humblest terms for the establishment of a separate State government, and have, in accordance with the provisions of the national constitution, presented to the General Congress a republican constitution, which was, without just cause, contemptuously rejected.

"It incarcerated in a dungeon for a long time one of our citizens for no other cause but a zealous endeavor to procure the adoption of our constitution and the establishment of a State government. It has failed and refused to secure on a firm basis the right to trial by jury—that palladium of civil liberty and only guarantee for the life, liberty, and property of the citizen.

"It has failed to establish any system of public education, although possessed of almost boundless resources (the public domain), and although it is an axiom in political science that unless a people are educated and enlightened it is idle to expect the continuance of civil liberty or the capacity for self-government.

"It has suffered the military commandants stationed among us to exercise arbitrary acts of oppression and tyranny, thus trampling upon the most sacred rights of the citizen, and rendering the military superior to the civil power.

"It has dissolved by force of arms the State Congress of Coahuila and Texas, and obliged our representatives to fly for their lives from the seat of government, thus depriving us of the fundamental political right of representation.

"It has demanded the surrender of a number of our citizens, and ordered military detachments to seize and carry them into the interior for trial, in contempt of the civil authorities and in defiance of the laws and the constitution.

"It has made political attacks upon our commerce by commissioning foreign desperadoes, and authorizing them to seize our vessels and convey the property of our citizens to far-distant parts for confiscation.

"It denies us the right of worshipping the Almighty according to the dictates of our own conscience, by the support of a national religion calculated to promote the temporal interests of its human functionaries rather than the glory of the true and living God.

"It has demanded us to deliver up our arms, which are essential to our defence—the rightful property of freemen, and formidable only to tyrannical governments.

"It has invaded our country both by sea and by land, with the intent to lay waste our territory and drive us from our homes, and has now a large mercenary army advancing to carry on against us a war of extermination.

"It has, through its emissaries, incited the merciless savage, with the tomahawk and scalping knife, to massacre the inhabitants of our defenceless frontiers.

"It has been, during the whole time of our connection with it, the contemptible sport and victim of successive military revolutions, and hath continually exhibited every characteristic of a weak, corrupt, and tyrannical government.

"These and other grievances were patiently borne by the people of Texas until they reached that point at which forbearance ceases to be a virtue. We then took up arms in defence of the national constitution. We appealed to our Mexican brethren for assistance: our appeal has been made in vain; though months have elapsed, no sympathetic response has yet been heard from the interior. We are, therefore, forced to the melancholy conclusion that the Mexican people have acquiesced in the destruction of their liberty and the substitution therefor of a military government; that they are unfit to be free and incapable of self-government.

"The necessity of self-preservation, therefore, now decrees our eternal political separation.

"We, therefore, the delegates, with plenary powers, of the people of Texas, in solemn convention assembled, appealing to a candid world for the necessities of our condition, do hereby resolve and declare that our political connection with the Mexican nation has for ever ended; and that the people of Texas do now constitute a *free, sovereign, and independent republic*, and are fully invested with all the rights and attributes which properly belong to independent nations; and, conscious of the rectitude of our intentions, we fearlessly and confidently commit the issue to the Supreme Arbiter of the destinies of nations.

"In witness whereof we have hereunto subscribed our names:

Name	*Age*	*Place of Birth*	*Former Residence*
Richard Ellis	54	Virginia	Alabama
C. B. Stuart	30	South Carolina	Louisiana
James Collingsworth	30	Tennessee	Tennessee
Edwin Waller	35	Virginia	Missouri
Asa Brigham	46	Massachusetts	Louisiana
J. S. D. Byrom	38	Georgia	Florida

Francis Ruis	54	Bexar, Texas	
J. Antonio Navarro	41	Bexar, Texas	
J. B. Bladgett	29	North Carolina	Arkansas Ter.
W. D. Lacy	28	Kentucky	Tennessee
William Menefee	40	Tennessee	Alabama
John Fisher	36	Virginia	Virginia
M. Caldwell	38	Kentucky	Missouri
W. Motley	24	Virginia	Kentucky
L. de Zavala	47	Yucatan	Mexico
George W. Smythe	33	North Carolina	Alabama
S. H. Everitt	29	New York	New York
E. Stapp	53	Virginia	Missouri
Claiborne West	36	Tennessee	Louisiana
W. B. Scates	39	Virginia	Kentucky
M. B. Menard	31	Canada	Illinois
A. B. Hardin	38	Georgia	Tennessee
J. W. Bunton	28	Tennessee	Tennessee
Thomas G. Gazeley	35	New York	Louisiana
R. M. Coleman	37	Kentucky	Kentucky
S. C. Robertson	50	North Carolina	Tennessee
George C. Childress	32	Tennessee	Tennessee
B. Hardeman	41	Tennessee	Tennessee
R. Potter	36	North Carolina	North Carolina
Thomas J. Rusk	29	South Carolina	Georgia
Charles S. Taylor	28	England	New York
John S. Roberts	40	Virginia	Louisiana
R. Hamilton	53	Scotland	North Carolina
C. M. Kinney	70	New Jersey	Kentucky

A. H. Lattimer	27	Tennessee	Tennessee
James Power	48	Ireland	Louisiana
Sam Houston	43	Virginia	Tennessee
David Thomas	35	Tennessee	Tennessee
E. Conrad	26	Pennsylvania	Pennsylvania
Martin Parmer	58	Virginia	Missouri
E. O. Legrand	33	North Carolina	Alabama
S. W. Blount	28	Georgia	Georgia
James Gaines	60	Virginia	Louisiana
W. Clark, Jr.	37	North Carolina	Georgia
S. O. Pennington	27	Kentucky	Arkansas Ter.
W. C. Crawford	31	North Carolina	Alabama
John Turner	34	North Carolina	Tennessee
B. B. Goodrich	37	Virginia	Alabama
G. W. Barnett	43	South Carolina	Mississippi
J. G. Swisher	41	Tennessee	Tennessee
Jesse Grimes	48	North Carolina	Alabama
S. Rhoads Fisher*	41	Pennsylvania	Pennsylvania
Samuel A. Maverick*	29	South Carolina	South Carolina
John White Bower*	27	Georgia	Arkansas Ter.
James B. Woods*	34	Kentucky	Kentucky
Andrew Briscoe*			
John W. Moore*			
Thomas Barnett"			

* Not present at the signing.

"Members who failed to reach the convention in time: James Kerr, from Jackson County, born in Kentucky, Sept. 24, 1790; came to Texas in 1835. John J. Linn, from Victoria, born in Ireland in 1798; came to Texas in 1829. Juan Antonio Padilla, a Mexican citizen, from Victoria."—*From a statement furnished in the convention to Dr. B. B. Goodrich.*

On the 16th day of March the convention adopted the executive ordinance by which was constituted the government *ad interim* of the Republic of Texas.

The constitution of the Republic of Texas was adopted at a late hour on the night of the 17th of March, but was neither engrossed nor enrolled for the signatures of the members prior to the adjournment next day.

The secretary was instructed to enroll it for presentation. As I learned from Hon. Jesse Grimes, Mr. Kimble, the secretary, took it to Nashville, Tenn., where it was published in one of the papers, from which it was reproduced by a Cincinnati paper, and from the latter copied by the *Texas Telegraph* of August 3 of the same year, being its first publication in Texas. No enrolled copy having been preserved, this printed one was recognized and adopted as authentic, and became the constitution, thus adding another striking evidence of the wonderful capacity of our people for self-government, of their ability to establish order out of chaos, and of their power to enforce law and order even amid the turmoil of revolution.

During the sitting of the convention General Sam Houston took leave of the body in order to assume command of the army then concentrating at Gonzales.

At eight o' clock on the 18th day of March the convention assembled for the last time, and elected David G. Burnet president, *ad interim*, of the Republic, and Lorenzo de Zavala, a patriot Mexican exile, vice president. The members of the cabinet, heretofore given, were also elected at this sitting. Having consummated the ends for which it was designed, the convention adjourned, *sine die*, at eleven o'clock. The dissolution was hastened somewhat by the rapid advance of the enemy, as reported on the evening previous.

Some of the members repaired forthwith to the army and others to their respective homes.

President Burnet, with two members of the cabinet, remained in Washington three days after the adjournment of the convention. These were Mr. Hardeman and General Rusk. Late in the afternoon of the third day they took their departure, and spent the night and a portion of the ensuing day at the residence of Mr. Grace, from which point they proceeded to Harrisburg.

Before leaving Washington the president issued a proclamation stating that the new government would be organized at Harrisburg, on Buffalo Bayou. The president announced, also, that the enemy's advance had no influence in this selection of a capital, as he had, previous to the election, urged the eligibility of Harrisburg over the more distant town of Washington.

At the time his excellency left Washington there was but one family in the city—that of the hotel keeper, Mr. Lott; and, indeed, the whole population of Texas had by this time flown to the east of the Brazos River.

The foregoing statement to the effect that J. A. Padilla was from Victoria is incorrect. Mr. J. M. J. Carbajal and John J. Linn were the delegates-elect from Victoria, and were prevented from attending by the advance of the Mexican army. John J. Linn had proceeded en route to the convention as far as the Colorado River, when he was forced to return to care for his family, who were left defenceless in Victoria, liable to be entered by the enemy at any hour. J. A. Padilla was from San Antonio.

President Burnet and William Menefee gave me some diverting incidents during the last hours of the convention. The alarming reports of the atrocities perpetrated by the Mexicans had a demoralizing effect on some of the members. Many wished to leave before the constitution had been adopted. Such proposed to delegate the president, Mr. Ellis, to act for them. On the last day, Mr. Menefee informed me, several mounted their horses, and it was with difficulty that he persuaded them to wait a few minutes.

There were three declarations of Texan independence:

1. At San Felipe, which declared the autonomy of Texas and dissolved its relationship to Coahuila.

2. Ira Ingram drew up an instrument, purporting to be a declaration of independence, at Goliad, which was signed by the members of Captain Dimmitt's company and others. Among the signers were several boys fifteen or sixteen years of age. This instrument was forwarded to the Consultation at San Felipe, but that body refused to receive it, deeming it premature, as the matter of absolute independence could only be acted upon by delegates invested with plenary constituent powers. Therefore the solemn question came before the convention of March 1836, in the town of Washington, on the Brazos, with the result just before narrated.

Happy, thrice happy, had it been for Texas had she guarded with sleepless watch and eternal vigilance this inestimable jewel of her sovereignty! It was to her what the golden fruit of Hesperides was to the maidens who kept their ceaseless watch and ward; the jewel of their chastity depended upon their fidelity to the trust.

Note.—The author of the Texan Declaration of Independence was George C. Childress.

Chapter 4

Of the early settlement of Texas—establishment of religion, etc.

The Catholic missionaries were unquestionably the first white men who penetrated the primeval wilds of Texas proper. They came not to increase the domain of earthly potentates by the conquest of territory, but to subdue the savage heart by the beautiful and pure precepts of the Church, and to thus fit his soul for the spiritual kingdom of his God.

It was my fortune to meet the last remaining two of this pious band of devoted men in Texas—Father Diaz and Father Muro—who gave me much valuable information upon the subject of the labors of themselves and their predecessors. And in regard to the earliest settlement of the country I learned much in conversations with Don Antonio Navarro and Don Erasmo Seguin.

These, as may well be imagined, were enthusiastic in their descriptions of the country in the immediate vicinity of the spot where San Antonio now stands, as pictured to them by their predecessors at the time the first settlers arrived from the Rio Grande.

There were several tribes of Indians inhabiting the country, whose history, alas! we know nothing of.

The undulating bosom of the country was covered with an emerald sward of the waving, willowy mesquite grass, which is as sweet and generous to the taste of the dumb brute as is the famous water of the Nile to man. Every valley and hillside seemed to smile 'neath the weight of the thousand-hued wildflowers that were scattered by the bountiful hand of Nature in prodigal profusion. Like the arteries through which courses the current of life from its source—the heart—so murmured on, in seeming dalliance with a clime brighter and more genial than Italia's sky, the streams of limpid water throughout the sylvan scene.

'Neath the moss-covered limbs of the umbrageous live oak the red chieftains of the virgin domain held their councils. As yet they were uncontaminated by contact with the civilized stranger; but their minds were as fettered by the thongs of a heathen phantasmagoria as were their limbs and actions free.

The first duty of the missionaries upon their arrival was to plant corn and vegetables upon which to subsist in the future. Their second labor was to win the confidence of the Indians and make them their friends, so that the great blessings of religion could be inculcated into their minds and hearts. The missionaries also taught their savage pupils the necessity of cultivating the earth for their support, and not to depend upon the uncertainties of the chase for a hazardous and poor means of seeking sustenance at best.

In a remarkably short period of time the labors of these devoted men began to be rewarded by fruits. Many Indians abandoned their nomadic life and settled down into communities, determined to bear the restraints of civilization in order that they might also enjoy its great blessings.

The next step was the erection of church edifices and other buildings for the use of the community, all of which have long since disappeared by the decaying influences of time.

Domestic animals were introduced, and, favored by the genial climate and good care, multiplied rapidly in a few years.

As soon as the exigencies of the situation would admit, and the fathers had means to do so, more costly and durable edifices were built, as churches, convents, etc. These remain as monuments to the fidelity, the courage, and religious zeal of the good missionaries. Probably endowed with as much interest to the intelligent tourist to San Antonio as the renowned Alamo itself is the famous Mission of San José, which was commenced in the year 1717 by Father Margil and completed in 1771. The good and pious father, however, died before its completion.

In the execution of this great purpose the missionaries fraternized a number of men together, both Spaniards and Indians, who were called the "Children of San José." They obtained grants of land from the government in addition to the land now known as "The Labor of José," the princely domain of five leagues, or over twenty thousand acres, all of which was held by them in good faith. The cupidity of Mr. John McMullen led him to test in the courts the validity of this title. McMullen was a resident of San Antonio, and became acquainted with several of "The Children of San José," who were then old men, of whom he purchased their claims, interest, etc., in and to the land. He endeavored in vain to have the new claim recognized by the legislature. The lands remained vested in the original trustees, as they might properly enough be called.

This building is a wonder of architectural design and finish. The sculpture and other adornments bespeak a master's hand; and the work of the carpenters, in elegance and durability, remains today as a challenge to competition. Much of the fine work in wood, such as carving, etc., has been carried off by the relic hunters, who displayed a barbaric spirit of vandalism in defacing this magnificent edifice.

About the commencement of the present century the wild Indians, as they were called—the Comanches, Wacos, Tewaconies, etc.—began to extend their marauding migrations to the coast section of Texas in great numbers. These tribes had not yet learned the use of horses, and proceeded on foot. So frequent were their incursions that the detached settlements were broken up and the colonists sought refuge in the towns. Indeed, this deplorable state of affairs continued on the Rio Grande up to the inception of the Mexican revolution in 1807-8. In 1807 the Mexican government equipped an expeditionary force to operate against these Bedouins. Two hundred and fifty well-armed men were selected, and Colonel Uvalde placed in command. These took the field, prepared for a year's campaign against the Indians.

Colonel Uvalde succeeded in surprising quite a large party in what is now called, in honor of himself, "Uvalde Cañon," and in almost entirely destroying the entire band. The report was some years afterwards that three hundred of the Indians were killed outright, besides a great many who were wounded. I have conversed with responsible parties, who informed me that they had seen piles of bleached human bones in the upper end of the cañon. A county in Texas is also named in honor of the able and brave Uvalde. At the commencement of the revolution in 1809 he was preparing for a similar expedition, but graver affairs at home superseding all interest in the matter, it was abandoned.

The revolution, once under way, engrossed the attention of all. There was no vigor lacking on the part of either republican or royalist.

Unfortunately for a better cause than either of the contending factions could claim, the peaceful and religious hamlet of San Antonio, sequestered as it was in the distant wilds of Nature, was not suffered to escape the demoniacal presence of war. The soldiery preyed upon the fruits of the citizens' labor. Most of their livestock was killed, and the missions broken up in consequence. The civilized Indians were forced to espouse whichever side was in the ascendant for the hour, and the consequence of this was that they rapidly relapsed into their former modes of life. For the brutal conduct of the civilized soldiery gave the lie to the beneficent teachings of the good fathers; and as error is disseminated with more ease and rapidity than truth, the work of the faithful missionaries for years was dissolved like snowflakes in a summer sun. The missionaries, excepting two, were recalled to the principal house in Zacatecas, and all the archives of value sent to the same city.

I have often wondered how the missionaries, who were men poor in the goods of this world, succeeded in erecting such substantial edifices in the wilderness. Many thoughtless people have imagined that the Indians were made "hewers of stone and drawers of water" in this work. But the truth is, the Indians performed very little of the labor.

The Franciscans were a very numerous body in the Church at that time, and among them were many lay brothers who were skilful artificers and architects. The priests were all thoroughly educated men, and they drew the designs, made the plans, etc., and the lay brothers executed the material work.

The following extracts from a sermon delivered by the Very Rev. Canon Johnston, of the diocese of San Antonio, which was published in the Victoria (Texas) *Advocate*, July 7, 1877, will be found to contain *multum in parvo* on this interesting subject:

"The establishment of a mission on the Rio Grande in 1703 is an important fact in the ecclesiastical history of Texas. It was founded by the Franciscans, and was known as the 'Mission of San José.' In 1707 it was removed some distance into the interior, and there known as the 'Mission of San Ildefonso.' It was removed back to the Rio Grande and called the 'Mission of San Francisco de Solano.'

"In 1718 it was removed to within a short distance of the headwaters of the San Antonio River, and there known as the 'Mission of San Antonio de Valero.' It was placed under the invocation of St. Anthony of Padua. The name "Valero" was added in honor of the Marquis of Valero, viceroy of New Spain, as Mexico was then called, at the time of the removal of the mission. The superior of the mission was San Buenaventura y Olevaxes.

"The first stone of the mission now standing was laid on the 8th of May, 1745. This building is now famous all over the country as the 'Alamo.'

"Alamo means cottonwood tree, and, as many trees of this species stood around the church, it was called by the Mexicans the Alamo. This church was for the use of the Indians exclusively. The church for the Spaniards was on the west side of the river. In 1730 thirteen families settled on that side of the river. They came from the Canary Islands. They called the town that they built San Fernando, thus placing it under the invocation of St. Ferdinand, King of Spain. It was well laid out into streets and squares. The main square was called La Plaza de la Islas, in memory of the Canaries. In 1732 they built a handsome church in Moresque style, part of which still stands and forms the sanctuary and sacristy of the beautiful new cathedral of San Antonio. This church was built facing the Plaza de las Islas, or main plaza; in its rear was the Military Plaza, so called because the garrison were on it. It was known as the Presidio de Bexar. The name of Bexar was added in honor of the Duke of Bexar, viceroy of Mexico.

"1715-16 was an important era in the Church history of Texas, for in that year Antonio Margil began his labors in Texas. This truly great man and apostolic missionary was born in Spain. He was a Franciscan of strict observance. He came to America when yet a young man. The superior that brought him out was delighted at his good fortune, and joyfully told his companion that he had secured St. Anthony of Padua. Venerable Antonio Margil began his missionary labors in Central America and different parts of Mexico. Fruit of his labor was great. It is stated in the history of his life that to secure that fruit he established colleges in all the missions he founded.

"His labors fill volumes. He labored in Texas and Louisiana. He founded the missions of the 'Conception,' 'San José,' 'San Juan Capistrano,' and 'San Francisco de Espada.' These missions are a few miles from San Antonio. Some of the churches of the missions are strikingly beautiful. Hundreds of tourists annually visit them. They are monuments of the energy, zeal, and tastes of the Franciscan fathers. The enlightened government of Mexico took these missions away from them, and the result was ruin.

"Father Margil founded the mission of Nacogdoches, in Texas, and performed missionary labors in Louisiana. This meagre sketch will give but an imperfect idea of the strenuous efforts of this great servant of God. He died and was buried in the city of Mexico.

"The Indians of Mexico cherish the memory of their great benefactor. Father Margil had many who followed in his footsteps and copied his example. The last of these great Franciscan missionaries was Padre Diaz, who was killed on the Trinity River in 1839. This was a season of struggle and strife, and turmoil and disorder, during which the independence of Texas was secured. At this time an event took place very favorable to the English-speaking Church in Texas. Quite a number of families went to Texas from Perry County, Missouri. They were mostly of Kentucky stock and Catholics. They were without a priest. Father Edward Clark and Father Hayden, natives and residents of Kentucky, hearing of their spiritual condition, volunteered to go to their assistance. Father Clark lived and labored eighteen years in Texas. Father Hayden hardly lived as many months. He was able and learned, and a preacher of remarkable eloquence. His early death was a heavy loss to the Church of Texas. In 1838 Father Timon, then at the college called The Barrens, in Perry County, Missouri, first visited Texas. He was appointed prefect apostolic of Texas. He visited Texas again in 1840. He is the first priest that ever said Mass in Galveston, Houston, and Austin. He travelled over a large part of eastern Texas.

"In 1840 Rev. John Murry Odin went to Texas from Perry County, Missouri. He visited San Antonio and all the old missions of western Texas. He went to Victoria, Seguin, Gonzales, and other points. He visited the Lavaca settlement, made by the Missouri Catholics. He received a joyful welcome from them, for they had known him in Missouri. Here he saw Father Clark for the first time. Father Odin was appointed vicar apostolic, then bishop of Galveston."

Bishop Odin was ordained bishop of Galveston in 1847, and in 1861 he was appointed archbishop of Louisiana by the pope. This promotion was by no means in conformity to his wishes, as he did not desire to be removed from his dear Texas; but as an obedient child of the Church he entered willingly into this new field of duty. He was received with joy and delight by the people of Louisiana. He visited Rome and France several times in the performance of his duties. He attended the Vatican Council, but ill health forced him to retire to his native town in France, where he died, surrounded by friends and relatives, in the year 1870.

His successor was Bishop Dubuis, a prelate in every respect worthy to fill the place of the lamented Bishop Odin, and to discharge the arduous duties incumbent upon the bishop of the largest diocese in the United States.

Texas has lately been divided into three dioceses, and Bishop Dubuis in a measure relieved of much of his onerous duties.

In 1840 the number of Catholics in Texas was thirty thousand in round numbers. The showing for the year 1880 shows that they number one hundred and twenty thousand. But this statement falls below the correct number.

Mr. Thrall (*History of Texas*) states that Bishop Timon, of Missouri, appointed Father Odin a bishop. Mr. Thrall is mistaken again, as the pope only can make the appointment of a bishop, after the candidate has been duly recommended by the clergy of the diocese. The memory of Bishop Odin is revered by the Catholics of Texas, where the many schools, colleges, convents, hospitals, and other institutions of public benefit that rose through his influence, zeal, and labor stand today commemorative of his memory and of his sterling worth.

Chapter 5

Letter of Hon. Guy M. Bryan in regard to Austin's first colony—General Long's expedition—fate of Captain Perry, etc.

"Peach Point, Brazoria Co.
July 1, 1852

"Editor *Texas Planter*:

"Dear Sir: In the last number of the *Planter* I noticed an article under the caption, "Austin's First Colony," in which I detected several errors, which I respectfully beg leave to correct. You say that Austin arrived on the banks of the Brazos River on the first day of August, 1821, with Edward Lovelace, Neel Gaspar, _____ Bellow, H. Holstien, William Little, Joseph Polley,[9] James Beard, _____ Beard, _____ Maple, William Wilson, Dr. Hewitson, _____ Irwine, W. Smithers, and _____ Barre. These were the hardy men with whom Austin first blazed his way through the Brazos bottom. They were the first of the old "three hundred." None preceded them. Austin arrived at San Antonio with his little party in company of the commissioner, Don Erasmo Seguin, on the 17th day of August, 1821, and not in January 1822, as stated by you. In justice to the name of Seguin let me add that no Mexican ever did more for Texas and the colonists than did that

---

[9] Mr. Polley resided some time in Brazoria County.

true-hearted man. In the infancy of Texas, in the days of her weakness and his strength, he was the faithful friend of the Americans.

"Would that I could say as much of the Americans towards him! He was a man of intelligence and position, having the confidence of his government. Through his instrumentality Austin obtained many favors for the colonists. In San Antonio whenever an American got into difficulty Seguin was the first and best friend he had; and those who lived in Texas at the time of Mexican supremacy know something of the value of such a friend at that time.

"Austin, through the representations of Seguin and Beremendis, was received with great kindness by General Martinez. He obtained permission of the governor to explore the country on the Colorado and Brazos rivers, and to sound the entrances of harbors, etc., lying adjacent to the mouths of those streams.

"With nine of his men he made these explorations sufficiently to satisfy himself of the great fertility of the land along the rivers. He then returned to Louisiana preparatory to the execution of his colonization scheme.

"In December 1821 he arrived on the Brazos, where the La Bahia road crosses that river, with his settlers, the first females of the "old three hundred." On New Year's eve he encamped on "New Year's Creek." Andy Robinson was the first permanent settler on the Brazos, near where the town of Washington now stands. In the March following Austin went to San Antonio to report to the governor, when he was informed that it would be necessary for him to proceed to Mexico, to procure from Congress, then in session, confirmation of the grant to his father, Moses Austin, and to receive special instructions as to the distribution of the land, issuance of titles, etc. This trip to Mexico was totally unexpected and very embarrassing; for, not anticipating anything of the kind, he was totally unprepared.

"But there was no time for hesitation. Preparations were made at once. Mr. Josiah H. Bell took charge of the settlements, and Austin departed for Mexico, a distance of twelve hundred miles by land.

"The greater portion of this distance he performed on foot, dressed in the garb of a mendicant soldier to avoid robbers. Mrs. Mary Bell, widow of Josiah H. Bell, now lives in this county, and a purer, nobler-minded woman never breathed the air. Not an old Texan lives who does not love and revere this estimable lady, this Good Samaritan of Austin's colony.

"Guy M. Bryan"

General Long's expedition.

The late John McHenry's account of the same.

"In the autumn of the year 1818 General Long landed at Pass Cavallo with fifty-two men recruited in the United States for service in the republican army of Mexico. From this point he proceeded by water to Mesquite Landing on the San Antonio River. A forced march was made from this point to La Bahia, opposite the present town of Goliad, on the west bank of the San Antonio River, where a royalist garrison was stationed.

"The command halted in front of the Spanish guardhouse at daybreak, and were hailed by the '*Qui vive!*' of the sentinel on duty.

"'*Republicanos!*' was the response of the Americans, who at the same time made a rush for the south entrance to the fort, and the Spaniards for the north one. Some few shots were exchanged in the hurly-burly of the moment, but all became quiet when the Americans gained possession of the place. The royalist commander, Don Francisco Garcia, turned his political coat at this unexpected and sudden turn of affairs, and announced himself a thorough republican. In the course of two or three days a body of Spanish troops, commanded by Captain Parris, came down from San Antonio. The first intimation that we had of the near presence of an enemy was the full view obtained of Captain Juan Parris[10] marshalling his legions for battle on the opposite bank of

---

[10] Ed. Note: Ignacio Perez

the river. General Long ascended to the roof of Garcia's house to reconnoitre the enemy's position, when the new convert to republican principles perfidiously attempted to shoot him. But fortunately the dastardly attempt resulted in no worse consequences than 'the rape of a lock' which the whizzing lead cut from the general's head.

"The Spanish troops opened fire as soon as they had entered the street that passes the northeast bastion. Lieutenant Du Val, one of the republican officers, had charge of that station, which he was gallantly defending with one piece of artillery, which effectually swept the street. The firing continued on both sides for two days, when it suddenly ceased in consequence of a flag of truce which Captain Juan Parris sent in to General Long. The redoubtable Captain Don Juan Parris wished to announce the newly discovered fact that the contestants were sinfully imbruing their hands in fraternal blood, as he and his men were also republicans. But General Long would not listen to Don Juan's soft impeachment, and doubtless thought that warlike worthy was poking fun at him.

"But the determined Don Juan persisted in his wooing for three days, and finally suggested that General Long and some of his officers should visit the authorities at San Antonio and ascertain the correctness of his statements for themselves; in the meantime the Americans should feast upon the fat of the land at the expense of the republic that they had come so far to serve. General Long eventually consented to receive his cast in the serio-comic drama at the prompting of Don Juan, and set out for San Antonio, accompanied by Major Burns and escorted by a guard of honor. It was announced that the Americans were to be billeted among the inhabitants of the town, and, ostensibly as a necessary preliminary to this purpose, they were all assembled in one house, in order that their names could be taken down and each man assigned to comfortable quarters. But no sooner were 'Los Americanos' corralled than a guard of cavalry surrounded the house, and whatever anticipations they may have indulged in regard to epicurean feasts evanished, as did the hope of personal liberty itself.

"The poor fellows, thus shorn of their strength by a treachery equaled only by that of Dalila, were treated with a rigor that but seldom even falls to the lot of prisoners of war.

"General Long had left an aged man at Mesquite Landing to guard the batteaux left there. Don Juan despatched a guard for him. The old man was physically unable to endure the fatigue of a rough horseback ride, and fell exhausted from the animal. The inhuman guard, to spare themselves farther trouble, despatched him where he fell, and left the body to be devoured by wolves.

"After three days spent under guard at La Bahia the Americans were started under a heavy guard for San Antonio. The bill of fare at this place consisted of corn and beef. The latter was haggled into 'chunks,' and, with the shelled corn, thrown into a pot of water, which, after simmering awhile, was served *rare*; the latter word is susceptible of two definitions, but not entitled to the general meaning that the orthography conveys.

"On this regimen the poor fellows subsisted eight days, and then took their doleful departure for Laredo under the command of the facetious Captain Don Juan Parris. It is unnecessary to remark that there was no amelioration of their condition during the march to the Rio Grande.

"Upon arriving at Laredo they were transferred to another officer, who treated them in a humane and kind manner by distributing them among the citizens. Here they tarried some seven or eight days, and somewhat recuperated their strength and spirits, when they were ordered to the city of Monterey. Each man was given one dollar with which to purchase necessaries along the route. But the kind-hearted Mexican ladies of Laredo said they would need the money and should not spend it in their town. Consequently they supplied the poor fellows with whatever they desired, who departed with full haversacks and breathing blessings upon the Christian sisterhood of Laredo. Arriving at Monterey they were quartered in the barracks under guard. Every fourth day each man was given one dollar with which to purchase the necessaries of life. To make these purchases one or two men with a guard were allowed to leave the barracks at a time. This programme continued about one month, when the authorities informed us that we could go our own way in peace. Some of the men, who had learned a bit of wisdom from their sad experience, immediately set out for the United States. The Mexicans, notwithstanding the fact that the Americans were their republican allies, wished to be rid of them. But a goodly number of the unwelcome visitors remained waiting for something to turn up.

"General Long preceded his unfortunate comrades in Mexico, and while they were yet at Monterey Colonel Milam and Colonel Christy came through the city just from the capital, and brought the sad intelligence of General Long's assassination, which occurred in the city of Mexico.

"General Trespalacios, having been appointed governor of Texas, arrived about this time at Saltillo. The new governor stated that Captain John Austin and others had conspired to intercept him on his way to Texas and assassinate him.

"Trespalacios caused the arrest of Austin and the other officers, and had them closely confined. But shortly after this affair the Americans were all ordered to the city of Mexico. We halted at San Luis, en route, one week to rest, and again at Queretaro. The officer who had us in charge had served under the ill-fated General Mina, and, being doubtless chastened by misfortunes himself, treated us with the greatest possible kindness. Finally the city of the Montezumas was reached. Mr. Poinsett, the United States minister, called to see the prisoners—for prisoners they were, whatever else the magnanimous (?) Mexican Republic might choose to denominate their anomalous condition. Through the influence of Mr. Poinsett they were released after a sojourn of six weeks in the city of Mexico, and forthwith were started, under the direction of an officer, for Tampico, at which port passage was engaged for them on board the American ship *John Adams* for Havana, the paramount desire of the Mexicans being to get rid of their troublesome allies, in utter disregard of their destination or destiny. From Havana some of them shipped for New York and others for New Orleans.

"During the semi-state of siege to which General Long was subjected in La Bahia, the forces of Captain Parris cut off their communication with the river, which afforded their sole supply of water. In this emergency the Mexican ladies vied with one another in stealing to the river under the friendly cover of night to fetch water to the thirsting garrison.

"The only casualties among the Americans were Lieutenant Burns and John McHenry wounded."

Upon reading the *Life and Adventures of L. D. Lafferty*, by Hon., A. H. Abney, I became struck with the discrepancy between the statements of this "historical" publication and the reports that I had been accustomed to hear passing current as the true story of General Long's expedition.

I took occasion to hand the book to Mr. McHenry, who participated in that expedition throughout, with the request that he peruse its contents with care and attention; to which he assented, and stated as the result of the perusal that he was morally convinced that Lafferty could not possibly have been a participant in General Long's expedition. He said that the battle so graphically detailed by Mr. Abney as having occurred on Aransas was purely a myth—no such fight had any existence in fact; the only fighting took place at La Bahia (Goliad), as stated in the foregoing narrative, which is substantially the statement of Captain John McHenry. Equally fictitious is Lafferty's account of the so-called surrender.

But on the principle, *falsus in uno, falsus in omnibus*, we will dismiss the Abney-Lafferty concoction for better game.

Soon after his return to New Orleans from Havana Captain McHenry made his way back to Texas and settled on the Lavaca River, where he opened a farm and settled down to the humdrum life of a farmer.

One morning he and his partner went into the woods to cut some timber, and in a hollow tree they discovered two young bear cubs.

As they were about to appropriate the prize the old mother bear approached in the angriest of moods down the river bank. McHenry seized his axe, and, aiming a blow at the enraged brute, he threw the whole force of his body into the stroke, and, missing the bear, fell headlong down the precipitous bank, closely followed by the brute, who, losing her centre of gravity, came turning end over end. Mac and the bear fell into one inextricably confused heap, and luckily for him his axe accompanied him in the rapid descent and fell close to his side. Seizing this a second time, he wielded a more correct blow and despatched his formidable adversary. Returning to the upper bank, his companion, who had climbed a tree, came down, and together they bore the cubs in triumph home.

Becoming tired of the monotony of the farm. Captain McHenry and his partner concluded to go to Louisiana shortly after the episode with the bear, and so without circumlocution they struck out on foot with their "budgets" on their backs. In passing through a prairie near Attakapas the cattle, unaccustomed to pedestrians, attacked them in furious style. The infuriated beasts came charging upon them in hundreds, tossing their heads high in air, bellowing, switching their tails, and, with other devilish indications of fright and anger, seemed ready to engulf them. Fortunately a friendly tree stood close at hand, and the excited men lost no time in mounting to its upper branches.

McHenry dropped a bundle of clothes, and upon these innocent articles the angry bovines proceeded to wreak their vengeance, not leaving Mac an extra shirt to his back; but he saved his bacon and accounted his loss as all gain.

Chapter 6

As before stated, these reminiscences do not purport to be a history of Texas, but rather a narrative of the events connected therewith that passed under the immediate observation of the author. For the concise historical statement the reader is referred to the works of Yokum, Morphis, Thrall, and others. But in this connection the author would say that, while contenting himself with a more modest title than that of historian, he has felt it to be his duty to attempt an elucidation of all vexed questions of which there are disparaging accounts, though immediately unconnected therewith himself.

The angry indications of the Mexican government, heretofore briefly adverted to, finally converged into an ominous war cloud in the year 1835. The Consultation of San Felipe had been held, and Committees of Safety appointed in each of the municipalities, and a general or executive council formed of one member from each Committee of Safety. On this latter committee the author of these reminiscences had the honor of serving. The incomparable memorial of the Texan Convention to the United Mexican States is here reproduced, as serving to elucidate the causes that led to the final rupture:

"The inhabitants of Texas, by their representatives-elect in convention assembled, would respectfully approach the national Congress and present this their memorial, praying that the union which was established between Coahuila and Texas, whereby the two ancient provinces were incorporated into one free and independent state under the name of 'Coahuila and Texas,' may be dissolved, abrogated, and perpetually cease; and that the inhabitants of Texas may be authorized to institute and establish a separate State government which will be in accordance with the federal constitution and the constitutive act, and the State so constituted shall be incorporated into the great confederation of Mexico on terms of equality with the other States of the union.

"To explain the grounds of this application your memorialists would respectfully invite the attention of the general Congress to the following considerations:

"The consolidation of the late provinces of Coahuila and Texas was in its nature provisional and in its intention temporary. The decree of the sovereign constituent Congress, bearing date of the 7th May, 1824, contemplates a separation, and guarantees to Texas the right of having a separate State government whenever she may be in a condition to ask for the same. That decree provides 'that as soon as Texas shall be in a condition to figure as a State of itself it shall inform Congress thereof for its resolution.' The implication conveyed by this clause is plain and imperative, and vests in Texas as perfect a right as language can convey, unless it can be presumed that the sovereign constituent Congress, composed of the venerable fathers of the republic, designed to amuse the good people of Texas by an illusory and disingenuous promise clothed in all the solemnity of a legislative enactment. Your memorialists have too high a veneration for the memory of that illustrious body to entertain any apprehensions that such a construction will be given to their acts by their patriotic successors, the present Congress of Mexico.

"The decree is dated anterior to the adoption of the federal constitution, and therefore, by a clear and fundamental principle of law and justice, it obviates the necessity of recurring to the correspondent provision in the fiftieth article of that instrument, which requires "the ratification of three-fourths of the other States" in order "to form a new State out of the limits of those that already exist." And it assures to Texas, by all the sanctity of a legislative promise in which the good faith of the Mexican nation is pledged, an exemption from the delays and uncertainties that must result from the multiplication of such legislative discussions and resolution. To give to the federal constitution, which is the paramount law of the land, a retrospective operation would establish a precedent that might prove disastrous to the whole nation's system of jurisprudence, and subversive of the very foundations of the government.

"The authority of precedents is decidedly in favor of the position which your memorialists would respectfully sustain before the general Congress. By the constitutive act adopted January 31, 1824, Coahuila, New Leon, and Texas were joined together and denominated the *Internal Eastern State.* By a law passed by the constituent Congress on the 7th May, 1824, that union was dissolved, and the province of New Leon was admitted into the confederacy as an independent State. It is on the second article of this law that the people of Texas now predicate their right to a similar admission. The constitutive act above mentioned consolidated the late provinces of Chihuahua, Durango, and New Mexico under the style of the *Internal Northern State*; and on the 22nd May, 1824, a summary law decreed that 'Durango should form a State of the Mexican confederation,' and she was admitted accordingly. The same privilege was extended to Chihuahua by a decree the 6th July of the same year. These conjunct provinces stood, at the period of their separation, in precisely the same relation to the federal government that Texas and Coahuila now occupy. They have been separated and erected into free and independent States in a summary manner; and the same right was guaranteed 'whenever she should be in a condition to accept it.' The other case, of Sonora and Sinaloa, is materially variant in matter of fact. Those provinces were originally incorporated into the confederation as one State, without any antecedent condition or guarantee, and at the adoption of the present constitution they justly became liable to all the forms and restrictions prescribed in the national pact.

"We would further suggest to the honorable Congress that the present juncture is exceeding felicitous for dispensing with interminable and vexatious forms. The federal government is wisely employed in adopting important organic improvements and aiming at a salutary renovation of the political system. The disasters of an eventful civil convulsion are yielding to the regenerating influences of domestic concord and improved experience; and every department of the confederacy is open to such needful modifications as the wisdom of the renewed Congress may designate. Texas solicits, as her part in the general reformation, to be disenthralled from her unhappy connection with Coahuila; and she avails herself of this opportunity, by means of her chosen delegates, who are the authorized organs of the people, to communicate to the general Congress that she is now 'in a suitable condition to figure as a State by herself.'

"The general Congress may possibly consider the mode of this communication as informal. To this suggestion we would with great deference reply that the events of the past year have not only violated the established forms and etiquette of the government, but have suspended at least its vital functions; and it would appear exceedingly rigorous to exact from the inhabitants of Texas, living on the remote frontier of the republic, a minute conformity to unimportant punctilios. The ardent desire of the people is made known to the Congress through their select representatives—the most direct and unequivocal medium by which they can possibly be conveyed; and surely the enlightened Congress will readily concur with us in the sentiment that the wishes and wants of the people form the best rule for legislative guidance. The people of Texas consider it not only an absolute right, but a most sacred and imperative duty to themselves and to the Mexican nation, to represent their wants in a respectful manner to the general government, and to solicit the best remedy of which the nature of their grievances will admit. Should they utterly fail in this duty, and great and irremediable evils ensue, the people would have to reproach themselves alone; and the general Congress, in whom the remedial power resides, would also have occasion to censure their supineness and want of fidelity to the nation. Under this view we trust the Congress will not regard with excessive severity any slight departure which the good people of Texas may in this instance have made from the ordinary formalities of the government.

"And we would further suggest to the equitable consideration of the federal Congress that, independent of, and anterior to, the express guarantee contained in the decree of the 7th May, 1824, the right of having a separate State government was vested in and belonged to Texas by the fact that she participated as a distinct province in the toils and sufferings through which the glorious emancipation of Mexico was achieved and the present happy form of government was established. The subsequent union with Coahuila was a temporary compact, induced by a supposed expediency arising from an inadequate population on the part of Texas 'to figure as a State of itself.'

"This inducement was transient in its nature; and the compact, like all similar agreements, is subject to abrogation at the will of either party whenever the design of its creation is accomplished or is ascertained to be impracticable. The obvious design of the union between Coahuila and Texas was, on the one part, at least, the more effectually to secure the peace, safety, and happiness of Texas. That design has not been accomplished, and facts piled upon facts afford a melancholy evidence that it is utterly impracticable. Texas never has and never can derive from the connection benefits in any wise commensurate with the evils she has sustained, and which are daily increasing in number and magnitude. But our reasons for the proposed separation are more explicitly set forth in the subjoined remarks.

"The history of Texas, from its earliest settlement to the present time, exhibits a series of practical neglect and indifference to all her peculiar interests on the part of each successive government which had the control of her public destinies. The recollection of these things is calculated to excite the most pungent regrets for the past and the most painful forebodings for the future.

"Under the several regal dominions Texas presented the gloomy spectacle of a province, profusely endowed by Nature, abandoned and consigned to desolation by the profligate avariciousness of a distant despot. The tyrants of Spain regarded her only as a convenient barrier to the mines of the adjacent provinces, and the more waste and depopulated she was the more effectually she answered their selfish and unprincipled purpose. Her agricultural resources were either unknown or esteemed of no value to a government anxious only to sustain its wasting magnificence by the silver and gold wrung from the prolific bosom of Mexico. To foster the agricultural interests of any portion of her splendid viceroyalty or her circumjacent conquests was never the favorite policy of Spain.

"To have done so would have nurtured in her remote dominions a hardy and industrious population of yeomanry, who have ever proved the peculiar dread of tyrants and the best assurance of a nation's independence.

"It was natural, then, that the royal miscreants of Spain should regard Texas with indifference, if not with a decided and malignant aversion to her improvement. But it would be both unnatural and erroneous to attribute similar motives to independent, confederate, republican Mexico. She can have no interest averse to the public weal; can feel no desire to depress the agricultural faculties of any portion of her common territory, and can entertain no disquieting jealousies that should prompt her to dread the increase or mar the prosperity of any portion of her agricultural population. These are the best, the broadest, and the most durable bases of her free institutions.

"We must look to other causes, therefore, for the lamentable negligence that has hitherto been manifested toward the prosperity of Texas. The fact of such negligence is beyond controversy. The melancholy effects of it are apparent in both her past and present condition. The cause must exist somewhere. We believe it is principally to be found in her political annexation to Coahuila. That conjunction was in its origin unnatural and constrained; and the longer it is continued the more disastrous it will prove.

"The two territories are disjunct in all their prominent respective relations. In point of locality they approximate only by a strip of sterile and useless territory, which must long remain a comparative wilderness and present many serious embarrassments to that facility of intercourse which should always exist between the seat of government and its remote population. In respect to commerce and its various intricate relations there is no community of interests between them. The one is altogether *interior*; is consequently abstracted from all participation in maritime concerns, and is naturally indifferent, if not adverse, to any system of polity that is calculated to promote the diversified and momentous interests of commerce. The other is blest with many natural advantages for extensive commercial operations, which, if properly cultivated, would render many valuable accessions to the national marine and a large increase to the national revenues. The importance of an efficient national marine is evinced not only by the history of other and older governments, but by the rich halo of glory which encircles the brief annals of the Mexican navy. In point of climate and of natural productions the two territories are equally dissimilar. Coahuila is a pastoral and a mining country; Texas is characteristically an agricultural district.

"The occupations incident to these various intrinsic properties are equally various and distinct, and a course of legislation that may be adapted to the encouragement of the habitual industry of the one district might present only embarrassment and perplexity, and prove fatally deleterious, to the prosperity of the other.

"It is not needful, therefore, neither do we desire, to attribute any sinister or invidious design to the legislative enactments or to the domestic economical policy of Coahuila (whose ascendency in the joint councils of the State gives her an uncontrolled and exclusive power of legislation), in order to ascertain the origin of the evils that affect Texas, and which, if permitted to exist, must protract her feeble and dependent pupilage to a period coeval with such existence. Neither is it important to Texas whether those evils have proceeded from a sinister policy in the predominant influences of Coahuila, or whether they are the natural results of a union that is naturally adverse to her interests. The effects are equally repugnant and injurious, whether emanating from the one or the other source.

"Bexar, the ancient capital of Texas, presents a faithful but a gloomy picture of her general want of protection and encouragement. Situated in a fertile, picturesque, and healthful region, and established a century and a half ago (within which period populous and magnificent cities have sprung into existence), she exhibits only the decrepitude of age—sad testimonials of the absence of that political guardianship which a wise government should always bestow upon the feebleness of its exposed frontier settlements. One hundred and seventeen years have elapsed since Goliad and Nacogdoches assumed the distinctive name of towns, and they are still entitled only to the diminutive appellation of villages.

"Other military and missionary establishments have been attempted, but, from the same defect of protection and encouragement, they have been swept away, and scarcely a vestige remains to rescue their locations from oblivion.

"We do not mean to attribute these specific disasters to the union with Coahuila, for we well know they transpired long anterior to the consummation of that union. But we do maintain that the same political causes, the same want of protection and encouragement, the same mal-organization and impotency of the local and minor faculties of the government, the same improvident indifference to the peculiar and vital interests of Texas, exist *now* that operated then. Bexar is still exposed to the depredations of her ancient enemies, the insolent, vindictive, and faithless Comanches. Her citizens are still massacred, their cattle destroyed or driven away, and their very habitations threatened by a tribe of erratic and undisciplined Indians, whose audacity has derived confidence from success, and whose long-continued aggressions have invested them with a fictitious and excessive terror. Her schools are neglected, her churches desolate; the sounds of human industry are almost hushed, and the voice of gladness and festivity is converted into wailing and lamentation by the disheartening and multiplied evils that surround her defenceless population. Goliad is still kept in constant trepidation, is paralyzed with all her efforts for improvement, and is harassed on all her borders by the predatory incursions of the Wacos and other insignificant bands of savages, whom a well-organized local government would soon subdue and exterminate.

"These are facts, not of history merely, on which the imagination must dwell with an unwilling melancholy, but they are events of the present day, which the present generation feel in all their dreadful reality. And these facts, revolting as they are, are as a fraction only in the stupendous aggregate of our calamities. Our misfortunes do not proceed from Indian depredations alone, neither are they confined to a few isolated, impoverished, and almost tenantless towns. They pervade the whole territory, operate upon the whole population, and are as diversified in character as our public interests and necessities are various. Texas at large feels and deplores an utter destitution of the common benefits which have usually accrued from the worst system of internal government that the patience of man ever tolerated. She is virtually without a *government*, and if she is not precipitated into all the unspeakable horrors of anarchy it is only because there is a redeeming spirit among the people which still infuses some moral energy into the miserable fragments of authority that exist among us. We are perfectly sensible that a large portion of our population, usually denominated 'the colonists' and composed of Anglo-Americans, have been greatly calumniated before the Mexican government. But could the honorable Congress scrutinize strictly into our real condition, could they see and understand the wretched confusion in all the elements of government which we daily feel and deplore, our ears would no longer be insulted nor our feelings mortified by the artful fictions of hireling emissaries from abroad, nor by the malignant aspersions of disappointed military commanders at home.

"Our grievances do not so much result from any positive misfeasance on the part of the present State authorities as from the total absence of, or the very feeble and futile dispensation of, those restrictive influences which it is the appropriate design of the social compact to exercise upon the people, and which are necessary to fulfil the ends of civil society. We complain more of the want of all the important attributes of government than of the abuses of any. We are sensible that all human institutions are essentially imperfect. But there are relative degrees of perfection in modes of government as in other matters, and it is both natural and right to aspire to that mode which is most likely to accomplish its legitimate purpose. This is wisely declared in our present State constitution to be 'the happiness of those who compose it.' It is equally obvious that the happiness of the people is more likely to be secured by a local than by a remote government. In the one case the governors are partakers, in common with the governed, in all the political evils which result to the community, and have, therefore, a personal interest in so discharging their respective functions as will best secure the common welfare.

"In the other supposition, those vested with authority are measurably exempt from the calamities that ensue an abuse of power, and may very conveniently subserve their own interests and ambition while they neglect or destroy 'the welfare of the associated.'

"But, independent of these general truths, there are some impressive reasons why the peace and happiness of Texas demand a local government. Constituting a remote frontier of the republic and bordering on a powerful nation, a portion of whose population, in juxtaposition to hers, is notoriously profligate and lawless, she requires, in a peculiar and emphatic sense, the vigorous application of such laws as are necessary not only to the preservation of good order, the protection of property, and the redress of personal wrongs, but such also as are essential to the prevention of illicit commerce, to the security of the public revenues, and to the avoidance of serious collision with the authorities of the neighboring republic. That such a judicial administration is impracticable under the present arrangement is too forcibly illustrated by the past to admit of any rational hope for the future.

"It is an acknowledged principle in the science of jurisprudence that the prompt and certain infliction of mild and humane punishment is more efficacious for the prevention of crime than a tardy and precarious administration of the most sanguinary penal code. Texas is virtually denied the benefit of this benevolent rule by the locality and character of the present government. Crimes of the greatest atrocity may go unpunished, and hardened criminals triumph in their iniquity, because of the difficulties and delays which encumber her judicial system and necessarily intervene a trial and conviction and the sentence and execution of the law.

"Our supreme tribunal of justice holds its sessions upward of seven hundred miles from our centre of population, and that distance is greatly enlarged, and sometimes made impassable, by the casualties incident to a 'mail' conducted by a single horseman through a wilderness often infested by vagrant and murderous Indians. Before sentence can be pronounced by the local courts on persons charged with the most atrocious crimes, a copy of the process must be transmitted to the assessor resident at Leona Vicario (Saltillo), who is too far removed from the scene of guilt to appreciate the importance of a speedy decision, and is too much estranged from our civil and domestic concerns to feel the miseries that result from a total want of legal protection in person and property. But our difficulties do not terminate here. After the assessor shall have found leisure to render his opinion, and final judgment is pronounced, it again becomes necessary to resort to the capital to submit the tardy sentence to the supreme tribunal for 'approbation, revocation, or modification' before the judgment of the law can be executed. Here we have again to encounter the vexations and delays incident to all governments where those who exercise its most interesting functions are removed by distance from the people on whom they operate and for whose benefit the social compact is created.

"These repeated delays, resulting from the remoteness of our courts of judicature, are pernicious in many respects. They involve heavy expenses, which, in civil suits, are excessively onerous to litigants, and give to the rich and influential such manifold advantages over the poor as to operate to an absolute exclusion of the latter from the remedial and protective benefits of the law. They offer seductive opportunities and incitements to bribery and corruption, and endanger the sacred purity of the judiciary, which, of all the branches of the government, is most intimately associated with the domestic and social happiness of man, and should, therefore, be not only sound and pure, but unsuspected of the venal infection. They present insuperable difficulties to the protective right of recusation, and virtually nullify the constitutional power of impeachment.

"In criminal actions they are no less injurious. They are equivalent to a license to iniquity, and exert a dangerous influence on the moral feelings at large. Before the tedious process of the law can be complied with, and the criminal, whose hands are perhaps imbrued in a brother's blood, be made to feel its retributive justice, the remembrance of his crime is partially effaced from the public mind, and the righteous arbitrament of the law, which, if promptly executed, would have received universal approbation and been a salutary warning to evil-doers, is impugned as vindictive and cruel. The popular feeling is changed from a just indignation of crime into an amiable but mistaken sympathy for the criminal, and an easy and natural transition is converted into disgust and disaffection toward the government and its laws.

"These are some of the evils that result from the annexation of Texas to Coahuila, and the exercise of legislative and judicial powers by the citizens of Coahuila over the citizens of Texas. The catalogue might be greatly enlarged, but we forbear to trespass on the time of the honorable Congress (confiding to the worthy citizens who shall be charged with the high duty of presenting this memorial, and the protocol of a constitution which the people of Texas have framed as the basis of their future government, the more explicit enunciation of them). Those evils are not likely to be diminished, but they be exceedingly aggravated by the fact that the political connection was formed without the cordial approbation of the people of Texas, and is daily becoming more odious to them. Although it may have received their reluctant acquiescence in its inception, before its evil consequences were developed or foreseen, the arbitrary continuance of it now, after the experience of nine years has demonstrated its ruinous tendencies, would invest it with some of the most offensive features of usurpation. Your memorialists entertain an assured confidence that the enlightened Congress of Mexico will never give their high sanction to anything that wears the semblance of usurpation or of arbitrary coercion. The idea may possibly occur, in the deliberations of the honorable Congress, that a territorial organization would cure our political maladies and effectuate the great purposes which induce this application; and plausible reasons may be advanced in favor of it. But the wisdom of Congress will readily detect the fallacy of these reasons and the mischief consequent to such vain sophistry. In this remote section of the republic a territorial government must of necessity be divested of one essential and radical principle in all popular institutions—the immediate responsibility of public agents to the people whom they serve. The appointments to office would in such case be invested in the general government; and although such appointments should be made with the utmost circumspection, the persons appointed, when once arrayed in the habiliments of office, would be too far removed from the appointing power to feel the restraints of a vigilant supervision and a direct accountability. The dearest rights of the people might be violated, the public treasures squandered, and every variety of imposition and iniquity practised, under the specious pretext of political necessity, which the far-distant government could neither detect nor control.

"And we would further present, with great deference, that the institution of a territorial government would confer upon us neither the form nor the substance of our high guarantee. It would, indeed, diversify our miseries by opening new avenues to peculation and abuse of power; but it would neither remove our difficulties nor place us in the enjoyment of our equal and vested rights. The only and adequate remedy that your memorialists can devise, and which they ardently hope the collective wisdom of the nation will approve, is to be found in the establishment of a *local State government.* We believe that if Texas were endowed with the faculties of a State government she would be competent to remedy the many evils that now depress her energies and frustrate every energy to develop and bring into usefulness the natural resources which a beneficent Providence has bestowed upon her. We believe that a local legislature, composed of citizens who feel and participate in all the calamities that encompass us, would be able to enact such conservative, remedial, and punitive laws, and so to organize and put into operation the municipal and inferior authorities of the country, as would inspire universal confidence; would encourage the immigration of virtuous foreigners, prevent the ingress of fugitives from the justice of other countries, check the alarming accumulations of ferocious Indians whom the domestic policy of the United States of the North is rapidly translating to our borders; would give impulse and vigor to the industry of the people, secure a cheerful subordination and a faithful adhesion to the State and general governments; and would render Texas what she ought to be—a strong arm of the republic, a terror to foreign invaders, and an example of peace and prosperity, of advancement in the arts and sciences, and of devotion to the union, to her sister States.

"We believe that an executive chosen from among ourselves would feel a more intense interest in our political welfare, would watch with more vigilance over our social concerns, and would contribute more effectually to the purposes of his appointment. We believe that a local judiciary, drawn from the bosom of our own peculiar society, would be enabled to administer the laws with more energy and promptitude, to punish the disobedient and refractory, to restrain the viciousness of the wicked, to impart confidence and security of both person and property to peaceable citizens, to conserve and perpetuate the general tranquillity of the State, and to render a more efficient aid to the co-ordinate powers of the government in carrying into effect the great objects of its institution.

"We believe that if Texas were admitted to the union as a separate State she would soon figure as a brilliant star in the Mexican constellation, and would shed a new splendor around the illustrious city of Montezuma. We believe she would contribute largely to the national wealth and aggrandizement, would furnish new staples for commerce and new materials for manufactures.

"The cotton of Texas would give employment to the artisans of Mexico, and the precious metals which are now flowing into the coffers of England would be retained at home to reward the industry and remunerate the ingenuity of native citizens. The honorable Congress need not be informed that a large portion of the population of Texas is of foreign origin. They have been invited here by the munificent liberality and plighted faith of the Mexican government; and they stand pledged by every moral and religious principle, and by every sentiment of honor, to requite that liberality, and to reciprocate the faithful performance of the guarantee to 'protect their liberties, property, and civil rights,' by a cheerful dedication of their moral and physical energies to the advancement of their adopted country. But it is also apparent to the intelligence of the honorable Congress that the best mode of securing the permanent attachment of such a population is to incorporate them into the federal system on such equitable terms as will redress every grievance, remove every cause of complaint, and insure not only an identity of interests, but an eventual blending and assimilation of all that is now foreign and incongruous.

"The infancy of imperial Rome was carried to an early adolescence by the free and unrestricted admission of foreigners to her social compact. England never aspired to the dominion of the seas until she had united the hardiness of Scotland and the gallantry of Ireland to her native prowess. France derives greatness from the early combination of the Salii, the Franks, and the Burgundians; and Mexico may yet realize the period when the descendants of Montezuma will rejoice that their coalition with the descendants of Fernando Cortez has been strengthened and embellished by the adoption into their national family of a people drawn by their own gratuitous hospitality from the land of Washington and of freedom. For these and other considerations your memorialists would solemnly invoke the magnanimous spirit of the Mexican nation, concentrated in the wisdom and patriotism of the federal Congress; and they would respectfully and ardently pray that the honorable Congress would extend their remedial power to this obscure section of the republic, would cast around it 'the sovereign mantle of the nation,' and adopt it into a free and plenary participation of that constitutional regime of equal sisterhood which alone can rescue it from the miseries of an ill-organized, inefficient, internal government, and can reclaim this fair and fertile region from the worthlessness of an untenanted waste or the more fearful horrors of a barbarian inundation.

"Your memorialists, on behalf of their constituents, would, in conclusion, avail themselves of this opportunity to tender to the honorable Congress their cordial adhesion to the *plan* of *Zavaleta* and to express their felicitations on the happy termination of the late unhappy conflict. They would also declare their gratitude to the patriot chief and his illustrious associates, whose propitious conquests have saved from profanation 'the august temple in which we have deposited the holy ark of our federal constitution,' and have secured the ultimate triumph of the liberal and enlightened principles of genuine republicanism. And they would unite their fervent aspirations with the prayers that must ascend from the hearts of all good Mexicans, that the Supreme Ruler of the universe, 'who doeth his will in the army of heaven and among the inhabitants of the earth,' would vouchsafe to this glorious land the blessings of peace and tranquillity, would preserve it in all future time from the horrors of civil discord, and would shed down upon its extended population the increased and increasing effulgence of light and liberty which is fast irradiating the European continent and extirpating the relics of feudal despotism, of the antiquated errors of a barbarous age, from the civilized world.

"David G. Burnet
Chairman of the Committee"

The foregoing "memorial," as well as the draft of the proposed State constitution, was presented to the Mexican Congress by General Stephen F. Austin in the month of June, A.D. 1833.

General Santa Anna now dominated Mexico, and it was his policy to centralize the functions of government in himself as far as possible. Therefore the "memorial" of the Texans, which advocated a policy diametrically the opposite of his own, met no favor at the hands of the ambitious chieftain, who caused General Austin to be arrested and thrown into prison. Here *The Father of Texas* languished in durance vile until September 1835.

In the spring of 1834 Colonel Juan Almonte was commissioned to proceed to Texas and "report the result of his observations to the executive, etc." Almonte's report, although confessedly imperfect, is worthy of reproduction here, as tending to illustrate by statistical evidence the giant strides that our commonwealth has made on the road to progress since 1834, or near half a century ago. We pass over the introductory remarks of his report, as belonging more to the domain of ostensible history, to arrive at his observations in regard to specific matters, which will furnish the data that we desire to be enabled to institute the comparison referred to. One remark of Almonte's, however, should not be passed over without some notice, as it now sounds as if uttered under the inspiration of prophecy. "I do not hesitate," he says, "particularly to assure retired officers and invalids that the best way to provide for their families is to solicit permission of the government to capitalize their pay and go and colonize Texas. There they will find peace and industry, and obtain rest in their old age, which, in all probability, will not be found in the centre of the republic."

Texas in 1834 was divided into three departments: Bexar, the Brazos, and Nacogdoches.

From San Antonio, on the west, the population extended to the Sabine River on the east, there being "not more than twenty-five leagues of unoccupied territory to occasion some inconvenience to the traveller." "In 1806 the department of Bexar contained two municipalities—San Antonio de Bexar and Goliad, the former containing a population of 5,000 souls, and the latter 1,400; total, 6,400. In 1834 there were four municipalities, with the following population respectively—San Antonio de Bexar, 2,400; Goliad, 700; Victoria, 300; San Patricio, 600, the latter an Irish settlement. Thus the Mexican population had declined from 6,400 to 3,400 between 1806 and 1834." "This is the only district of Texas in which there are no Negro laborers." "Of the various colonies introduced into it but two have prospered: one, of Mexicans, on the river Guadalupe, by the road which leads from Goliad to San

Felipe; the other, of Irish, on the road from Matamoras to Goliad. With the exception of San Patricio the entire district of Bexar is peopled by Mexicans."

"Extensive undertakings cannot be entered on in Bexar, as there is no individual capital exceeding $10,000. All the provisions raised by the inhabitants are consumed in the district. The wild horse is common, so as rarely to be valued at more than twenty *reals* [about $2.50], when caught. Cattle are cheap, a cow and calf not being worth more than $10, and a young bull or heifer not more than $5. Sheep are scarce, not exceeding 5,000 head. The whole export trade is confined to from 8,000 to 10,000 skins of various kinds, and the imports to a few articles from New Orleans, which are exchanged in San Antonio for peltry or currency.

"There is one school in the capital of the department, supported by the municipality, but apparently the funds are so reduced as to render the maintenance of even this useful establishment impossible. What is to be the fate of those unhappy Mexicans who dwell in the midst of savages without hope of civilization? Goliad, Victoria, and even San Patricio are similarly situated, and it is not difficult to foresee the consequences of such a state of things. In the whole department there is but one curate; the vicar died of cholera morbus in September last.

"The capital of the department of the Brazos is San Felipe de Austin, and its principal towns are San Felipe, Brazoria, Matagorda, Gonzales, Harrisburg, Mina, and Velasco. The district containing these towns is that generally called 'Austin's Colony.' The following are the municipalities and towns of the department, with the population: San Felipe, 2,500; Columbia, 2,100; Matagorda, 1,400; Gonzales, 900; Mina, 1,100; total, 8,000. Towns: Brazoria, Harrisburg, Velasco, Bolivar. In the population are included 1,000 Negroes, introduced under certain conditions guaranteed by the State government (*introducidos baso ciertas condiciones, guarantizadas por el gobierno del estado*); and although it is true that a few African slaves have been imported into Texas, it has been done contrary to the opinion of the respectable settlers, who were unable to prevent it. It is to be hoped that this traffic has already been stopped; and it is desirable that a law of the general Congress and of the State should fix a *maximum* period for the introduction of Negroes into Texas as servants to the impresarios, which period ought not, in my opinion, to exceed ten or twelve years, at the end of which time they should enjoy absolute liberty. The most prosperous colonies of this department are those of Austin and De Witt. Towards the northwest of San Felipe there is now a new colony, under the direction of Robertson—the same that was formerly under the charge of Austin.

"In 1833 upwards of 2,000 bales of cotton, weighing from 400 to 500 pounds each, were exported from the Brazos; and it is said that in 1832 not less than 5,000 bales were exported. The *maize* is all consumed in the country, though the annual crop exceeds 50,000 bushels. The cattle, of which there may be about 25,000 head in the district, are usually driven for sale to Natchitoches. The cotton is exported regularly from Brazoria to New Orleans, where it pays two and one-half per cent duty, and realizes from ten to ten and one-half cents per pound for the exporter after paying the cost of transportation, etc. The price of cattle varies but little throughout Texas, and is the same in the Brazos as in Bexar. There are no sheep in this district; herds of swine are numerous, and may be reckoned at 50,000 head. The trade of the department of the Brazos has reached $600,000. Taking the estimate from 1832 (the settlements having been ravaged by the cholera in 1833), the exports and imports are estimated thus: 5,000 bales of cotton, weighing 2,250,000 pounds, sold in New Orleans, and producing, at ten cents per pound, $225,000 net; 50,000 skins, at a net average of eight reals each, $50,000; value of exports, $275,000, exclusive of the sale of livestock. The imports are estimated at $325,000.

"In this department there is but one school, near Brazoria, erected by subscription, and containing from thirty to forty pupils. The wealthier colonists prefer sending their children to the United States, and those who have not the advantages of fortune care little for the education of their sons, provided they can wield the axe and cut down a tree or kill a deer with dexterity.

"The department of Nacogdoches contains four municipalities and four towns. Nachidoches municipality has a population of 3,500; that of San Augustine, 2,500; Liberty, 1,000; Johnsburg, 2,000; the town of Anahuac, 50; Bevil, 140; Teran, 10; Tanaha, 100; total population, 9,900, in which is included about 1,000 Negroes, introduced under special arrangements. Until now it appears that the New York Company are only beginning to interest themselves in settling their lands, bought or obtained by contract with Messrs. Zavala, Burnet, and Vehlein, impresarios, who first undertook the colonization of the immense tracts which they obtained of the State of Coahuila and Texas, and which are laid down on the maps of the North as 'Lands of the Galveston Bay Company.' In consequence of that transaction the company are proprietors of nearly three-fourths of the department of Nacogdoches, including the twenty leagues of boundary from that town to the Sabine. Of the contracts of Zavala, Burnet, and Vehlein some expired last year, and others will expire during the present year. The supreme government, if at all anxious to do away with a system of jobbing so ruinous to the lands of the nation at the hands of a few Mexicans and foreigners, ought, without loss of time, to adopt means to obviate the confusion daily arising out of contracts with the speculators, which create a feeling of disgust among the colonists, who are dissatisfied with the monopoly enjoyed by companies or contractors that have acquired the lands with the sole object of speculating in them. The settlements of this district have not prospered, because speculators have not fulfilled their contracts, and the scattered population is composed of individuals who have obtained one or more leagues of land from the State, and of others who, in virtue of the law of colonization inviting strangers, have established themselves wherever it appeared most convenient. But the latter have not even the titles to their property, which it would be only fair to extend for them, in order to relieve them from that cruel state of uncertainty in which some of them have been placed for several years as to whether they appertain to Mexico or the United States. And as these colonists have emigrated at their own expense, it seems just that the contractors on whose lands they have settled, and who were not instrumental to the introduction of their families, should not receive the premium allowed by law. In stipulating with those contractors (*empresarios*) both the general and State government have hitherto acted with too much negligence, and it would be well that they now seriously turn their attention to a matter so deeply important.

"There are three common schools in this department: one in Nacogdoches, very badly supported, another at San Augustine, and the third at Johnsburg.

"Texas wants a good establishment for public instruction where the Spanish language may be taught, otherwise the language will be lost. Even at present English is almost the only language spoken in this section of the republic.

"The trade of this department amounts for the year to $470,000; the exports consist of cotton, the skins of deer, otter, beaver, etc., Indian corn, and cattle. There will be exported during this year about 2,000 bales of cotton, 90,000 skins, and 50,000 head of cattle, equal in value to $205,000. The imports are estimated at $265,000; the excess in the amount of imports is occasioned by the stock which remains on hand in the stores of the dealers. There are about 50,000 head of cattle in the whole department, and prices are on a level with those in the Brazos. There are no sheep, nor pasturage adapted to them. There are about 60,000 head of swine, which will soon form another article of export. There are machines for cleaning and pressing cotton in the departments of Nacogdoches and the Brazos. There are also a number of sawmills. A steamboat is plying on the Brazos River, and the arrival of two more is expected; one for the Neches and the other for the Trinity. The amount of the whole trade of Texas for the year 1834 may be estimated at $1,400,000, tabulated as follows:

Department	Imports	Exports	Total
Bexar	$40,000	$20,000	$60,000
Brazos	325,000	275,000	600,000
Nacogdoches	265,000	205,000	470,000
Approximate contraband trade with the interior through the ports of Brazoria, Matagorda, and Copano			270,000
Grand total			$1,400,000

"Money is very scarce in Texas; not one in ten sales are made for cash. Purchases are made on credit or by barter, which gives the country the appearance of a continued fair. Trade is daily increasing, owing to the large crops of cotton and the internal consumption caused by the constant influx of emigrants from the United States."

Colonel Almonte estimated the population of Texas in 1834 at 36,300, of which 21,000 were civilized inhabitants and 15,300 Indians. The number of hostile Indians were estimated at 10,800, and of friendly tribes 4,500; of the former 9,900 are appropriated to the department of Bexar, and the remaining 900 to the Brazos.

Chapter 7

Stephen F. Austin, from his prison, wrote his countrymen on the 25th of August, 1834, in which he spoke of his vain efforts to have judicial action taken in his case. He warned his people against interfering in the political family quarrels of Mexico, as by doing so they had everything to lose and nothing to gain. He invoked the colonists to obey the president, Santa Anna, who professed to be friendly to Texas and himself, and cautioned the farmers against "inflammatory politicians," he having begun to lose confidence in all persons except those who sought their living between the handles of the plough.

Mr. Austin remained in prison from the spring of 1833 until the autumn of 1835, at which latter date he returned to Texas, and, at a public meeting in Brazoria, gave an account of his unhappy and unsuccessful stewardship. He also advised the holding of a "General Consultation," which was to deliberate upon the policy Texas ought to pursue, as elsewhere previously stated.

Previous to Austin's return the Texans had been about equally divided on the momentous question of submission or resistance to the centralization programme, which was now an accomplished fact west of the Rio Grande since the subjugation of Zacatecas. But now all parties united cordially in the manly determination of standing up for the vested constitutional rights of Texas. The émeute at Gonzales has been styled the "Lexington" of Texas. The military organization (Texan) at that town had a cannon which General Ugartechea, the commandant of San Antonio, in conformity to his purpose of disarming the Texans, wished to possess himself of. In pursuance of this object he despatched Captain Castonado with a force of men to seize the gun. The Texan force at Gonzales had been increased by volunteers from the Guadalupe, Lavaca, and Colorado rivers to one hundred and sixty-eight men, who were commanded by Colonel Moore. The affair terminated by the retreat of Castonado back to Bexar.

News of this engagement spread rapidly and electrified the people throughout the country. Volunteers hastened to Gonzales, and Captain Saviriago, who had commanded Goliad, came to Victoria to take possession of a small piece of cannon (a three-pounder) from the De Leon family. It was mounted on a pair of truck wheels, and was of little value for fighting purposes. This move was unexpected on the part of the citizens. Saviriago stated that he was acting by order of Colonel Ugartechea. Upon holding a conversation with him he informed me that he was also ordered to visit the Lavaca and Colorado settlements. He departed on his way to Lavaca River, this being late in the day. On his way he met two men and inquired of them where they were going; they replied, "Victoria." Each bore a gun. He asked why they were armed. They made some reply, but as neither could understand the others' language only a few disconnected sentences could be understood. He ordered his company to about-face and return with the men to Victoria, the men supposing by this movement that they were to be placed under a guard when they arrived in the town. They came to me to act as interpreter. I found the men were on a business trip to the town. I explained this to the captain, after which he appeared satisfied. He left the next morning and returned to Goliad. The arrested men had a letter from Captain Alley[11] informing me that his (Alley's) company would leave for Gonzales. By several men, who were soldiers of a company in Jackson County, I sent a letter to Captain Alley that I would meet him at Gonzales. I left about two days afterwards and was joined by Placido Benevidos, and arrived there safely. I found about one hundred and fifty men under different commanders. Benevidos and myself joined

---

[11] Ed. Note: There were two John Alleys among Austin's Old Three Hundred. This is the John Alley (not John C. Alley) who was not a member of the five-brother Alley family in Austin's Colony.

Captain Alley's company of about fifty men. We arrived there in the evening. Next morning it was agreed to have a grand parade. I had been a captain in New Orleans of a volunteer militia company, and had some knowledge of military drill. It was left to me to bring the company on parade, which I did. After the dismissal of the men that day I received a despatch from my friend in Goliad (Mr. T. G. Western) to the effect that the Mexican general, Cos, had arrived in Goliad with fifty cavalry and was on his way to San Antonio to take command of the place, and that he had about fifty or sixty thousand dollars in money for the purpose of paying off the Mexican army at San Antonio, which had not received pay for several months. If we could muster near one hundred men in Gonzales we could cut him off and capture him and the treasure, as Cos would leave in about two days after receiving some more money. I called a meeting of the principal officers and read my letter. Many were inclined to doubt it. Now, my friend and I had adopted an alphabet of our own to avoid detection if our messages should fall into the hands of the enemy. I produced the letter, which none could decipher; but with the key I made it plain to all. However, several objections were raised against the movement, and it was declared "a wild-goose chase." The only persons who were favorable to the affair were W. H. Jack, Colonel B. F. Smith, and Captain John Alley and his company. In the meantime I received another despatch, stating that Cos had left Goliad with about fifty-five men and the money on pack mules. I also made this letter public; but nothing was done, as only the Jackson County men were willing to take the field. Colonel Smith proposed to go and take Goliad. W. H. Jack agreeing, we started at sundown and travelled all night, and arrived at Cuero Creek next morning. Here we rested; then it was agreed that the main body should cross the Guadalupe at the old crossing. Myself and Benevidos returned to Victoria with the intention of meeting the company at the Manhuilla Creek, five miles from Goliad; but, on arriving at Victoria, we found that Collingsworth's company had passed on to Goliad and captured the place after a slight resistance.

The account of the battle of Gonzales, as given by some, would cause the world at large to believe that the engagement was a military display equal to any battle on record. The truth is this: Some of the Texas troops meeting the enemy in a thick fog, each party was taken by surprise; a few random shots were exchanged, and after the fog cleared up the Mexicans were nowhere to be found, only their trail in the direction of San Antonio, Captain Castonado thinking it safest to leave a wide space between him and the Texans. He had only twenty-five men, and was sent by Ugartechea to demand the cannon to be given up, but not to attempt to take it by force. These are the facts; notwithstanding all that has been said on the subject, there was not a man killed on either side.

Just after the men had been dismissed from Colonel Wallace's parade someone arrived in camp and reported that they had been chased by Indians within a short distance from Gonzales. Edward Burleson, who was always ready to join in an Indian fight, asked for men to follow him, and they would go in pursuit of the savages. Some twenty men responded, and came up with the Indians after going about four miles. The "red-skins," about twelve in number, retreated at once, and a running fight occurred for six or seven miles. Several Indians were unhorsed, they finally taking to the thick brush. A white boy that was with them as a prisoner was retaken. He was as ugly a specimen of humanity as I ever saw, being between fourteen and fifteen years of age, red curly hair, freckled from head to foot, and from sunburn had turned to a dark color, and from his general features it was judged he was of German descent. He was placed in charge of Mr. Beason, on the Colorado, and lived with him some months, but finally disappeared. It was supposed he returned to wild life with the Indians. The boy could speak only the Comanche language.

Captain George Collingsworth, at the head of forty men, marched to attack Goliad, which point he reached on the 9th October, 1835. Assisted by the gallant Milam, himself just from a prison in Mexico, the place was surprised and attacked. The commander, Lieutenant Colonel Sandoval, was taken prisoner when the Mexicans surrendered unconditionally. Kennedy says the Texans came into the possession of stores valued at $10,000 and two pieces of artillery by this victory.

General Austin hastily summoned volunteers, and proceeded at their head to the attack of San Antonio, where General Cos was in command of the Mexican army, he having superseded General Ugartechea. But having anticipated somewhat the thread of the narrative, I will now invite the reader's attention to other scenes before describing the stirring events that were to be enacted around the walls of San Antonio.

Of the Consultation mention has been hastily made. The duties of the members were onerous and laborious in the extreme. Continued demands upon the body were being made for clothing and subsistence for the men in the field. The mythical treasury of Texas contained not one cent, and many members of the Consultation were not on a much more solid pecuniary basis. More than one honorable member constituted himself a private committee of one to devise "ways and means" of meeting the demands of his landlord. The imperative and immediate wants of the army in front of San Antonio necessitated the adoption of the always unjust system of impressments. All food necessary for the army, as well as the means of transportation, were impressed. For all property so summarily appropriated by government the "press-master" gave orders or due-bills on the Consultation; and it is now a pleasure to be able to state that all those orders have been honored by payment, in some instances, it is true, after the lapse of considerable time.

During the sittings of the Consultation an effort was made, actuated by what motives I know not, to adjourn and the members retire to their homes. The body was convened in the early days of 1835 in San Felipe, Judge Martin of that municipality in the chair. E. Adams and others addressed the house on various topics, when Moseley Baker secured the floor. He had prepared a speech with some care, which he had privately read over to me, in which he held that the Consultation was illegally established, and that affairs would progress more satisfactorily without than through an intervention, and the sooner the members retired to their homes the better would it be for all concerned. I advised Baker not to deliver the speech, as it was calculated to distract the councils of the infant commonwealth at the moment that her destiny was hanging suspended on the issue of battle, and when, above all other times, union in the deliberative body was essential to her existence as a political entity. Baker's admirers called for him, and he delivered the remarkable and ill-timed oration.

At his conclusion General Sam Houston asked permission to submit a few remarks in regard to the political situation, which was granted him. General Houston commenced by saying that the people of Texas had assumed a grave and peculiar attitude, and that it would require the most profound thought and well-timed action on their part to be enabled to control the situation.

The people had held a convention, and the present status was in direct conformity to the specific utterances of their sovereign will. This body was the sole representative of the people. A solemn trust and confidence had been reposed in it. The Consultation could not abandon that trust with honor. A convention fresh from the people would be convened in the month of March. To that body the Consultation would be responsible for their stewardship. In the meantime no man having the best interests of Texas at heart, and who was anxious for the success of her cause, would advocate the dissolution of the Consultation and create anarchy in the midst of the desolations of war. To precipitate our unhappy condition into the miseries of chaos would be a deed of heartless depravity less excusable, and far more serious in its consequences, than the midnight application of the incendiary's torch. If there was any man present who would counsel such a suicidal course, the finger of scorn should single him out from his honorable fellows. General Houston then dwelt upon the situation of affairs at some length, and attempted to forecast the success of the patriots in the near future. Houston then turned toward Baker, and drawing his majestic figure up to its full height, and looking his writhing adversary full in the face, deliberately said, as he pointed his finger in close proximity to that gentleman's nose: "*I had rather be a slave, and grovel in the dust all my life, than a convicted felon!*"

Nothing more came of the matter. Baker tore the manuscript of his unfortunate speech into atoms, and said that designing men had made of him a "cat's paw" to draw the chestnuts out of the fire.

Houston's remark to Baker had allusion to the fact of his being a refugee from justice, he having fled his native State for the forgery of a check for $5,000, all of which he, however, subsequently paid. He was a man of some education, a very creditable lawyer, and, on the whole, Texas had within her confines much worse men than he. He afterwards became a religionist, and, after the death of his wife, took to preaching. He published a paper purporting to be his religious views, which the conference of his denomination (Methodist) pronounced heterodox and proceeded to enjoin silence upon him. But Baker declared that he could read the Bible as well as they, and that he had just as much authority to place his own construction thereon as any man.

He commanded a company at the battle of San Jacinto with marked gallantry, and died a few years afterwards.

The sittings of the Consultation, grave as was the situation of the country, were sometimes relieved of the monotonous tedium by facetious episodes. The sittings took place in a house owned by a Mr. Urbane, and which was in very close proximity to the one occupied by his family. The smoke from a stove in the "Consultation Hall" at times became intolerable, and members would be forced out into the open air for relief occasionally. Added to this nuisance was the exasperating noise of a steel mill through which Mr. Urbane passed the corn that was destined to become the daily bread of himself, family, and boarders, some of the latter of whom were members of the Consultation.

One day Mr. Martin, of Washington, better known by the sobriquet of "Ring-Tailed Panther," called the attention of the house to the intolerable annoyance occasioned by the smoke and mill. After various motions had been aimed at the subject it was finally decided to send for Mr. Urbane, whose name did not belie his polite and gentlemanly characteristics. Mr. Urbane made his appearance in obedience to the summons of the august body, and was forthwith made acquainted with the situation of affairs. He was interrogated whether he could not dispense with the active operation of the mill while the Consultation was wrestling with the fate of an infant empire. He replied that he knew of no other means whereby he could procure the "staff of life," but if his *boarders* signified their acceptance of a bill of fare in which bread was an unknown quantity, he could stand it, and all of his house. This was carrying the war into Africa, and a number of members became more disgusted with the discussion of the subject than they had been by the smoke. As to the smoke, Mr. Urbane supposed that if the stove was removed from the house the evil would be remedied. He further ventured the gratuitous observation that, impelled by his patriotism and commiseration for the poverty of his country, he had charged no rent for the use of his house, but that he did not doubt but that the august body could find better houses close at hand, etc.

The "Ring-Tailed Panther" got in a resolution or motion to the effect that Mr. Urbane be fined fifty dollars for contempt of the Consultation. But he was spared that demand upon his exchequer. This Martin was a queer genius. Illiterate and uncouth, he had good "horse sense" and was in the main actuated by correct motives.

Yokum says (*vide* vol. I. page 207) that upon the death of a favorite bear-dog Martin despatched a messenger a distance of fifty miles for a minister to preach the funeral sermon.

The preacher actually responded to the summons, imagining that some member of the family of Colonel Palmer, a son-in-law of Walker, had died. His son, from whom this latter portion of the narrative was obtained, said he heard the sermon delivered.

A party of Carankua Indians visited Goliad this year (1835) and desired to have a "pow-wow" with the big captain of the whites. Captain Dimmitt appointed Major James Kerr and myself to meet them, which we did near the old graveyard. The Indians professed themselves as anxious to give their services in the field to the cause of Texas. We dissuaded them from this project, and told them their services would not be required by either of the parties to the quarrel, and advised them to go to the bays and lagunes along the coast and live peaceably, not visiting the settlements of the whites as long as the present war continued; to all of which they assented and took their departure. We subsequently ascertained, however, that they killed several straggling white men soon after the execution of this informal treaty.

During the months of August and September, 1835, there was much uneasiness felt in regard to the threatened loss of the slave property; and the owners of slaves were disposed to favor the peace policy, although there was for them little more to hope from that horn of the dilemma than from war, if indeed as much.

The proclamation of Santa Anna announced his purpose to emancipate the slaves.

About this time I wrote a letter to an old friend living in Brazoria, Sterling McNeil, in which I stated that the emergency in which we found ourselves involved admitted of but three courses: bend to the storm and receive the iron yoke of usurpation and tyranny; "take the Sabine chute," as flying to the United States was called; or fighting it out like men. The latter alternative I took occasion to advocate in most earnest terms. Mr. McNeil handed the letter to John A. Wharton, who read it to an assembly of the people; and I have been assured that it was instrumental in a marked degree in strengthening the fortitude of many who were in doubt as to the best course to pursue.

I should have stated that "taking the Sabine chute" did not at all solve the problem, in which the Negro was so important a factor, as the laws of the United States prohibiting the slave trade were enforced against such introductions into American territory.

Years afterwards, when time had demonstrated the correctness of the views I then advocated, I endeavored to regain possession of that letter, and would have been willing to have paid a handsome sum for it. But it had been irretrievably lost.

It is a pleasure now, however, unmixed with any sentiments of selfishness, to witness, in the full-blown prosperity of my beloved State, the fruition of all my patriotic hopes and wishes. I am happy in the proud consciousness of having contributed my mite upon her altar at a time when her storm-tossed cradle was threatened by all the elements of a vindictive destruction.

My snowy locks and faltering footsteps, which have borne me far beyond the ordinary limits of human existence, admonish me that I may never live to see Texas the empire she is destined to be. But I have lived to witness her pass through the most dangerous vicissitudes that can ever beset her pathway, and I know intuitively that her destiny is no common one.

My ardent wish is that wisdom and unity shall preside over her councils, and all will be well.

Zavala succeeded Austin as chairman of the Committee of Public Safety when the latter set out at the head of his army for Bexar. This patriotic Mexican gentleman used his best endeavors to assist his compatriot by hastening to the front volunteers and material of war.

Austin arrived on the banks of the Salado, five miles east of San Antonio, on the 20th, and under flag of truce to General Cos, who refused to receive Austin's communication or to recognize Austin in military capacity, and threatened to fire on a second flag, should one be sent him.

Not being satisfied with his position on the Salado, Austin moved his camp to the Mission de Espada, ten miles south of the city, and on the San Antonio River. Austin was awaiting promised reinforcements, as giving greater hope of success.

He despatched Colonels Bowie and Fannin with ninety-two men, on the 27th, to select suitable ground for a camp nearer the city. These officers, after completing a reconnaissance of the missions below the city, encamped for the night in a bend of the river, and not two miles distant from the city, occupied by the Mexican army. The Mexicans surrounded the camp during the night, as should have been expected. Colonel Bowie says:

"The men were called to arms, but were for some time unable to discover their foes, who had entirely surrounded the position and kept up a constant firing at a distance, with no other effect than a waste of ammunition. When the fog rose it was apparent to all that we were surrounded and that a desperate fight was inevitable, all communication with the main army being cut off. Immediate preparation was made by extending our right flank (first division) to the south, and placing the second division on the left on the same side, so that they might be prepared for the enemy, should they charge into the angle, and avoid the effect of a cross-fire of our own men, and likewise form a compact body, so that either might reinforce the other at the shortest notice without crossing the angle, an exposed ground, which would have occasioned certain loss. The men, in the meantime, were ordered to clear away bushes and vines under the eminence in the rear and along the margin of the river, and at the steepest places to cut steps for foothold, in order to afford them space to form and pass, and at suitable places ascend the bluff, discharge their rifles, and fall back to reload. The work was not completed to our wish when the Mexican infantry were seen to advance, with arms trailed, to the right of the first division, and form the line of battle about two hundred yards distant from the right flank. Five companies of cavalry supported them, covering our whole front and flank.

"The engagement commenced about eight o'clock a.m. by the deadly crack of a rifle from the extreme right. The action was immediately general. The discharge from the enemy was one continued blaze of fire, while that from our own lines was more slowly delivered, but with good aim and deadly effect, each man retiring under the cover of the hill and timber to give place to others while he reloaded. The battle had not lasted more than ten minutes when a brass six-pounder was opened upon our line at a distance of eighty yards from our right flank, and charge sounded. But the cannon was cleared as if by magic, and a check put to the charge. The same experiment was resorted to, with like success, three times; the division advancing under cover of the hill at each fire, and thus approximating near the cannon and victory. 'The cannon and victory!' was truly the war cry; the enemy only fired it five times, and it had been three times cleared and their charge as often broken, when a precipitate and disorderly retreat was sounded by the Mexicans, and most readily obeyed, leaving the cannon to the victors. Thus a detachment of ninety-two men gained a complete victory over part of the main army of the central government, being at least four to one, with only the loss of one brave soldier (Richard Andrews) and none wounded."

Morphia, in his "comic" history of Texas, states that Colonel Bowie estimated the Mexican loss at about sixty killed and forty wounded, the list of killed including many officers.

The main Texan army reached the field about an hour after the enemy's retreat.

At noon the next day General Cos sent a flag of truce to General Austin, requesting permission to bury his dead, which request was granted.

This must have been a great humiliation to the proud Cos, who had so lately refused to recognize Austin in a military capacity and refused to receive his flags of truce. But the hand of war is a great leveller of pride and distinctions.

This was the "battle of Concepcion," and the Texan army encamped on the field of battle until November 2, when Austin moved to a position north of the city and encamped near San Pedro Springs. Occasional skirmishing was indulged in between detachments of the two armies. In the "Grass Fight," which almost attained the dimensions of a battle, fifty Mexicans were killed, besides a number wounded; while the Texans had two wounded and one missing.

Immediately upon the capture of Goliad by the Texans the Mexican commandant at Lapantitlan, on the Rio Nueces, near San Patricio, stopped all the traders and travelers coming east. Among these were a number of citizens of Victoria. The consequence of this action was that Lapantitlan drew down upon itself a doom which its insignificance would else have averted. The capture of this place having been decided upon by the men at Goliad, Captain Dimmitt detailed some forty men under the command of Captain Westover.

The author of this book was in Goliad at the time, and I was one of the forty who followed the lead of Captain Westover. We proceeded from Goliad to the mission of Refugio, where a few volunteers joined our party. This was on the 4th or 5th of November. We proceeded from this point to a rancho four or five miles below San Patricio.

Here a Mexican informed us that Captain Rodriguez, the commandant of Lapantitlan, was on the Goliad road, at the head of his men, expecting to intercept us. His force was estimated at eighty men or more. We immediately proceeded up the river a short distance, and with the aid of a canoe crossed the river, which was considerably swollen in volume. We arrived in front of the "formidable" fortress of Lapantitlan about dark. We proceeded to invest the place, stationing guards all around it, expecting to assault in the morning. Soon after the guards were posted two citizens of San Patricio, who knew nothing of our presence, came straggling into camp. Of course they were quite surprised and somewhat frightened, but were soon placed at ease. One of these, O'Reilly, offered to go to the fort and say to the garrison that if they would surrender they should be treated with kindness and immediately liberated, to all of which they readily complied, and we took possession of Lapantitlan. The "garrison" consisted of several Mexican soldiers; there were also a few Texan prisoners of war in the fort.

The "fort" was a simple embankment of earth, lined within by fence rails to hold the dirt in place, and would have answered tolerably well, perhaps, for a second-rate hog pen. The captured munitions of war consisted of two four-pounder cannon, eight "escopets," or old Spanish guns, and three or four pounds of powder; but no balls for the guns were discovered.

Captain Rodriguez, after learning the situation of affairs, retreated across the Nueces and took up position some miles north of us. We had pickets posted to give intelligence of the enemy's movements.

In the afternoon one-half of our men were crossed to the east bank of the river, so as to be able to meet the Mexicans, should they elect to attack from that quarter. About four o'clock in the afternoon our guards came in with the news that the enemy was advancing. We immediately made preparations to receive him by forming a line of battle near the river in some scattering timber that there abounded.

The Mexicans opened fire at a distance of two hundred yards, which we returned and with more accurate aim. A Mexican officer—a brave fellow—stood on the declivity of a slight elevation and fired guns at us as fast as his men could load and hand them to him. Major James Kerr, of Jackson County, made him the special target of his practice, and succeeded in wounding the cool fellow, who was borne from the field by two of his comrades. Very few shots were fired after this. We remained masters of the field, and the enemy retired. We had only one man wounded—William Bracken, who had just shot down a Mexican, and was reloading his rifle when he received a shot in the right hand, sweeping away three fingers. A very fine horse, bearing a splendid saddle and other accoutrements, that had escaped from some Mexican officer, came into our camp. Our entire force was crossed to the east bank of the river, after consigning the cannon, which we could not remove, to the channel of the Nueces. The night was extremely dark, and soon after crossing the river we were drenched to the skin by a heavy rain, and that was succeeded by a cold norther, which was the reverse of agreeable.

A council of war was convened, and it was decided that we should go to the edge of the prairie and camp for the night. Subsequently, however, we headed for the town of San Patricio. The citizens of this village hospitably vied with one another in their efforts to render us comfortable. A number of the men of the place had been impressed into the Mexican service by Captain Rodriguez, and their anxious wives and relatives were mourning their—supposed—unfortunate fate, as they feared that they had been killed in the battle. But the next day the patriotic citizens of "Saint Patrick" returned to their homes and wives unscathed. The next morning a flag of truce was sent in, asking permission to send in the Mexican wounded to receive surgical attention, they having no surgeon. In compliance with our permission the wounded arrived a few hours later, and among them the second officer in command, Lieutenant Marcilleno Garcia, who was mortally wounded and died the next day. Lieutenant Garcia was a particular friend of the author, who did all that was possible to mitigate his excruciating pains the few hours that his lamp of life was permitted to burn. He presented me the horse that had borne him through the battle.

With his last breath Lieut. Garcia deplored the unhappy relations existing between Texas and the mother-country in consequence of Santa Anna's ambitious purposes. He was opposed to the schemes of the wily and unreliable president-general, and at heart a sympathizer with the Texans; but, being an officer of the regular service, had no option in the premises.

Lieutenant Garcia's remains were interred by his generous enemies with the honors of war.

Some of the men discovered an oven full of tempting bread and cakes, which, in the absence of the owner, they appropriated to their own use. But presently an aged female made known her loss, and the company decreed that she should be repaid; and I, being the only Texan present who had any money, was forced to send the good woman on her way rejoicing in the possession of four silver dollars.

An uncompleted building, intended for a barrack, was burned, and we despatched a courier to Rodriguez, inviting him to another pleasant meeting; but that gentleman replied that he could not cope with the Texan rifles and could not accept the invitation. He soon after departed for Matamoras.

Before the engagement at Lapantitlan I entered the office of Captain Rodriguez, and among other papers discovered one from the authorities in Mexico, directing Rodriguez to keep a sharp lookout for Linn and Dwyer on their return from Mexico, and to embargo their money. The supposition was that we had sold our goods in Saltillo and were making home overland with the proceeds. I had sold my goods, but, as elsewhere stated, knew how to take care of both my person and funds. Dwyer, who was a partner of Captain Dimmitt, had a large stock unsold at Saltillo. He went to Zacatecas, where he remained nearly two years, claiming British protection, as he was a native of Ireland.

On our return to Goliad we were overtaken on the Aransas by Governor Viesca, late constitutional executive of Coahuila and Texas, accompanied by his secretary of state, Señor Irela, who had been recently imprisoned at Monterey by order of General Santa Anna. The governor was escorted by a company of cavalry who had made good their escape from centralized Mexico.

On arriving at Goliad I left the army for home in order to attend the Consultation, of which I was a member. I proceeded to San Felipe, where that august body was in session, and upon presenting my credentials was sworn in and took a seat.

Mr. Viesca expected on arriving at San Felipe to be recognized as governor of Texas, as he had been so elected by the popular vote and his term had not expired. The Consultation, however, thought otherwise. The governor, despairing of official recognition, retired with his secretary of state to the United States, where he remained two years, when he was permitted to return to his home.

Governor Viesca was an affable gentleman, a thorough scholar, an elegant writer, and a sagacious statesman. His publication on the impending crisis portrayed with prophetic foresight the events that would necessarily follow Santa Anna's usurpation, in so far as Texas was concerned. He cited the parallel causes that produced the revolution that severed the American colonies from Great Britain, and ventured the prediction that if Santa Anna persisted in his autocratic course that Texas would be irremediably lost to Mexico.

I remained at San Felipe, attending the sittings of the Consultation, until intelligence reached us that Santa Anna was en route for Texas at the head of a formidable army, when I applied for leave of absence and returned home.

At the pending election, and against my will, I was chosen alcalde of Victoria. I caused the name of Garcia to be placed in nomination, and worked to secure his election; but he did the same thing for me, and caused my election by a majority of sixteen votes.

The Consultation now ordered the election of delegates to the convention which was to be convened at Washington on the 1st March,

1836. I was elected a member of that body, together with José M. J. Carbajal.

We were kept in a constant state of excitement and apprehension during the months of January and February by the reported movements and intentions of Santa Anna. We maintained regular communications with Goliad and San Antonio; and as the prevailing opinion was to the effect that Santa Anna could not possibly arrive sooner than the 1st of April, I took my departure for the town of Washington, where the convention was to be held; and on reaching the Lavaca River I met a courier from the town of Gonzales with the startling intelligence that Santa Anna had entered San Antonio. I, in company with others, returned home to look after our families. This episode precluded me from sharing the honor with others of signing "The Declaration of Independence."

On my arrival at Victoria I found the news of Santa Anna's arrival confirmed, and that his army was estimated at between four and five thousand men; opinions were various as to the number, some placing it as high as six thousand men. There were in Victoria two or three companies en route to Goliad, where Colonel Fannin, at the head of some American volunteers, was posted. No movement was made in this vicinity, so far as my observation extended, until the sad intelligence came of the fall of the Alamo. During this interval, however, an order passed to Colonel Fannin from General Sam Houston directing him to retire to Victoria with his command, and there await further orders. This order was conveyed through a Captain Tarleton, who stated that it was General Houston's intention to concentrate all the available forces of Texas, so as to be able to encounter the legions of Santa Anna with success. Fannin made no attempt to execute this command for ten or twelve days. The major portion of his command were volunteers from the United States, who had come, they said, to have a brush with the Mexicans, and they feared that by leaving Goliad they would lose the opportunity for so doing. In justice to the lamented Fannin it may be said, doubtless with truth, that he found himself utterly powerless to control his insubordinate though brave and generous men. This total disregard for the primary duty of a soldier must have been excruciatingly galling to the high and sensitive spirit of the gallant Fannin.

I, as alcalde of Victoria, directed the citizens to avail themselves of all means of transportation in order to remove their families to a place of safety. The citizens responded that they had twenty yoke of oxen in readiness for the emergency. The following communications speak for themselves:

"Fort Goliad, February 14, 1836

"Señor J. J. Linn:

"Please let the bearer have the corn which I contracted for from Mr. King, and on delivery it shall be paid for.
"Y. Dedrick, *Commissariat*
Lieut. Thornton, *Commandant*
Approved:
J. W. Fannin
Colonel Commanding Army of Texas

"P.S. Mr. Linn: You will hasten the corn forward, as we are without bread. Also recommend to me some suitable person, well acquainted on the Guadalupe and Lavaca, for contractor and wagonmaster, to aid in forwarding provisions and ammunition from Dimmitt's Landing. In the meantime please take some measures to furnish us some, and the army at Bexar as well. Push forward all mounted volunteers to aid me in driving in all the stock to the east.
"J. W. Fannin
Colonel Commanding Army of Texas
Goliad, February 14, 1836"

The foregoing letter was handed me by an officer in charge of a company of twenty-five men. I objected to the demands at first, regarding my first duty as due to my immediate townspeople. Should we send Fannin all our means of transportation, and disaster should befall his command, our own people would be left at the mercy of the invader. But finally twenty yoke of oxen were delivered to the officer, who proceeded with them to Goliad. But Fannin was now compelled to await the return of the companies of King and Ward, whom he had sent to Refugio to escort persons wishing to seek safety in flight to Goliad. This occupied seven or eight precious days, and was the immediate cause of the deplorable disaster that was so soon to befall him.

(Copy of letter written by Fannin)
"Goliad, 28th February, 1836

"Mr. Jos. Mims:

"The advice which I gave you a few days ago is too true. The enemy have the town of Bexar, with a large force, and I fear will soon have our brave countrymen in the Alamo. Another force is near me, and crossed the Nueces yesterday morning and attacked a party by surprise under Colonel Johnson, and routed them, killing Captain Pearson and several others after they had surrendered. I have about four hundred and twenty men here, and, if I can get provisions in tomorrow or next day, can maintain myself against any force. I will never give up the ship while there is a pea in the dish. If I am whipped it will be well done, and you may never expect to see me. I hope to see all Texans in arms soon. If not we shall lose our homes and must go east of the Trinity for a while. Look to our property; save it for my family, whatever may be my fate. I expect some in about this time by Coagly, and wish you would receive and take care of it. I now tell you, be always ready. . . . If my family arrive, send my wife this letter. Inquire of McKinney. Hoping for the best, and prepared for the worst, I am, in a devil of a bad humor.

"Farewell,
J. W. Fannin, Jr."

Chapter 8

Recurring to the thread of the narrative, dropped in a former chapter, regarding Austin's operations in front of San Antonio: The army lay around the walls of the city from the 2nd November, with the exception of a few skirmishes and partial engagements, in inglorious idleness until December 4, when an order was given to break up camp and retire into winter quarters.

"*Glorious old Ben Milam*" called for volunteers, and, three hundred responding, himself and Colonel Frank W. Johnson led them to the attack. After several days of terrible fighting, General Cos surrendered and departed for the Rio Grande with one thousand one hundred and five of his men, the remaining one thousand four hundred electing to remain in San Antonio.

The brave Milam fell in this glorious battle.

Much that is highly interesting must now be passed over relative the history of those stirring events, which were to prove but the precursors of events yet more stirring, more sadly fatal, than Texas in her eventful career had ever known. We left the gallant Fannin uttering his last words to the outside world at Goliad, where the meshes of fate were silently but surely encircling him, yet, with the spirit of the brave and generous, commiserating the probable destiny of his beleaguered compatriots in the Alamo. Of that more than "*the Thermopylae*" of Texas, first; and then its twin sister in sad and pathetic history—The *Massacre of Fannin* and his men!

In presenting the details of the Alamo tragedy I unhesitatingly adopt the narrative of my friend Reuben M. Potter, Esq., as being the most correct version extant. Mr. Potter estimates the entire force of Santa Anna, upon entering Texas, at seven thousand men of all arms. The subdivisions consisted of two regiments of horse and thirteen battalions of foot. The main army, commanded by Santa Anna in person, advanced from Laredo upon San Antonio in four successive detachments. This was rendered necessary by the scarcity of pasturage and water on certain portions of the route. The lower division, commanded by Brigadier General Urrea, moved upon Goliad from Matamoras in one body. It consisted of the cavalry regiment of Cuatla, the infantry battalion of Yucatan, and some companies of permanent militia.

Potter says:

"The aforesaid battalion, which I counted, numbered three hundred and fifty-odd men; the regiment of dragoons about the same; and the whole made nine hundred or one thousand.

"The advanced detachment from Laredo, consisting of the dragoon regiment of Dolores and one or two battalions, arrived in San Antonio in the latter part of February; I think the 21st. The Alamo was at that time garrisoned by one hundred and fifty-six men, under Lieutenant Colonel Travis. James Bowie was, I think, considered his second in command. David Crockett, of Tennessee, also belonged to this garrison, having joined it a few weeks before; but whether he ever had any command or not I have never heard.

"One of the most estimable and chivalrous men attached to it was J. B. Bonham, Esq., of South Carolina, who had recently come to volunteer in the service of Texas; but what his position was in the fortress I am unable to say. Travis had been commissioned by the provisional government of Texas a lieutenant colonel of regular cavalry; but his corps had not been raised, and the men whom he now commanded were volunteers. Some of them had been engaged in the recent siege of San Antonio, when Cos capitulated, and others had more lately arrived from the United States. Among them were only three Mexicans of San Antonio; and what proportion the old residents of Texas bore to the newly arrived among them I am unable to say. No regular scouting service seems to have been kept up from Travis's post; for, though the enemy was expected, his near approach was not known till his advance of dragoons were seen descending the slope west of the San Pedro. The guard in town is said to have retired in good order to the fort; yet so complete was the surprise of the place that one or more American residents, engaged in mercantile business, fled to the Alamo, leaving their stores open. After the enemy entered the place a cannon shot from the Alamo was answered by a shell from the invaders; and I think little more in the way of hostility was done that day.

"The fortress was not immediately invested, and the few citizens who had taken refuge in it succeeded in leaving it that night.

"On the 23rd Santa Anna, with the second division, arrived, and on the same day a regular siege was commenced. Its operations, which lasted eleven days, are, I think, correctly given in Yokum's *History of Texas*, though he did not succeed in getting a true account of the assault. Several batteries were opened on successive days on the north, south, and east of the Alamo, where there were then no houses to interfere with the operations. The enemy had no regular siege train, and only light field pieces and howitzers. A breach was opened in the northern barrier, but the buildings seem not to have been severely battered. The operations of the siege consisted of an active, though not very efficient, cannonade and bombardment, with occasional skirmishing by day and frequent, harassing alarms by night, designed to wear out the garrison for want of sleep. No assault was attempted, as has often been asserted, till the final storming of the place; neither was the investment so close as to prevent the passage of couriers and the entrance of one small reinforcement, for on the night of the 1st March a company of thirty-two men from Gonzales made its way through the enemy's lines and entered the Alamo, never again to leave it. This raised the force of the garrison to one hundred and eighty-eight men, as none of the original number had yet fallen. There could have been no great loss on either side until the final assault. Santa Anna, after calling a council of war on the 4th March, fixed upon the morning of Sunday, the 6th, as the time for the final assault. Before narrating it, however, I must first describe the Alamo as it then existed. It had been founded soon after the first settlement of the vicinity, and, being originally built as a place of safety for the settlers and their property in case of Indian hostility, with sufficient room for that purpose, it had neither the strength nor compactness, nor the arrangement of dominant points, which belong to a regular fortification. As its area contained between two and three acres, a thousand men could have barely sufficed to man its defences, and before a heavy siege train its walls would soon have crumbled. It was resolved by Santa Anna that the assault should take place at early dawn. The order for the attack, which I have read, but have no copy of, was full and precise in its details, and was signed by Brigadier General Amador as chief of staff. The besieging force consisted of the battalions of Toluca, Jimenes, Matamoras, *los zapadores* (the sappers), and another, which I think was that of Guerrero, and the dragoon regiment of Dolores. The infantry were directed, at a certain hour between midnight and dawn, to form at a convenient distance from the fort in four columns of attack and a reserve. This disposition was not made by battalions, for the light companies of all of them were incorporated with the zapadores to form the reserve, and some other transpositions may have been made. A certain number of scaling ladders and axes were to be borne by particular columns. The cavalry were to be stationed at various points around the fortress to cut off fugitives. From what I have learned of men engaged in the action, it seems that these dispositions were changed on the eve of attack so far as to combine the five bodies of infantry into three columns of attack. This included the troops designated in the order of attack as reserves; and the only actual reserve that remained was the cavalry. The immediate command of the assault was entrusted to General Castrillon, a Spaniard by birth, and a brilliant soldier. Santa Anna took his station, with a part of his staff and all the regimental bands, at a battery south of the Alamo, and near the old bridge, from which a signal was to be given by a bugle note for the columns to move simultaneously at double-quick time against various quarters of the fortress. One, composed mainly of the battalion of Toluca, was to enter the north breach, the other two to move against the southern side; one to attack the gate of the large area, the other to storm the chapel. By the timing of the signal it was calculated the columns would reach the foot of the wall just as it became light enough to operate.

"When the hour came the batteries and the music were alike silent, and a single blast of the bugle was at first followed by no sound save the rushing tramp of soldiers. The guns of the fortress soon opened upon them, and then the bands at the south battery struck up the assassin notes of *deguello*! But a few and not very effective discharges from the works could be made before the enemy was under them; and it is thought that the worn and wearied garrison was not till then fully mustered. The Toluca column arrived first at the foot of the wall, but was not the first to enter the area. A large piece of cannon at the northwest angle of the area probably commanded the breach. Either this or the deadly fire of the riflemen at that point, where Travis commanded in person, brought the column to a disordered halt, and its leader, Colonel Duque, fell dangerously wounded; but while this was occurring one of the other columns entered the area by the gate or by an escalade near it. The defence of the outer walls had now to be abandoned, and the garrison took refuge in the buildings. It was probably while the enemy were pouring in through the breach that Travis fell at his post, for his body was found beside the gun just referred to. All this passed within a few minutes after the bugle sounded. The early loss of the outer barrier, so thinly manned, was inevitable; and it was . . . till the garrison became more concentrated as to the space, not as to unity, for there was no communicating between the buildings, nor, in all cases, between the rooms. There was now no retreating from point to point, and each group of defenders had to fight and die in the den in which it was brought to bay. From the doors, windows, and loopholes of the several rooms around the area the crack of the rifle and hiss of the bullet came fierce and fast; as fast the enemy fell and recoiled in his first efforts to charge. The gun by the side of which Travis lay was now turned against the buildings, as were also some others, and shot after shot in quick succession was sent crashing through the doors and barricades of the several rooms. Each ball was followed by a storm of musketry and a charge, and thus room after room was carried at the point of the bayonet, when all within them died fighting to the last. The struggle was made up of a number of separate and desperate combats, often hand-to-hand, between squads of the garrison and bodies of the enemy. The bloodiest spot about the fortress was the long barrack and the ground in front of it, where the enemy fell in heaps.

"In the meantime the turning of Travis's gun had been imitated by the garrison. A small piece on the roof of the chapel or one of the other buildings was turned against the area while the rooms were being stormed. It did more execution than any other cannon of the fortress, but, after a few effective discharges, all who manned it fell under the enemy's fire. Crockett had taken refuge in a room of the lower barrack near the gate. He either garrisoned it alone or was left alone by the fall of his companions, when he sallied forth to meet his fate in the face of the foe, and was shot down. Bowie had been severely hurt by a fall from a platform, and, when the attack came on, was confined to his bed in a room of the upper barrack. He was there killed on his couch, but not without resistance, for he is said to have shot down with his pistols one or more of the enemy as they entered his chamber.

"The church was the last point taken. The column which moved against it, consisting of the battalion of Jimenes and other troops, was at first repulsed, and took refuge among some old houses outside of the barrier, near its southwest angle, till it was rallied and led on by General Amador. It was soon joined by the rest of the force, and the church was carried by a *coup de main*. Its inmates, like the rest, fought till the last, and continued to fire from the upper platforms after the enemy occupied the floor of the building. A Mexican officer told of seeing a man shot in the crown of the head in this melee. During the closing struggle Lieutenant Dickinson, with his child in his arms—or tied to his back, as some accounts say—leaped from an upper window, and both were killed in the act. Of those he left behind him the bayonet soon gleaned what the bullet missed, and in the upper part of the church the last defender must have fallen. The morning breeze which received his parting breath probably still fanned his flag above that fabric ere it was pulled down by the victors.

"*The Alamo had fallen!*

"The action, according to Santa Anna's report, lasted thirty minutes. It was certainly short, and possibly no longer space passed between the moment the enemy fronted the breach and that when resistance died out. Some of the incidents, which have to be related separately, no doubt occurred simultaneously and occupied very little time. The account of the assault which Yokum and others have adopted as authentic is evidently one which popular tradition has based on conjecture. By a rather natural inference it assumes that the enclosing wall of the fortress was its principal work, that in storming this the main conflict took place, and that after it was entered nothing more than the death struggle of a few occurred. The truth is, that extensive barrier proved to be nothing more than the outworks, speedily lost, while the buildings constituted the citadel and the scene of the sternest resistance. That Santa Anna himself was under the works urging on the escalade in person is exceedingly fabulous.

"A Negro boy belonging to Travis; the wife of Lieutenant Dickinson; Mrs. Alsbury, a native of San Antonio; and a Mexican woman and two children, were the only inmates of the fortress whose lives were spared. The children were those of the two females whose names are given. Lieutenant Dickinson commanded a gun in the east upper window of the church. His family was probably in one of the two small upper rooms of the fort. This will account for his being able to take one of his children to the rear platform while the building was being stormed. A small irrigating canal runs below the window referred to, and his aim in the desperate attempt at flight was probably to break his fall by leaping into the water; but the shower of bullets that greeted him rendered the precaution as needless as it was hopeless.

"About the time the outer barriers were carried a few men leaped from them and attempted to escape, but were all cut down by the cavalry. Half an hour or more after the action was over a few men were found concealed in one of the rooms under some mattresses; General Houston, in a letter of the 11th, says as many as seven, but I have generally heard them spoken of as only three or four. The officer to whom they were first reported entreated Santa Anna to spare their lives; but he was sternly rebuked and the men ordered to be shot, which was done. Owing to the hurried and confused manner in which the mandate was obeyed a Mexican soldier was accidentally killed with them.

"Castrillon was the soul of the assault. Santa Anna remained at the south battery, with the music of the whole army and a part of his staff, till he supposed the place was nearly mastered, when he moved up with that escort towards the Alamo, but returned again upon being greeted by a few rifle balls from the upper windows of the church. He, however, entered the area towards the close of the scene, and directed some of the last details of the butchery."

General Bradburn informed Mr. Potter that about five hundred Mexicans were killed and wounded. Of these he estimated that three hundred were permanently lost to the service, including with those slain outright the disabled and those who died of their wounds subsequently. Says Mr. Potter in his admirable pamphlet, *The Fall of the Alamo, etc.*:

"Santa Anna, when he marched for Texas, had counted on finding a fortified position in the neighborhood of San Antonio, but not at the Alamo; for he supposed, with good reason, that the 'Mission of Concepcion' would be selected. The small area of that strong building, which had room enough for Travis's force, and not too much, and its compactness, which would have given better range for his cannon, would have made it a far better fortress than the Alamo, and earthworks of no great extent would have covered the garrison's access to the river. The advantages of the position must have been known to Travis, and that he did not avail himself of it was probably owing to his imperfect command of men unwilling to leave their town associations. An attempt to move might break up the garrison. The neglect of scouting service, before alluded to, indicates a great lack of subordination; for

Travis, who, during the late siege of Bexar, had been the efficient head of that branch of duty, must have been aware of its importance. On the 24th February he thus wrote: 'When the enemy appeared in sight we had not three bushels of corn. We have since found in deserted houses eighty or ninety bushels, and got into the walls twenty or thirty beeves.' This omission to provide, remedied so late by accident, must have been owing more to the commander's lack of control, and to the occupation of his mind incident to it, than to his want of foresight. His men were willing to die by him, but, I infer, not ready to obey in what did not immediately concern fighting.

"I am tempted here to speculate briefly on the bearing which it might have had on the campaign had Travis changed his post to the 'Mission,' strengthened it to the best of his ability, and secured a supply of provisions for a few weeks. The great importance Santa Anna attached to an early blow and rapid movement would probably have induced him to make an assault there as early, or nearly so, as he did at the Alamo; and there, even had his force been stronger, I am confident the result would have been different.

"Instead of the panic which the fall of the Alamo spread through the land, sending fugitives to the Sabine, a bloody repulse from Concepcion would have filled Texas with exultation and sent men in crowds to Houston's camp. The fortress could then have held out till relieved, and the war have been finished probably west of the Guadalupe. Its final results could not have been more disastrous to the invaders than they eventually were, but a large extent of country would have been saved from invasion and partial devastation. Of the foregoing details that do not refer to documentary authority I obtained many from General Bradburn, who arrived at San Antonio a few days after the action and gathered them from officers who were in it. A few I had, through a friend, from General Amador. Others, again, I received from three intelligent sergeants, who were men of fair education, and, I think, truthful. One of these, Sergeant Becero, of the battalion of Matamoras, who was captured at San Jacinto, was for several years my servant in Texas."

The Mexicans made three piles of the bodies of the slaughtered garrison a few hours after the action, and burned them.

On the 25th of February, a year afterwards, Colonel Seguin collected the remaining bones, and, placing them in a coffin, had them interred with due solemnity and with military honors.

It will certainly not be necessary for me to make any excuses for appropriating in so great a measure Mr. Potter's incomparable account of the "Fall of the Alamo," as in correctness of detail and purity of style it cannot be surpassed.

The soul-stirring "Hymn of the Alamo" that follows is from the same gifted pen:

Hymn of the Alamo

By Reuben M. Potter

Rise! Man the wall! Our clarion blast
Now sounds its final reveille;
This dawning morn shall be the last
Our fated band shall ever see.
To life—but not to hope—farewell!
Yon trumpet's clang, and clarion's peal,
And storming shout, and clash of steel
Is ours, but not our country's knell!
Welcome the Spartan death!
'Tis no despairing strife.
We fall! We die! But our expiring breath
Is Freedom's birth of life.

Here, on this new Thermopylae,
Our monument shall tower on high,
And "*Alamo*" hereafter be
On bloodier fields the battle cry!

> Thus Travis from the ramparts cried,
> And, when his warriors saw the foe
> Like whelming billows move below,
> At once each dauntless heart replied:
> Welcome the Spartan death!
> 'Tis no despairing strife.
> We fall! but our expiring breath
> Is Freedom's dawn of life.
>
> They come! Like autumn's leaves they fall,
> Yet hordes on hordes still onward rush;
> With gory tramp they mount the wall,
> Till numbers the defenders crush,
> And earth drank blood like copious rain!
> Well may the ruffians quake to tell
> How Travis and his hundred fell
> Amid a thousand foemen slain!
> They died the Spartan's death,
> But not in hopeless strife;
> Like brothers died, and their expiring breath
> Was Freedom's dawn of life.

Notes on the fall of the Alamo

"Deguello."—No quarter.

"It is a fact not often remembered that Travis and his men died under the Mexican federal flag of 1824, instead of the 'Lone Star,' although the independence of Texas, unknown to them, had been declared four days before. They died for a republic whose existence they never knew."

Of the force that attacked Fannin, Mr. Potter considers that it consisted simply of this lower division. It consisted of about three hundred cavalry, three hundred regular infantry, and three hundred permanent militia, or nine hundred, and certainly not exceeding one thousand, men.

Travis encountered much the superior force, but at long range he had a much better position than Fannin. After the assault, however, Travis's was as lamentable a situation as that occupied by the heroic Fannin, surrounded by enemies, and rendered inactive by the Plutonian darkness of that fatal *noche* tryst.

The last words of Travis were, "*No rendirse muchachos!*" I obtained this from "Old Borgarra," who was among them till the last, and who escaped and arrived at Gonzales to give the news that the "Alamo had fallen." He was an aged man, an admirer of Travis and a friend to Texas, though upon his arrival at Gonzales he was imprisoned as a spy when he gave the information above stated.

The subjoined account of the visit of Mrs. Hannig, the widow of Captain Dickinson, to the scene of the terrible tragedy of the fall of the Alamo, after an interval of forty years, will prove of interest to the reader.

Alas! What must have been her emotions upon once more pressing with her feet the soil that so greedily drank up the blood of heroes, and viewing again the self-same walls that stood the centre of attack and defence on that frightful day? To us the scene is pathetic; but to *her*?

The Heroine of the Alamo.

The *San Antonio Express* chronicles a visit to the tragic scene of her infancy of Mrs. Susan J. Hannig, of Austin, the only survivor of the massacre at the fall of the Alamo:

"She is a Tennesseean by birth, is now sixty-six years of age, and, when the Alamo fell, lost her husband, Captain Dickinson. Just before the Mexicans arrived, headed by Santa Anna, she was, together with her child, at the Musquiz house, near Main Plaza. The enemy appeared first in swarms early in the morning in the southwestern suburbs of the city. Their forces were from ten to thirteen thousand strong. As soon as they were announced to be coming her husband rode up to the door of her abode, and called to her to seize her child and take refuge in the Alamo. She mounted the bare back of the horse he rode, behind his saddle, and, holding her child between her left arm and breast, soon reached the old church. An apartment was assigned her, while her husband turned away, after an embrace and a kiss, and an eternal adieu, to meet his obligations to his fellow men and his country. By this time the Mexican bugles were sounding the charge of battle, and the cannon's roar was heard to reverberate throughout the valley of the San Antonio. But about one hundred and sixty sound persons were in the Alamo, and when the enemy appeared overwhelmingly upon the environs of the city to the west, and about where the International depot now stands, the noble Travis called up his men, drew a line with his sword, and said: 'My soldiers, I am going to meet the fate that becomes me. Those who will stand by me, let them remain; but those who desire to go, let them go—and who crosses the line that I have drawn shall go!' The scene is represented by Mrs. Hannig to have been grand. The heroes defied the Mexicans, though the former were but a handful and the Aztec horde came on like the swoop of a whirlwind. Organized into divisions, they came in the form of a semicircle that extended from northeast to southeast, but the strongest attack was from about where the military plaza is, and from a division that marched up from the direction of the Villita. Three times they were repulsed, and the two cannon, planted high upon the ramparts, carried dismay with their belches of fire and lead. There was indeed a resolution to battle to the end. And that fatal end came, and brought with it horrors of which even the vivid conception of Crockett could not have dreamed. She can give but little of the struggle, as she was in a little dark room in the rear of the building. The old lady recognized almost every stone, however, and the arch overhead and the corners, she said, with tears in her eyes, came back as vividly to memory as though her experiences of yore had been but yesterday. She showed the reporter where her couch had stood, and the window through which she peeped to see the blood of noble men seeping into the ground and the bodies of heroes lying cold in death. It was in this room that she saw the last man fall, and he was a man named Walker, who had often fired the cannon at the enemy. Wounded, he rushed into the room and took refuge in a corner opposite her own. By this time the Alamo had fallen and the hordes of Santa Anna were pouring over its ramparts, through its trenches and its vaults. The barbarous horde followed the fated Walker, and, as Mrs. Hannig describes the scene, 'they shot him first, and then they stuck their bayonets into his body and raised him up like a farmer does a bundle of fodder with his pitchfork when he loads his wagon.' Then she says they dropped the body. They were all bloody, and crimson springs coursed the yard. What became of her husband, Al Marion[12] Dickinson, she cannot tell, but saw him last when he went from her presence with gun in hand to die for his country. She says that for a while she feared her own fate, but soon was assured by an English colonel in the Mexican army that the Mexicans were not come to kill women but to fight men. Through the intervention of Almonte she was permitted to leave the city on a horse and carry her child with her.

"After leaving on the horse she proceeded a short distance beyond the Salado, when she met with Travis's servant, who had escaped from the guard and was lurking in the brush. The servant recognized her and followed after her, and when about fifteen miles distant three men were observed approaching. The heart of the woman did not fail, but the servant feared Indians. Said she, under these circumstances: "This is a bald prairie, and if it is an enemy we must meet them face to face." But the apprehensions of the party were assuaged when it was discovered that the dreaded forms were Deaf Smith, Robert E. Handy, and Captain Karnes, sent out by General Sam Houston to ascertain the condition of the garrison of the Alamo. It was a meeting of friends, and soon Mrs. Dickinson, now Mrs. Hannig, reached Gonzales."

---

[12] Ed Note: Almaron Dickinson.

List of the heroes of the Alamo

W. B. Travis, James Bowie, David Crockett, J. B. Bonham

M. Autry	_____ Cockran
R. Allen	G. W. Cottle
M. Andress	J. Dust
_____ Ayres	J. Dillard
_____ Anderson	A. Dickinson
W. Blazeby	C. Déspalier
J. B. Bowman	L. Davell
_____ Baker	J. C. Day
S. C. Blair	J. Dickens
_____ Blair	_____ Devault
_____ Brown	W. Dearduff
_____ Bowin	I. Ewing
_____ Balentine	T. R. Evans
J. J. Baugh	D. Floyd
_____ Burnell	J. Flanders
_____ Butler	W. Fishbaugh
J. Baker	_____ Forsyth
_____ Burns	G. Fuga
_____ Bailey	J. C. Goodrich
J. Beard	J. George
_____ Bailess	J. Gaston
_____ Bourn	J. C. Garrett
R. Cunningham	C. Grimes
J. Clark	_____ Gwyn
J. Cane	J. E. Garwin
_____ Cloud	_____ Gillmore
S. Crawford	_____ Hutchason
_____ Cary	S. Hollaway
W. Cummings	_____ Harrison
R. Crossan	_____ Hieskell

J. Hayes
_____ Horrell
_____ Harris
_____ Hawkins
J. Holland
W. Hersie
_____ Ingram
_____ John
J. Jones
L. Johnson
C. B. Jamison
W. Johnson
T. Jackson
D. Jackson
_____ Jackson
G. Kemble
A. Kent
W. King
_____ Kenney
J. Kenney
_____ Lewis
W. Linn
Wm. Lightfoot
J. Lonly
_____ Lanio
W. Lightfoot
G. W. Linn
_____ Lewis
W. Mills
_____ Micheson
E. T. Mitchell
E. Melton
_____ McGregor
T. Miller

J. McCoy
E. Morton
R. Mussulman
_____ Milsop
R. B. Moore
W. Marshall
_____ Moore
R. McKenney
_____ McCaferty
J. McGee
G. W. Main
M. Querry
G. Nelson
_____ Nelson
J. Noland
_____ Nelson
Wm. G. Nelson
C. Ostiner
_____ Pelone
C. Parker
N. Pollard
G. Paggan
S. Robinson
_____ Reddinson
N. Rough
_____ Rusk
_____ Robbins
W. Smith
_____ Sears
C. Smith
_____ Stockton
_____ Stewart
A. Smith
J. C. Smith

_____ Sewall
A. Smith
_____ Simpson
R. Star
_____ Starn
N. Sutherland
W. Summers
J. Sumerline
_____ Thompson
_____ Tomlinson
E. Taylor
G. Taylor
J. Taylor
W. Taylor
_____ Thornton
_____ Thomas
J. M. Thurston

_____ Valentine
L. J. Wilson
_____ Williamson
D. Walsh
_____ Washington
D. Wilson
W. Wells
C. Wright
R. White
T. Walters
J. White
J. Wilson
_____ Warner
J. Washington
_____ Warnall
D. Wilson
A. Wolf

<u>Mexicans</u>

_____ Badilla
Antonio Fuentes
Gerogorea Esparza
Toribio Losoya

Andres Nava
José Maria Guerrero
Juan Abamello

Chapter 9

The curtain now rises upon the second act of the tragedy, with the ill-fated Fannin and his comrades in the cast of characters. Dr. Barnard's account of the "Goliad Massacre" is doubtless the most correct and complete extant; and, desiring to place in more durable form so invaluable a chapter in Texas history, I cheerfully transcribe from the columns of the *Goliad Guard* for 1875 the verbatim report:

"Whenever he had an enterprise of activity that required prompt courage to overcome danger and win success, he [Fannin] had sustained himself and acquired the confidence of his men. But his position was getting perplexed now and dangerous. The loss of Grant and Johnson's men, the now certain anticipation of the loss of the Alamo, and the delay of the people in turning out to defend the frontier, where so much was at stake, served to cover our prospects with a gloom that deepened more and more, and was destined not to be expelled until after unparalleled scenes of barbarity and murder had been perpetrated and the country deluged with blood.

"Thursday, March 10, 1836, a party of sixteen or eighteen men of Captain Shackelford's company, under command of Lieutenant Francis, were ordered down to the ranchos occupied by the citizens of Goliad, and about fifteen miles below the town. The principal object was to investigate some reports of there being Mexican soldiers among them as spies, who were gaining intelligence of our movements and designs, to report the same to the enemy. Tired of the monotony of life in the fort, and wishing for some exercise in the open country, I obtained leave to go with them. The expedition was of no importance in itself, and would have passed into oblivion had it not been that I preserved the notes I then made, which thus enable me with certainty to fix the dates of subsequent occurrences. I had kept a regular journal up to this time, but afterwards lost it, together with all other papers and some clothing, at the time of our battle and capture. These notes had remained in my pocket, where I providentially discovered them after losing everything else, and have carefully preserved them until this time. We left the fort and went down on the west side of the river six miles to a creek called the Candia, and halted. We here met some teams conveying corn to the fort. A drove of beeves for the same destination was also driven by. We went on about three miles further, and camped in a thicket. We left early on the morning of Friday, the 11th, and went to some cabins, but discovered nothing to confirm our suspicions. We then, after procuring something to eat, went down a few miles farther and crossed over the river to where the absconded citizens of Goliad were living. They received us kindly and treated us with hospitality, professing the warmest sympathy for our cause, and denied having any communication with the Mexican army. They gave as a reason for leaving town and coming here that many of the volunteers were unruly and turbulent, and disposed to impose on them and their families, and that to avoid any quarrels with them they had removed. They succeeded in blinding us as to their real disposition, and we remained with them that night.

"Saturday, March 12—After getting breakfast we turned our faces towards the fort, and went up on the east side of the river. We arrived a little past noon, and found that some important movements had been made during our absence—to wit: After our party left the fort on the evening of the 10th, either that evening or the next morning an urgent message came from a Mr. Ayres, of Refugio, requesting that a guard might be sent down to assist him in bringing off his family, as Mexican soldiers were making their appearance in the vicinity, and he was apprehensive of danger without some protection. Why he had not removed before, or whether any blame could be justly attached to him for not doing so, I never learned. Still, Fannin felt it to be his duty to afford all the protection in his power, and forthwith despatched Captain King, of the Georgia battalion, with his company of twenty-three men, to his assistance. The distance to Refugio was thirty miles, and King on his arrival found himself confronted by a superior force that drove him into the church of the old Mission. Here he made a stand, and contrived to send a messenger back to Goliad for a reinforcement. The messenger came in; and early this morning, before daylight, the Georgia battalion, of about one hundred and fifty men, commanded by Colonel Ward, was on its way to King's relief. When that was effected they were to return immediately, and they were looked for back on the morrow. News had also come in of the fall of the Alamo and the slaughter of every one of its defenders. About this time, certainly before today, arrived the order from General Houston to Colonel Fannin to retreat to Victoria. This was the first and only communication had from General Houston while Fannin was at Goliad; in fact, it was the first intimation we had of his whereabouts. The necessity of a retreat was now palpable to all. So far from Colonel Fannin wishing to disobey the order, I know from his own lips that he intended to conform to it as soon as the Georgia battalion should return; and I had heard him before this express a wish that General Houston would come on and take command of the troops. The alleged disobedience of Colonel Fannin to Houston's order is an undeserved censure on a gallant soldier; and that he wrote back a refusal I know to be false. Circumstances have enabled me to possess a positive knowledge on these points, and justice to both the dead and the living requires of me thus to state it. Sunday was passed in vain anticipation of Ward's return. On Monday, the 14th, expresses were sent out to obtain intelligence of Ward, but the day passed without any tidings of him. Colonel Horton, of Matagorda, now arrived with about thirty horsemen to assist us in our retreat. On Tuesday, the 15th, still no tidings of Ward had been received. Other expresses were sent; but the day passed without any intelligence being received of the Georgians.

"Wednesday, 16th—No expresses have returned. Another was sent today, but, after going a short distance, his fears induced him to return. It was now that Captain Frazer, who lived at and was acquainted about Refugio, proposed to Colonel Fannin that if he could be furnished with a good horse he would go down and ascertain the state of affairs, and pledged himself, if alive, to return in twenty-four hours with intelligence. A horse was procured, and he left.

"Thursday, 17th—We were now in a state of intense anxiety respecting the fate of our comrades. Nothing had been heard from them since they left us on Saturday morning, and none of our messengers had returned. We were convinced that some calamity had befallen them, and of its nature and extent we now had gloomy apprehensions. At length, about four p.m., Captain Frazer, true to his word, arrived and gave us full and explicit information, and to the following purport: Colonel Ward had reached Refugio and relieved Captain King. Instead of immediately turning back they unfortunately delayed their return, and Captain King started off with his company to destroy some ranches where the people had shown some hostility. Colonel Ward was soon after attacked by some Mexican troops, and driven into the church from which he had but a short time before released Captain King. He now found that Urrea, with his whole division, was about him and endeavoring to dislodge him from his position in the church. Ward and his men gallantly defended themselves, and repulsed all attacks made upon them. When night came, finding their ammunition exhausted, they succeeded in eluding the vigilance of the Mexicans, and, silently leaving the church, retreated to the coast. Captain King, upon reaching the ranches that he intended to destroy, met with opposition and got rather worsted in the fight. He made a circuit to get back to Refugio, which he reached in the night, and found the town occupied by the Mexicans. They then crossed the river and endeavored to retreat from the place, but got lost on the prairie, and, after wandering about all night, found themselves in the morning at a place called Malone's ranch. They had been watched and followed by a party of spies, and soon a force was around them that made resistance hopeless.

"They surrendered, and were immediately started in the direction of Goliad. They had proceeded but a few hundred yards when a halt was made in the prairie. King and his comrades were taken out and shot. Such were the results of this expedition. Fannin and his officers immediately held a council, and without any hesitation resolved to commence our retreat the next morning. Hardly had they left the council room when some of our scouts came in with the information of a large force of the enemy in the vicinity. Preparations were made for leaving, and patrols were kept out all night to watch and give notice of any movement that might be made by the enemy.

"Friday, 18th—This morning, while taking the necessary measures for a retreat in accordance with the officers in council last evening, a party of the enemy were discovered reconnoitring in the vicinity of the fort. Colonel Horton and a few horsemen sallied out to engage them. They did not wait for an attack, but fled, followed by Horton, until a large body of the enemy appeared, who in turn chased the Texans back. Horton then sent for all the horsemen in the fort, who turned out to his assistance and enabled him to resume the offensive.

"As the affair was nearly all visible from the fort, it produced considerable excitement, and all left their work to witness the "sport." I went with several others to the top of the church, which commanded a fine view of the country for several miles around. Colonel Horton, now giving chase to his late pursuers, followed them over to the north side of the river and on over the prairie; occasionally a shot was fired, until the parties were lost from our view in the distance.

"After a time they made their appearance coming back; but now the condition of affairs had changed: the Mexicans were pursuing our men and pressing them rather hard. But they succeeded in reaching the old *Acanama*, a mission, and, getting under shelter of its walls, made a stand. This was one of the old Spanish missionary stations, now in ruins, and standing about three-fourths of a mile northerly from the fort of La Bahia, and on the north side of the river. The Mexicans, numbering about one hundred, drew up in front at a safe distance, and opened fire, which was returned. Captain Shackleford now started out with his company to relieve Horton, and our artillerymen got one of their guns mounted on the wall and brought to bear on the Mexican party. A shot was fired at them, which fell short; but they deemed it wise to withdraw. They soon disappeared, and we saw no more of them.

"Colonel Horton left his position to return, and met the company going to his relief with warm greetings (they had forded the river and gone about half way to him), and with them returned to the fort in the highest spirits. The events of the day had animated all, and good humor and cheerfulness for a while prevailed. Thus far the events of the day were, perhaps, beneficial; but, alas! other considerations were forced unwillingly on our minds. The day was spent, when time with us was precious, and our retreat was necessarily postponed until the morrow. The horses were tired and jaded down, and our oxen that had been gotten up to draw the cannon and baggage carts were left all day without food; and we had given the enemy a day of our invaluable time in which to select his positions and perfect his arrangements for our destruction. I never heard that any man had been injured on either side in the foregoing skirmishing. Although fully determined, from the necessity of the case, on retreating, we were by no means disposed to run. We confidently counted on our ability to take ourselves and all our baggage, etc., to Victoria. We still had about two hundred and seventy men, besides Colonel Horton's company of about thirty horsemen, numbering in all about three hundred; and, though mishaps had come on thick and fast, we still had confidence and determination. The necessary guards were posted for the night, during which we had some rain. Some alarms occurred, but they proved groundless.

"Saturday, 19th—The morning opened with a heavy, impenetrable fog. We left the fort as early as possible, with all our artillery and baggage, which was drawn by oxen. We fully expected an attack at the ford of the river. Colonel Fannin had, however, despatched Colonel Horton at an early hour to go down and occupy such position as would most effectually prevent the enemy from interrupting us in the passage.

"We succeeded in crossing the river without molestation, but with some delay arising from the weak condition of our teams. After all had passed, Colonel Horton's company was directed to scout around and give us notice should any of the enemy appear; for as yet none of them had appeared, and we were still favored by the fog, which was very heavy. We then marched on six miles to the Manhuilla Creek. After passing that about a mile we came upon a patch of green grass where the prairie had been recently burned, and we halted to allow the animals to graze, as well as for the men to partake of refreshments. Our scouts reported no enemy discoverable within four or five miles. No manifestations of an attack, nor even of a pursuit, were apparent. After an hour's halt we resumed the march, supposing that now the enemy did not intend to obstruct our retreat, as they had neglected to avail themselves of the most suitable position for harassing us; and relying on the alertness and fidelity of our horsemen for giving us timely notice of their approach, we proceeded about two miles. Our teams showed signs of weariness, and our march was necessarily slow. We had reached a low ridge when we discovered the enemy advancing in our rear. They had just emerged from the belt of timber that skirted along on this side of the creek, and consisted of two companies of cavalry and one of infantry. We halted, and a six-pounder was unlimbered, from which three shots were fired at them, but, as we perceived, fell short. It appears that four horsemen had been left in the rear, and that they, instead of keeping a lookout, had, under a false sense of security, lain down, and were only aroused by the close approach of the Mexicans. They now came up at full speed; one of them, and one only (a German of the name of Ehrenburg), joined us. The other three, in the greatest apparent terror, passed about a hundred yards on our right, without even stopping to look at us, and under the strongest appliances of whip and spur, followed by a few hearty curses from our men. Observing one or two more bodies coming from the woods, Colonel Fannin ordered his men to resume the march slowly, so as not to harass the jaded oxen, saying further that the enemy in sight were merely skirmishers, etc.; that Colonel Horton, being notified by our firing that the enemy were in sight, would immediately return and rejoin us, and that we had only to keep ourselves cool and collected, and we could easily foil such a party. The men all viewed the matter in the same light, and we marched on coolly and deliberately for about one mile further, expecting all the time to see our horsemen coming to join us. We had now come to a piece of low ground, and were yet about half a mile from the point of timber, when we were brought to a halt by the breaking down of our ammunition cart. One company of the enemy's cavalry had come up abreast of us on our right flank, and the others had got a little in advance on the left, their infantry coming up in our rear. Before we could make any disposition of our broken cart they closed around our front and opened fire, and in this way the battle commenced. Colonel Fannin directed the men to reserve their fire until the enemy was near enough to make sure shots. Soon, however, the fire became general on our side as well as on theirs. I judged the enemy to be about five hundred strong at the commencement, but other troops kept continually coming up during the engagement, and by night they had not less than one thousand men opposed to us. The enemy's cavalry made numerous attempts to charge us, forming behind a little rise in the ground about four or five hundred yards off, then galloping up at full speed. But they were always so warmly received by our rifles that they were obliged to fall back. So confident were we in the beginning of the affair that Colonel Horton and his men would come back and rejoin us that in several of their charges a number of our men, imagining the party to be Horton's troop, called out: 'Don't fire! They are our horsemen!'

"But neither Horton nor his men ever made their appearance. Our artillery did not appear to have as much effect on the enemy as we expected, and after the brave Petreswich, who commanded it, fell, and several of the artillery men wounded, the guns were not much used in the latter part of the fight. Our men behaved with the utmost coolness and self-possession; and when it is considered that they were undisciplined volunteers, and this the first time (in most cases) of their encountering an enemy, their order regularity would have reflected credit on veterans. The fight continued without intermission from about three p.m. until night caused a cessation. The enemy drew off to the timber and encamped, having us surrounded by numerous patrols.

"We now had time to look around and consider our situation. It was sunset, and a night of impenetrable darkness, such as is rarely to be witnessed, succeeded. We were without water, and many, especially the wounded, were suffering from thirst, and upon further inquiry we found, from some unaccountable oversight, we had left our provisions behind. Our teams, during the engagement, were killed or had strayed off beyond our reach. We had seven men killed and sixty wounded, about forty of whom were disabled. Colonel Fannin had committed a grievous error in suffering us to stop in the prairie at all. We ought to have moved on at all hazards and all costs until we reached the timber. We might have suffered some loss, but we could have moved on and kept them at bay as easily as we repulsed them while stationary. Fannin behaved with perfect coolness and self-possession throughout, and evinced no lack of bravery. He was wounded in the thigh, and had the cock of his rifle carried away by a musket ball while in the act of firing. His former experience in fighting Mexicans had led him to entertain a great contempt for them as soldiers, and led him to neglect to take such precautionary measures as were requisite from their great numerical superiority. On leaving Goliad I had taken my spare clothing and papers and rolled them up in my blanket, which I slung on my shoulders as a knapsack; and at the beginning of the action, finding that it somewhat embarrassed my motions, I took it off and threw it into the middle of the square. Now, on looking for it, it was gone, and I saw no more of it. On account of the excessive darkness and our having no lights, I found no chance to attend to the wants of our suffering men to any extent. The want of water was most severely felt, for all had become thirsty, and more especially the wounded, whose misery was greatly aggravated by it.

"It was determined by the officers to wait until morning before any further action was attempted; indeed, it was impossible to do otherwise under all the circumstances. In addition to the excessive darkness the air was misty, and not a breath of wind, and it would have been impossible to keep together or follow a straight course for two hundred yards.

"Weary and supperless, I lay down on the bare earth, without any cover, in order to obtain some repose; but the coldness of the ground soon benumbed my limbs and roused me from an unsatisfactory slumber to seek for warmth in some exercise. This was supplied by an order to make an entrenchment. During the fight, while drawn up in order of battle, which was a hollow square, we occupied about an acre of ground. When the firing ceased we had left the lines and congregated in the centre, where we lay down. The entrenchment was made around us as we then were, and did not enclose a fourth part of the ground we occupied in the battle.

"We set to work with our spades and dug a ditch two or three feet in depth. Our carts were then drawn up and disposed of upon the breastworks, so as to aid in our protection; and the carcasses of two horses, all that we had with us, and those of several oxen, were piled up for breastworks. Thus the night wore away, the enemy's patrol keeping up incessant music with their bugles to regale us; while the shrill and discordant scream of '*Sentinel alerto!*' which afterwards became so familiar, then first jarred upon my ear.

"I worked with the spade until fatigued, then lay down for a little troubled sleep until the chilly earth forced me to seek for warmth by using the spade again. In such alternations the dismal night wore away, and day at last dawned upon us. It was Sunday, March the 20th. Early in the morning, and before it was quite light, we perceived a reinforcement of three or four hundred men coming to the enemy, accompanied by a hundred pack mules. They brought up two pieces of artillery and a fresh supply of ammunition, and they directly commenced the business of the day by treating us to a few rounds of grape and canister. The enemy now being well supplied, their force so superior to our own—having at least one thousand three hundred men in good order, while we, exclusive of our wounded, could only muster about two hundred, and they worn out by the toils and exertions of the previous day—left our situation perilous in the extreme. The question was now agitated: 'Should we surrender?' We well knew their faithlessness and barbarity, as shown in the recent example of Johnson and King, and that we could not rely on any feelings of honor or humanity in them when once they had us in their power. The only chance for us to escape from them was by a desperate rush through their main body into the timber. This would necessarily involve the abandoning of our wounded to a certain death and leaving everything behind. We felt confident, indeed, in being able to keep them at bay; but without provisions or water it would only be to postpone without averting our fate, and we were now satisfied that no aid would come to us from Victoria or the settlements. The officers consulted together and then submitted the question to their respective companies. I was with my messmates in Shackleford's company when he submitted the proposition to us. After a cool discussion of the chance it was considered that if the enemy would agree to a formal capitulation there would be some chances of their adhering to it, and thus of saving our wounded men. Dr. Shackleford resolutely declared that he would not agree to any alternative course that involved an abandonment of his wounded men. It was finally agreed that we would surrender if an honorable capitulation would be granted, but not otherwise, preferring to fight it out to the last man in our ditches rather than place ourselves in the power of such faithless wretches without at least some assurance that our lives would be respected.

"These, as understood, were the sentiments of the party generally. When the matter was first proposed to Colonel Fannin he was for holding out longer, saying: 'We whipped them off yesterday, and we can do so again today.'

"But the necessity of the measure soon became obvious. He inquired if the sentiment was unanimous, and finding that all, or nearly all, had made up their minds, he ordered a white flag to be hoisted. This was done, and was promptly answered by one from the enemy. The flags met midway between the forces. Colonel Fannin, attended by Major Wallace, the second in command, and Captain Dusangue, as interpreter, went out and met the Mexican commanders. After some parley a capitulation with General Urrea was agreed upon, the terms of which were that we should lay down our arms and surrender ourselves as prisoners of war; that we should be treated as such according to the usage of civilized nations; that our wounded men should be taken back to

Goliad and properly attended to, and that all private property should be respected. These were the terms that Colonel Fannin distinctly told his men on his return had been agreed upon, and which was confirmed by Major Wallace and Captain Dusangue, the interpreter. I saw Colonel Fannin and his adjutant, Mr. Chadwick, get out his writing desk and paper and proceed to writing. Two or three Mexican officers came within our lines and were with Colonel Fannin and Chadwick until the writing was finished. We were told that the articles of capitulation were reduced to writing and signed by the commander of each side and one or two of their principal officers; that the writings were in duplicate, and each commander retained a copy.

"I am thus particular and minute in regard to all the incidents of this capitulation, and especially what fell under my personal observation, because Santa Anna and Urrea both subsequently denied that any capitulation had been made, but that we surrendered at discretion. We were also told, though I cannot vouch for the authority, that as soon as possible we should be sent to New Orleans under parole not to serve any more against Mexico during the war in Texas; but it seemed to be confirmed by an observation of the Mexican colonel, Holtzinger, who came to superintend the receiving of our arms. As we delivered them up he exclaimed: 'Well, gentlemen, in ten days liberty and home!' Alas! within that time the most of our men did reach their final homes. We now surrendered our arms, artillery, ammunition, etc., to the Mexicans, who took immediate possession. Our officers were called to put theirs by themselves, which we did, in a box which was nailed up in our presence, with the assurance that they should be safely returned to us on our release, which they flattered us would shortly take place.

"Now that our fate was decided, I gave all my attention to the wounded. I was assisted by Dr. J. E. Fields, who had joined us about ten days before; also by Dr. Shackleford, captain of the company of 'Red Rovers,' who was a surgeon and physician by profession; and by Dr. Ferguson, a student of his, who had come out with his company. The prisoners were now marched back to Goliad, the wounded being left on the field until carts could be sent for them. The loss of the enemy in the engagement I could never learn with precision. They had above a hundred wounded badly that we (the surgeons) were afterwards obliged to attend to. Fifteen of their dead were counted within a few hundred yards of our entrenchment early in the morning, besides an officer, badly wounded, who was brought into our camp and died shortly after. The accounts of the Mexicans themselves, of whom I subsequently inquired, varied in their statements of their dead from forty to four hundred.

"Thus terminated the battle of '*Encinal del Perdido*,' by which, from untoward events, we were placed in their power; yet they had but little cause to boast of their victory.

"Monday, March 21—Carts came out and took in a portion of our wounded men, attended by the other surgeons, while I remained on the ground with those left. This day, while dressing the wounds of our men, some of the soldiers stole my pocket case of instruments, and thus deprived me of the power of properly attending them.

"Tuesday, March 22—Carts came again today and took in the remainder of our wounded. Captains Dusangue, Frazer, and Pettus, and two or three other men who had been left with me on the ground, went also with the last of the wounded.

"At the Manhuilla Creek we met General Urrea with about one thousand men going to Victoria. The captain of the escort appeared to be a very gentlemanly man, and endeavored to cheer up our spirits. Finding that Captain Dusangue could speak Spanish, he engaged him in lively and cheerful conversation, dismounting and walking with us for several miles. We certainly were inspired with more confidence by his lively and cheerful manners. It was dark when we reached the San Antonio, which we waded, it being three feet deep. Perceiving some disorder among the carts which had not yet crossed, our Mexican captain went back to them, and the guard halted a moment on the east side. Captain Dusangue now remarked in a very serious tone that contrasted strangely with the cheerful voice in which he had been conversing: 'I am now prepared for any fate.' The words and his manner struck us with surprise, and he was asked if he had ascertained by anything the captain had said that treachery was meditated. 'No,' he replied, and ominously repeated his former remark. The idea struck me that here was a chance to escape by silently dropping into the water while the guard and their captain were on the other side, and from the darkness could not see me; in two or three minutes I would have floated beyond their reach, and, being a good swimmer, could then easily escape. I stopped to consider the matter more fully, and directly the captain and his guard were alongside of us; and thus by indecision in a critical moment lost the chance.

"After-events frequently called this matter to my mind and made me bitterly regret not having acted on the first impression of my mind. It was late when we reached the fort, and we were sent into the church, where we found all the prisoners were placed and crowded up in a very uncomfortable manner, strictly and strongly guarded.

"Wednesday, 23rd—My first effort was to see Colonel Fannin, and if by any possibility through him get hold of some of our surgical instruments and hospital dressings for the wounded, we having been robbed of everything of the kind. Most of such articles had belonged to individuals; and Colonel Fannin, at my request, addressed a note to the Mexican commandant, in which he claimed sundry instruments and other articles, not only as private property according to the articles of the capitulation, but from the necessity of the surgeons having them for the benefit of the wounded Mexicans as well as of the Americans. The application was of no avail, and I should not mention it except to show that the terms of the capitulation had been appealed to once by Colonel Fannin, which, of course, he never would have done had there been no capitulation. This day all the prisoners except the wounded were removed from the church and placed on the west side of the fort. The church being still too small, the American wounded were removed to the cuartels on the west wall.

"Thursday, March 24—We had been politely requested by the Mexican officers as a favor that we would attend to their wounded, as their surgeons had not arrived, which we, not to be outdone by them in politeness, replied that we would do so with the greatest pleasure.

We, however, found that we were not to be permitted to visit our own wounded until we had attended to all theirs. We remonstrated against this arrangement, but to no purpose.

"A Mexican surgeon at length arrived, but we had no assistance from him. It took us nearly the whole day to get through with the Mexicans before we could be allowed to see our own men; and then we had so little time that we could only dress some of the severest wounds and leave the rest altogether. Some of them up to this time had not the first dressing. We resolved to refuse attendance altogether upon the Mexicans, at all risks, unless we could be allowed time enough to properly attend our own men at least once a day. But at this time Major Miller, with seventy men, who had come from Nashville, Tennessee, and who had been made prisoners on their landing at Copano, were brought in. Major Miller immediately tendered his services to us as medical aid, as did some of his men, by which our labor was much lightened, and we thenceforward managed to get along without an open rupture with our taskmasters.

"Friday, March 25—Colonel Ward and the Georgia battalion were this day brought in as prisoners. After their retreat from the Mission of Refugio they had kept around by the coast, endeavoring to get to Victoria. They had expended all their ammunition in their last fight, and had been about ten days in getting to the Guadalupe River, in the vicinity of Victoria. They had been within hearing distance of our guns on the 19th, but were unable to reach us. They had succeeded in getting across to the east side of the Guadalupe when General Urrea, with a superior force, came upon them and offered them the same terms of capitulation that had been granted Colonel Fannin. Wearied out, dispirited, with no ammunition or provision, they had no other alternative, and surrendered and were conducted back to Goliad.

"Saturday, March 26—Colonel Fannin, who, with his adjutant, Mr. Chadwick, had been sent to Copano, returned this day. They were placed in the small room of the church which had been appropriated to the surgeons and their assistants and guard—rather crowded, to be sure, but we had become accustomed to that. They were in good spirits and endeavored to cheer us up. They spoke of the kindness with which they had been treated by the Mexican colonel, Holtzinger, who went with them, and their hopes of our speedy release. Fannin asked me to dress his wound, and then talked of his wife and children with much fondness until a late hour. I must confess that I felt more cheerful this evening than I had before since our surrender. We had reiterated assurances of a speedy release, it is true, by the Mexicans, though we placed but little reliance on them. Our fare had been of the hardest, being allowed no rations except a little beef or broth. Now we had been able to purchase from the camp followers a little coffee and bread, more grateful to me than any luxury I ever tasted; and, after sleeping on the ground without a blanket from the time of our capture, I had at last succeeded in getting an old worn-out one, upon which I had lain down to rest this evening with more pleasure and happier anticipations than I had before allowed myself to indulge in.

"Sunday, March 27—At daylight Colonel Gary, a Mexican officer, came to our room and called up the doctors. Dr. Shackleford and myself immediately rose (Dr. Field was at a hospital outside the fort) and went with him to the gate of the fort, where we found Major Miller and his men. Colonel Gary, who spoke good English, here left us, directing us to go to his quarters (in a peach orchard three or four hundred yards from the fort) along with Miller's company, and there wait for him. He was very serious and grave in countenance; but we took but little notice of it at that time. Supposing that we were called to visit some sick or wounded at his quarters, we followed on in the rear of Miller's men. On arriving at the place Dr. Shackleford and myself were called inside a tent, where were two men lying on the ground, completely covered up, so that we could not see their faces, but supposed them to be the patients that we were called in to prescribe for. Directly a lad came in and addressed us in English. We chatted with him for some time. He told us his name was Martinez, and that he had been educated at Bardstown, Kentucky.

"Beginning to grow a little impatient because Colonel Gary did not come, we expressed an intention of returning to the fort until he would come back; but Martinez said that the directions for us to wait there were positive, and that the colonel would soon be in, and requested us to be patient a little longer, which was, in fact, all that could be done. At length we were startled by a volley of firearms, which appeared to be in the direction of the fort. Shackleford inquired: 'What's that?' Martinez replied that it was some of the soldiers discharging their muskets for the purpose of cleaning them.

"My ears had, however, detected yells and shouts in the direction of the fort, which, although at some distance from us, I recognized as the voices of my countrymen. We started, and, turning my head in that direction, I saw through some partial openings in the trees several of the prisoners running at their utmost speed, and, directly after, some Mexican soldiers in pursuit of them.

"Colonel Gary now returned, and, with the utmost distress depicted on his countenance, said to us: 'Keep still, gentlemen; you are safe. This is not from my orders, nor do I execute them.' He then informed us that an order had arrived the preceding evening to shoot all the prisoners; but he had assumed the responsibility of saving the surgeons and about a dozen others, under the plea that they had been taken without arms. In the course of five or ten minutes we heard as many as four distinct volleys fired in as many directions, and irregular firing which continued an hour or more before it ceased. Our situation and feelings at this time may be imagined, but it is not in the power of language to express them. The sound of every gun that rung in our ears told but too terribly the fate of our brave companions, while their cries, which occasionally reached us, heightened the horrors of the scene. Dr. Shackleford, who sat by my side, suffered perhaps the keenest anguish that the human heart can feel. His company of 'Red Rovers,' that he had brought out and commanded, were composed of young men of the first families in his own neighborhood—his particular and esteemed friends; and besides two of his nephews, who had volunteered with him, his eldest son, a talented youth, the pride of his father, the beloved of his company, was there; and all, save a trifling remnant, were involved in the bloody butchery.

"It appears that the prisoners of war marched out of the fort in three different companies: one on the Bexar road, one on the Corpus road, and one towards the lower ford. They went one-half or three-fourths of a mile, guarded by soldiers on each side, when they were halted, and one of the files of guards passed through the ranks of the prisoners to the other side, and then all together fired upon them. It seems the prisoners were told different stories, such as they were to go for wood, to drive up beeves, to proceed to Copano, etc.; and so little suspicion had they of the fate awaiting them that it was not until the guns were at their breasts that they were aroused to a sense of their situation.

"It was then—and I proudly record it—that many showed instances of the heroic spirit that had animated their breasts through life. Some called to their comrades to die like men, to meet death with Spartan firmness; and others, waving their hats, sent forth their huzzas for Texas!

"Colonel Fannin, on account of his wound, was not marched from the fort with the other prisoners. When told that he was to be shot he heard it unmoved, and, giving his watch and money to the officer who was to superintend his execution, he requested that he might not be shot in the head and that his body should be decently buried.

"He *was* shot in the head, and his body stripped and pitched into the pile with the others.

"The wounded lying in the hospitals were dragged into the fort and shot. Their bodies, with that of Colonel Fannin, were drawn out of the fort about a fourth of a mile and there thrown down.

"We now went back to the hospital and resumed our duties. Colonel Gary assured us that we should be no longer confined, but left at large, and that as soon as the wounded got better we should be released and sent to the United States.

"We found that Dr. Field and about a dozen of Fannin's men had been saved. The two men who were concealed under the blanket in the tent were two carpenters by the names of White and Rosenbury, who had done some work for Colonel Gary the day before that pleased him so much that he sent for them in the night and kept them there until the massacre was over.

"We continued on attending the wounded Mexicans for about three weeks. The troops all left Goliad for the east the day after the massacre, leaving only seventy or eighty men to guard the fort and attend to the hospital. Major Miller, by giving his parole that his men would not attempt to escape, obtained for them leave to go at large.

"I must not here omit to mention the Señora Alvares, whose name ought to be perpetuated to the latest times for her virtues, and whose action, contrasted so strangely with those of her countrymen, deserved to be recorded in the annals of this country and treasured in the heart of every Texan. When she arrived at Copano with her husband, who was one of Urrea's officers, Miller and his men had just been taken prisoners; they were tightly bound with cords so as to completely check the circulation of the blood in their arms, and in this state had been left several hours when she saw them. Her heart was touched at the sight, and she immediately caused the cords to be removed and refreshments to be given them. She treated them with great kindness, and when, on the morning of the massacre, she learned that the prisoners were to be shot, she so effectually pleaded with Colonel Gary (whose humane feelings revolted at the barbarous order) that, with great personal responsibility to himself and at great hazard at thus going counter to the orders of the then all-powerful Santa Anna, he resolved to save all that he could; and a few of us, in consequence, were left to tell of that bloody day.

"Besides those that Colonel Gary saved, she saved by connivance some of the officers—gone into the fort at night and taken out some, whom she kept concealed until after the massacre. When she saw Dr. Shackleford a few days after, and heard that his son was among those sacrificed, she burst into tears and exclaimed: 'Why did I not know that you had a son here? I would have saved him at all hazards.' She afterwards showed much attention and kindness to the surviving prisoners, frequently sending messages and presents of provision to them from Victoria. After her return to Matamoras she was unwearied in her attention to the unfortunate Americans confined there. She went on to the city of Mexico with her husband. She returned to Matamoras without any funds for her support; but she found many warm friends among those who had heard of and witnessed her extraordinary exertions in relieving the Texas prisoners. It must be remembered that when she came to Texas she could have considered its people only as *rebels* and *heretics*, the two classes of all others the most odious to the mind of a pious Mexican; that Goliad, the first town she came to, had been destroyed by them recently, and its Mexican population dispersed to seek refuge where they might; and yet, after everything that had occurred to present the Texans to her view as the worst and most abandoned of men, she became incessantly engaged in contributing to relieve their wants and to save their lives. Her name deserves to be recorded in letters of gold among those angels who have from time to time been commissioned here by an overruling and beneficent Power to relieve the sorrows and cheer the hearts of men, and who have for that purpose assumed the form of helpless women, that the benefits of the boon might be enhanced by the strong and touching contrast with aggravated evils worked by fiends in human shape, and balm poured on the wounds they make by a feeling of pitying women.[13]

"During the ensuing three weeks we could ascertain but little of what was being done by the Mexican army, save the news that came in general terms that Santa Anna was ravaging the whole country and the Texans were flying before him to the Sabine; that Matagorda was taken,

---

[13] This noble woman, Señora Alvares, it was generally believed, had she known the day before of the order of Santa Anna, she would have informed the prisoners to that effect and aided them in rising on their guard, and, by so making a sudden movement, might have obtained some arms and possibly changed the result. During the time of the massacre she stood in the street, her hair floating, speaking wildly, abusing the Mexican officers, especially Portillo. She appeared most frantic. Colonel Miller informed me that the taking of the arms and overcoming the guard would have occupied but a few minutes, as the prisoners would have acted with desperation, and would also have been aided by Miller's men. Her words were: "Curse you, Santa Anna! What a disgrace you've brought on the country!"

and that San Felipe was burned by its own citizens and abandoned on the approach of the army.

"April 16—I now commenced a regular journal. By the request of Colonel Ugartechea, the commandant of Goliad, Dr. Shackleford and myself promised to go up to San Antonio to take in our charge the wounded officers there. The leaving of Goliad, where we had undergone such variety of fortune, and where every scene recalled such painful remembrances, was truly reviving. We crossed the river and rode through the day over a delightful country covered with patches of shrubbery, now in full verdure; and while our eyes were relieved by reposing on Nature's freshness, the fragrance of the numerous flowers that covered the prairies conveyed exquisite pleasure to another sense, and the balmy breeze seemed to infuse new vigor and give us the feeling of healthful and animated life. It was while riding along today that I became struck with the great alteration that six weeks had made in the appearance of my companion, Dr. Shackleford; then an active, hale man of forty, he now seemed at least ten years older and bending under the weight of his sorrows. I remarked the change to him, and he replied that the same idea had occurred to him in regard to myself. The last few weeks, though short, seem an age, and they have not only made us *look* but *feel* older.

"Sunday, 17th—Rode about twenty-five miles; prairie high and rolling, with mesquite trees scattered about. We occasionally today had glimpses of the San Antonio timber that winds along like a narrow belt four or five miles to our left. At night signs of rain; fixed a tent with our saddles, blankets, and some bushes. While engaged in camping, it now being dark, a wild goose in flying over became dazzled by the campfire and came fluttering down in a few feet of us. Our soldiers soon despatched it with their swords, and, as we had eaten supper, we dressed it for breakfast.

"Monday, 18th—After discussing our goose and a cup of coffee we again resumed our journey. About ten a.m. we came to a rancho and procured some milk, bread, and cheese, which now are the greatest luxuries to us. Passed two or three ranchos today; within a few miles of each we were sure to find two or three hundred head of cattle grazing. At one rancho today we saw goats. Came to a rancho and stopped for the night. These *rancheros* remind me forcibly of the patriarchs of old in their possessions and simplicity of life. It will not do, however, to trust to people's honesty because of their simplicity, as I found to my cost. I had managed to obtain one change of clothing since being a prisoner, and this night they stole that and left me to travel proudly on with all my wealth on my back. Went on a few miles to a rancho, where we stopped and took breakfast under a large live oak, the branches of which spread out and overshadowed the yard in front of the house. Rode on and crossed the Salado, a beautiful stream of water. Our guide refused to halt here for fear of Indians. Rode on a few miles further and halted to graze our horses on a post oak prairie. After making a fire and cooking, lay down under the shade of a tree; the trunk of another lay near us on the ground, through the crevices of which we presently discovered the folds of an enormous rattlesnake. We punched him with a stick to drive him out, but his snakeship only sounded his rattles and drew himself further in. We then set fire to the old trunk and burned up this representative of mankind's first great adversary. After the trunk was burned down we poked open the cinders and found two large rattlesnakes nicely broiled; the meat looked as nice and smelt as deliciously as trout, but we did not feel any inclination to taste it, notwithstanding its flavor.

"Rode on, and soon came in sight of the lower Mission, about three miles off to our left—a stately church, left tenantless and waste in the wilderness. Met a company of cavalry en route for Goliad. After passing by two or three other missions about the same distance off, we came in sight of Bexar, and arrived there a little before sunset.

"We were conducted to the commandant, General Andrade, who, with several of his officers, we found sitting before one of the houses on one side of the public square.

"The moment we entered the town the whole population, men, women, and children, began to flock around us, and by the time we had reached the commandant it appeared as if the whole town was about us and gazing with the greatest curiosity. Had we been tigers or captive Comanches there could not have been a greater stir. General Andrade, after reading our letters, addressed us, inquiring if we spoke Spanish or French. I answered him in the latter language. He observed that Colonel Ugartechea had written to him as if we had come of our own accord; we were not to be considered as prisoners, but were entitled to our release, and that he had promised us passports to leave as soon as the wounded could get along without our assistance.

"The general appeared pleased at our coming, and pledged his honor that what had been promised us should be strictly fulfilled. We were then conducted to our quarters. Dr. Shackleford was placed in the house of Don Ramon Musquies, and I went to that of Angelo Navarro.

"April 21—Yesterday and today we have been round with the surgeons of the place to visit the wounded; and a pretty piece of work 'Travis and his faithful few' have made of them. There are about a hundred here now of the wounded.

"The surgeons inform us that there were four hundred brought into the hospitals the morning they assaulted the Alamo; but I should think from appearances that there were more. I see many around the town who were crippled there, apparently two or three hundred such; and citizens inform me that three or four hundred have died of their wounds. We have two colonels, one major, and eight captains under our charge who were wounded in the assault. We have taken one ward of the hospital under our charge. Their surgical departments are shockingly conducted; not an amputation performed before we arrived, although there were several cases even now that should have been operated upon from the first; and how many have died from the want of operations it is impossible to tell, though it is a fair inference that there have been not a few. There has been scarcely a ball cut out as yet, almost every patient carrying the lead he received on that morning.

---

[14] Ed Note: Not to be confused with other Navarros, this is Jose Angel Navarro (1784-1836); son of Angel Navarro and Maria Josefa Gertrudis Ruiz y Pena.

"In the course of a week after we came to town a party of Comanches were here. They brought in hams and things to trade to the Mexicans, who made much of them and treated them with a great deal of deference. They are large men and very muscular.

"This evening (27th) a family of rancheros coming into town with a cart were attacked two or three miles out by the Tawacana Indians (as they say, but I strongly suspect the Comanches who left two or three days ago). Two or three men and women were killed, one woman dangerously wounded in the stomach, one woman slightly wounded in the back and scalped, and one girl severely wounded. We have taken them in our care and dressed their wounds. I am told that Indians frequently kill people in a few miles of the town. We get on very comfortably here; these people show us much respect and courtesy. We meet with much simple and unaffected kindness of heart from the citizens, particularly the females; we are also well treated by the officers. It is evident that they have a high opinion of our skill, and if the surgeons that I have seen among them are fair samples of the medical talent in the nation I can safely say, without the least degree of vanity, that they have reason to think well of us. The surgeon of the garrison came for me the other day to visit his wife, who was in the greatest distress and he did not know what to do for her. On going to his house I found that she had the *tooth ache*. He amputated a leg the day we arrived, and the man died the next. We have as yet amputated but one, and the patient is doing well. There are about a half-dozen more that should have received operations, but *now* they will die anyhow.

"Today I got some clothes from the tailor—the first change that I have been able to get since coming here.

"Thursday, 28th—One of the men killed by the Indians yesterday was brought in today, stabbed in several places and scalped. Three or four of our hospital patients died last night. A courier from Goliad, but no news of interest. We hear nothing of what is doing on the Brazos or beyond. The officers here appear to know no more than ourselves, and if they do they keep it to themselves. Three Negroes brought in from Tenexticlan, on the Brazos; a drove of cattle and hogs brought in from the Colorado.

"Friday, May 6—Several Negroes brought in from the Brazos, belonging to Groce and Donahue. Observed this evening, as I walked out, the people collecting in small groups, talking anxiously together and seeming to have some great news that agitated them. I was walking with an officer, and did not think proper to inquire of him what it was; but on meeting some Negroes he requested me to ask of them the news. I did so, and they informed me that Santa Anna had lost a battle and was taken. At first I could not credit it, but reflected a moment on the agitation that was visible among the people, which suggested forcibly to my mind at the moment the commencement of Byron's celebrated enigma:

'Twas whispered in heaven, and muttered in hell,
And echo caught softly the sound as it fell!'

"It must be true, then! And now what torturing anxiety, what racking suspense, till the news is confirmed or falsified! And now what will my countrymen do in the way of reprisal for the outrages perpetrated by this monster? What ought they to do? The few who fell here fell in open fight, it is true, and, fighting to the last, they asked no quarter; and yet does not an order to give no quarter deserve to be retaliated? Does not the killing of Grant and his men, taken by surprise and unable to fight; and the wanton murder of King and his dozen after they could fight no longer; and that worst of outrageous atrocities, the massacre at Goliad in violation of pledged faith and solemn stipulations, deserve, I will not say retaliation, but just vengeance on the author of these enormities, and by whose special order they were perpetrated?

"Certainly, now that they have him in their hands, they are bound by every sentiment of regard for their families driven from their homes, and their houses pillaged and burned; by the blood of their brothers and sons, which has flowed like rivers; and by the manes of those whose chivalry led them to meet the foe at the onset, whose bones and ashes lie here and at Goliad, bleaching in the sun, preyed upon by the vulture and the wolf, and when the soil is yet black from their blood that saturated it—they are bound to execute judgment! It may be dangerous for me, but I have faced too many dangers of late for that to influence any sentiments in regard to a principle of right and wrong or a matter of duty and obligation.

"Saturday, 7th—The news of yesterday seems to be confirmed, and also that there is an armistice, or suspension of hostilities, agreed upon; and the Mexicans are to retreat to this river at least, if not wholly to evacuate the country. Today Don José Lombardus, the owner of the wagons and their equipage in this army, showed me a letter he received from Matamoras, dated 21st of April, in which was written: "Tomorrow the American prisoners, fourteen in number, are to be shot." Poor fellows! You are to suffer as hundreds of others besides you have done; but, in my humble opinion, there will soon be a stop put to this shooting of prisoners, or the tables will be turned with a vengeance. Don José is in great trouble about the wagons Santa Anna has lost for him. He fears, and, I suspect, truly enough, that the government of Mexico will never pay him for them.

"Monday, 9th—Wrote to Dr. Field and Dr. Hale, and also to Dr. Hurtado, at Goliad, by a courier.

"Tuesday, 10th—We have many flying reports that tantalize us by their uncertainty and want of credibility: 'The Mexican array is coming to San Antonio, where it will fortify and send to the interior for reinforcements, so as to take the field early in the fall.' Again: 'Santa Anna has escaped and regained his liberty'; 'Santa Anna and Houston are coming on to San Antonio together in perfect amity.' Today we hear, with some appearance of probability, that the Mexican army will not come here, but go to Goliad, and that this place, with all its artillery, ammunition, etc., is to be given up, and that the Texan troops are now on their way here to take possession. Last night there was much riding about town. It is evident that they are agitated about something. Time will show.

"Sunday, 15th—Nothing more of news. A Mexican surgeon from Nondova arrived. His name is Nioran, and he seems something more respectable for a surgeon than the others I have seen. Yesterday I strolled over to the Alamo with our hospital captain, Martinez. They are hard at work fortifying. Went along through some of the old gardens; many of the most beautiful flowers now in bloom; mulberries are ripening, and the fruit of the fig trees begins to appear; but everything of nature's productions looks wild and neglected.

"Tuesday, 17th—Dr. Alabery came into town today with a pass from General Fillasola, now commander in chief. He (Dr. A.) is son-in-law to Angelo Navarro, with whom I live. His wife and sister, together with a Negro, Bowies, were in the Alamo when it was stormed. He had come in in order to look after his family and take them off. He gave us all the particulars of the battle of San Jacinto, the capture of Santa Anna and the retreat of the Mexican army, the number of volunteers pouring into Texas, stimulated thereto by the tale of Fannin and Travis. Now I am truly revived; our cause is prospering and the blood of so many heroes has not been shed in vain.

"19th—Dr. Alabery, in his narrative, related Santa Anna's complimentary speech to General Houston, where he modestly compares himself to Napoleon, and Houston, Wellington. There is a sprightly little Frenchman, here who is armorer, and I could not forbear relating to him the anecdote. He sprang up in the greatest excitement. "What!" said he, "does Santa Anna compare himself to Napoleon, the *foudre*, because he can run about with two or three thousand ragged Indians and take a few mud towns? Does he think that his greatest exploit will bear any comparison to the least thing done by our hero?" He stormed and raved for a considerable time before he could cool down, so indignant was he; and I was much amused at his idea of the comparison. General Andrade has received orders to destroy the Alamo and proceed to join the main army at Goliad. The troops have hitherto been busy in fortifying the Alamo. They are now as busy as bees—soldiers, convicts, and all—tearing down the walls, etc. We were promised our passports a few days ago, but there being some difficulty in the way of getting them, finding that the troops were about retreating from here, we have, by means of our friend, Don José Lombardus, and Don Ramon Musquies, induced the commandant to leave us here when he goes out, ostensibly in charge of the sick he is obliged to leave behind."

❧

List of officers and men, under command of Colonel J. W. Fannin, who surrendered to the Mexican forces under General Urrea in March 1836, and afterwards shot in violation of the terms of surrender, March 27, 1836:

The * indicates those who were marched out to be shot with the others, but made their escape; the † those who were spared for laborers and surgeons, and the ‡ those who escaped from Colonel Ward's division on his retreat and did not fall into the hands of the enemy.

J. W. Fannin, colonel, commandant
William Ward, lieutenant colonel
Benjamin C. Wallace, major Lafayette Battalion
Warren Mitchell, major Georgia Battalion
Staff: _____ Chadwick, adjutant; J. S. Brooks, adjutant; Gideon Rose, sergeant major; David I. Holt,‡, quartermaster; James Field,† James H. Barnard,† surgeons.

CAPTAIN DUVAL'S COMPANY
FIRST REGIMENT VOLUNTEERS

Captain, B. H. Duval; lieutenants, Samuel Wilson, J. Q. Merifield; sergeants, G. W. Daniel, J. S. Bagly, E. P. G. Chisem, W. Dickerson; corporals, N. B. Hawkins, A. B. Williams, A. H. Lynd, R. C. Breshear. Privates: T. G. Allen, J. M. Adams, J. F. Bellows, William S. Carlson, Thomas S. Churchill, William H. Cole, John C. Duval,* H. M. Dawnman, John Donohoe, George Dyer, John Holliday,* C. R. Heaskill, _____ Johnson, L. P. Kemps, A. G. Sermond, William Mayer, J. McDonald, William Mason, Harvey Martin, Robert Owens,

R. R. Rainey, _____ Sharpe,* L. S. Simpson, _____ Sanders, C. B. Shaine,* L. Tilson, B. AV. Tolover, J. Q. Volckner, John Van Bibber,† _____Batts, _____ Woolrich, William Waggoner.

CAPTAIN KING'S COMPANY
AUXILIARY VOLUNTEERS

Captain, Aaron B. King; sergeants, Samuel Anderson, George W. Penny, J. H. Callison, William R. Johnson. Privates: J. P. Humphries, H. H. Kirk, L. C. Gibbs, L. G. H. Bracy, J. C. Stewart, T. Cooke, James Henley, F. Davis,‡ Jackson Davis, J. Coleman, Gavin H. Smith, Snead Leadbeatter, R. A. Toler, William S. Armstrong, Benjamin Oldum,† Joel Heth, _____ Deadrick,† _____Johnson.

CAPTAIN PETTUS'S COMPANY
SAN ANTONIO GRAYS

Lieutenant, John Grace; sergeants, E. S. Heath, William L. Hunter,* _____ James, Samuel Reddell. Privates: C. J. Carriere, Allen O. Kenney, Joseph P. Riddle, F. H. Gray, George Green, Charles Seargent, _____ Holland, _____ Cozart, William G. Preusch, John Wood, Dennis Mahoney, Noah Dickerson, George M. Gillaud, George Voss,† David J. Jones,* _____ Wallace, William Harper, William Brennan,* Edward Moody, _____ Escott, John Reese,* Manuel Carabajal, R. J. Scott, _____ Gould, W. P. Johnson, A. Bynum, _____ Hodge, Charles Philips, _____ West, J. M. Cass, _____ Perkins, Peter Griffin,† _____ Logan, Milton Irish.*

CAPTAIN BULLOCK'S COMPANY
First Regiment Texas Volunteers

Captain U. J. Bullock, left sick at Velasco; F. M. Hunt,* first sergeant; Bradford Fowler, second sergeant; Allison Arms, third sergeant; J. R. Munson, first corporal; T. S. Freeman, second corporal; S. T. Brown, third corporal;* G. M. Vigal, fourth corporal. Privates: Joseph Andrews,‡ George Washington Cummings, Isaac Adredge, William A. J. Brown, W. S. Butler,‡ Joseph Dennis, _____ Michael, J. H. Barnwell,† Devraux Ellis, Charles Fine, _____ Gibbs, Pearce Hammock,† Samuel G. Hardaway,‡ Perry H. Minor, John O. Moore, Benjamin H. Mordecat,† John Moat, _____ McKennie, L. T. Pease,‡ Robert A. Pace, Austin Perkins, Samuel Rowe, John T. Spellers,† John S. Scully, Thomas Stewart,† Joseph H. Stovall, _____ Trevesant,‡ William L. Wilkerson,† _____ Weeks, _____ Wood, James McCoy, Moses Butler, A. H. Osborne (left wounded in the church at the Mission, afterward escaped), J. Bridgman.†

CAPTAIN JAMES C. WINN'S COMPANY
First Regiment Texas Volunteers

Wiley Hughs, first lieutenant; Daniel B. Brooks, second lieutenant; Antony Bates, first sergeant; John S. Thorn, second sergeant; J. H. Callaghan,† third sergeant; Wesley Hughes, fourth sergeant; John McKemble, first corporal; Walter W. Davis, second corporal; Abraham Stevens, third corporal; J. M. Powers, fourth corporal; _____ Ray, fifth corporal. Privates: John Aldredge, John M. Bryson, Michael Carrol, Thomas H. Corbys, John Ely, George Eubanks, Dominic Gallagher, Wilson Helms, Grier Lee, Joseph Loving, Alexander J. Loveely, Martin Moran,‡ Aaron S. Mangum, Watkins Nobles, John M. Oliver, Patrick Osburn, William Parvin, Gideon S. Ross, Anderson Ray, Thomas Rumley, William Shelton, James Smith, Christopher Winters,

Harrison Young, Josias B. Beall, John Bright,‡ Reason Banks, H. Shults.

CAPTAIN WADSWORTH'S COMPANY
FIRST REGIMENT TEXAS VOLUNTEERS

Thomas B. Ross, first lieutenant; J. L. Wilson, second lieutenant; Samuel Wallace, third sergeant;* J. H. Weely, fourth sergeant;† Josiah McSherry, first corporal; J. S. Brown, second corporal; J. B. Murphy, third corporal. Privates: George Rounds,‡ William Abercrombie, T, S. Barton, J. H. Clark, W. J. Cowan, E. Durrain,† J. A. Foster, Joseph Gamble,† F. Gelkerson, William Gilbert, Thomas Horry,† A. J. Hitchcock,† Allen Ingram,‡ John C. P. Kennymore,† J H. Moore, C. C. Milne, M. K. Moses,‡ J. B. Rodgers, R. Slatter, J. H. Sanders, W. S. Tuberville, E. Wingate, H. Rogers.‡

CAPTAIN TICKNOR'S COMPANY
FIRST REGIMENT TEXAS VOLUNTEERS.

Memory B. Tatom, first lieutenant; William A. Smith, second lieutenant; Edmund Patterson, first sergeant;† Nicholas B. Waters, second sergeant; Richard Rutledge, third sergeant;‡ Samuel C. Pelman, fourth sergeant; Joseph B. Tatom, first corporal;‡ James C. Jack, second corporal; Perry Ruse, third corporal; Thomas Rieves, fourth corporal; Thomas Weston, musician. Privates: D. Green,‡ John McGowen, David Johnson, Samuel Wood, W. Welsh,† Isaac N. Wright, William L. Alison, Washington Mitchell, Stephen Baker, Henry Hasty, James A. Bradford, Cornelius Rooney, Seaborne A. Mills, Cullen Conrad, James O. Young, Edw. Fitsimmons, Hezekiah Fist, C. F. Hick,† O. F. Leverette, William Comstock, John O'Daniel, Charles Lantz, Evans M. Thomas, A. M. Lynch, G. W. Carlisle, Leven Allen, Jesse Harris, _____ Swords, _____ Williams, William P. B. Dubose.

CAPTAIN P. S. WYANT'S COMPANY
LOUISVILLE VOLUNTEERS

Captain, P. S. Wyant, on furlough; B. T. Bradford, first lieutenant;‡ Oliver Smith, second lieutenant; William Wallace, first sergeant; George Thayer, second sergeant; Henry Wilkins, third sergeant; J. D. Rains, fourth sergeant;‡ Oliver Brown, quartermaster; Peter Allen, musician. Privates: Bennett Butler,* Gabriel Bush, Ewing Caruthers, N. Dembrinski, Perry Davis,‡ Henry Dixon, T. B. Frizee, I. H. Fisher, Edw. Fuller, Frederick Gebenrath, James Hamlinton, E. D. Harrison, H. G. Hudson,‡ J. Kortickey, John Lumkin,† C. Nixon, _____ Clennon, J. F. Morgan, F. Petreswich, William S. Parker, Charles Patton, John R. Parker, William R. Simpson, Frederick Siveman, Allen Wren.

CAPTAIN WESTOVER'S COMPANY
OR SAN PATRICIO COMPANY, REGULAR ARMY

Ira Westover, captain; Louis W. Gates, second lieutenant; W. S. Brown, first sergeant; George McNight, second sergeant; John McGloin, third sergeant. Privates: Augustus Baker, Matthew Byrne, John Cross, John Fagan, William Harris, John Kelly, Dennis McGowan, Patrick Wevin, A. M. Boyle,† George Pettick,† Thomas Quirk, Edw. Ryan, Thomas Smith, E. J. A. Greynolds, Daniel Buckley, Marion Betts, G. W. Goglan, Matthew Eddy, Robert English, John Gleeson, William Hatfield, John Hilchard, Charles Jenson, William Mann, John Numlin, Stephen Pierce, Sidney Smith, Daniel Syers, Lewis Shotts, Charles Stewart, Joseph W. Watson, James Webb, William Winningham, Ant. Siley, John James.

CAPTAIN BURKE'S COMPANY
MOBILE GRAYS

David N. Burke, captain, on furlough; J. B. Manomy, second lieutenant; James Kelly, orderly sergeant; H. D. Ripley, sergeant. Privates: Kneeland Taylor, C. B. Jennings, P. T. Kissam, John Richards, Orlando Wheeler, J. D. Cunningham, William Rosenbury,† William McMurray, A. E. White,† John Chew, M. P. King, Jacob Coleman, W. P. Wood, William Stephens, Peter Mattern, H. Ehrenberg,* Conrad Egenour, G. F. Courtman, J. H. Sphon,† Thomas Kemp,* N. J. Dwenny,* James Reid, William Hunter, M. G. Frazier, S. M. Edwards, William J. Green, A. Swords, Z. O'Neil, Charles Linley, William Gatlin, Randolph T. Spain.

CAPTAIN JACK SHACKLERFORD'S† COMPANY
RED ROVERS

T. S. Shackleford, orderly sergeant; J. D. Hamlinton,* second sergeant; A. G. Foley, third sergeant; Z. H. Short, fourth sergeant; H. H. Hintty, first corporal; D. Moore, second corporal; J. H. Barkley, third corporal; A. Winter, fourth corporal. Privates: P. H. Anderson, Joseph Blackwell, Z. S. Brooks,* B. F. Burts, Thomas Burbridge, J. N. Barnhill, W. C. Duglass, J. W. Cain, D. Cooper,* Harvey Cox, Seth Clark, J. G. Coe, Alfred Dorsey, G. L. Davis, H. B. Day, H. Dickson, J. W. Duncan, R. T. Davidson, J. E. Ellis, Samuel Farney, Robert Finner, E. B. Franklin, Joseph Ferguson, M. C. Garner, D. Gamble, William Gunter, J. E. Grimes, William Hemphill, John Eiser, John Jackson, H. W. Jones, J. N. Jackson, John Kelly, D. A. Murdock, Charles W. Kinley, J. H. Miller, W. Simpson,‡ J. N. Seaton, W. J. Shackleford, B. Strunk, W. F. Savage, W. E. Vaughn, James Vaughn, Robert Wilson, James Wilder, William Quinn, Henry L. Duglass.

PART OF CAPTAIN HORTON'S COMPANY

Privates: Ellis Yeamans, Erastus Yeamans, Daniel Martindale,* William Haddon,* Charles Smith,* Francisco Garsear,† Ranson O. Graves, Napoleon B. Williams, Lewis Powell, Hughs Witt, George Pain, Thomas Dasher, John J. Hand, _____ Duffield, _____ Spencer, _____ Cash.

The following persons, who had not attached themselves to any company, were with Fannin: Captain William Shurlock; Lieutenant _____ Hurst, _____ Bills, Nathaniel Hazen,* William Murphy,* Captain Dusangne, John Williams,* Samuel Sprague, _____ Hughes,† James Pitman, C. Hardwick, R. E. Petty, Charles Hec,‡ Nathaniel R. Brester, _____ Spann.

Lieutenant John Grace,[15] of Captain Pettus's company, was a brother to the present Rt. Rev. Thomas L. Grace, Bishop of St. Paul, Minnesota. A. M. O'Boyle, a member of Captain Westover's company, was saved by Colonel Gary of the Mexican army. When the men under General Urrea crossed the river at San Patricio, Colonel Gary stopped at the first house, which was owned by Mr. Edward O'Boyle. Mrs. O'Boyle, being at home, was asked by Colonel Gary to be permitted to stay overnight, as it was late in the day, to which Mrs. O'Boyle consented. Next morning, when the colonel was about leaving, he thanked her for her kind hospitality and said that any service he could return he would do so cheerfully. She remarked that he was quite welcome, and knew of nothing, only that she had a brother in Fannin's command at Goliad; that if, in the fortunes of war, he could do him a favor was all she asked, to which he agreed and asked for the name, which he wrote down in his memoranda. Colonel Gary was a Greek by birth, whom an

---

[15] Lieutenant John Grace gave up a fine situation in Memphis and came to Texas with fifteen men, principally at his own expense. They joined the "New Orleans Grays" at Goliad, and he was elected lieutenant.

adventurous nature had led from the classic East to seek his fortune on the shores of the distant occident.

On the morning that the prisoners were led forth to execution he rode up to the line and asked if there was a man present named Michael O'Boyle. O'Boyle replied in the affirmative, when Colonel Gary instructed him to follow him, which he did as well as his wounded ankle would permit. Colonel Gary placed him with Miller's men, and saved his life, thus keeping the promise made to the sister of O'Boyle.

Escape of Judge W. L. Hunter

Hunter made an extraordinary escape from the "Fannin massacre." He was a member of the "New Orleans Grays"; he was shot down at the first fire, and remained for a considerable time unconscious. Upon reviving he could not move his body, as a dead comrade had fallen upon him. Being very weak from the loss of blood, he extricated himself with difficulty, and discovered that he had been stripped of his clothing, retaining only undershirt and drawers. He summoned all his strength for one supreme effort to reach the river, and nearly failed in doing so. He submerged himself in the water, and remained in that position all day. At night he crossed the river and struck out in an easterly direction. He came to a small stream the next morning, upon the banks of which he remained nearly all day, suffering excruciating pains from his wounds, and being rendered weak from the loss of blood and hunger. He finally made another start, and soon came to another stream, and in following the course of this he came across his own tracks where he had crossed before. He then took down the creek, and came to a house, near the Coletto, where he found some Mexicans who could speak a few words of English, and received of them some clothing and food. These people treated him with the utmost kindness and did all that they could to alleviate his pains. The owner of the *jacol*, Juan Reynea, had previously lived at the Goliad crossing, but had removed to avoid the unwelcome visits of the soldiers, who were continually passing between Goliad and Victoria.

With the aid of these Good Samaritans Hunter speedily recovered sufficient strength to resume his journey, when Señor Reynea himself accompanied him to the house of Mrs. Margaret Wright, wife of David R. Wright, five miles above Victoria, on the Guadalupe River. This good old mother in Israel died very recently, in the city of Victoria, at the advanced age of eighty-seven years. She nursed Hunter with a mother's care, and sheltered him from the Mexicans until after the battle of San Jacinto.

This statement I have from the lips of Judge Hunter himself, who now resides in Goliad, near the spot of that most terrible episode in his life.

A Coincidence of the Foregoing

The Fate of Captain Perry

All who have read Kennedy's *History of Texas* will recall the charm of romance and chivalry with which he invested the American heroes of the "Gauchapin war."

Conspicuous among these was Perry, whom the author represents as attacking La Bahia with forty men; that a Spanish force that had pursued him from the Rio Grande came up and attacked the indomitable adventurer in the rear; that Perry, after all his men had fallen around him, drew his pistol and blew his own brains out.

It is a pity, perhaps, to destroy such a heroic detail, but as truth sometimes cannot be arrived at but by the way of iconoclastic assaults, the idols must give way.

Perry came to Texas with the expedition headed by Colonel Magee in 18—. Magee captured La Bahia and died there. Colonel Kemper succeeded to the command, met the royalists on the field of Salado, and inflicted a crushing defeat upon them. Many of the prisoners captured in this engagement were butchered in cold blood by order of Guttierez, the nominal leader. In consequence of this cruel act of barbarism Kemper retired in disgust from the service and from the country. Ross succeeded to the command and achieved another victory over the royalists near San Antonio, but soon retired, which placed

Perry in command; and under his lead the Americans encountered the royalists in considerable numbers, under General Arredondo, on the fatal field of Medina, where they were disastrously defeated and many killed. Perry escaped the massacre, however, and joined the expedition of General Mina into Mexico. With this chieftain he saw much service and participated in several sharply contested engagements. Despairing of Mina's eventual success, or being forced to comply with the demands of his men—it is not absolutely certain which—he left the army of Mina in Mexico, and at the head of forty men retreated to La Bahia, which was occupied by a royalist garrison. Perry pitched his camp at the old crossing on the river, and sent in a flag of truce to the Spanish officer, demanding a surrender. The demand of Perry was indignantly rejected. Perry desired to attack the place, but his men, who regarded him of late as a madman, refused to march to the assault. The men prepared for their march to the Sabine; Perry would not leave, but insisted that the fort should surrender to him. After all means of persuasion had failed they left him standing on the bank of the river.

Too late he followed on the trail of his men. A company sent out from the fort to ascertain the movements of the Americans discovered Perry near the locality subsequently to be made famous as "Fannin's Battleground."

They made short shrift with the daring adventurer, and hanged him to the most convenient black-jack tree.

There is somewhat of a coincidence in the fate of Perry and Fannin upon the same ground after an interval of years. I was shown the identical tree upon which he was hanged, by one of the followers of Perry at the time, a Dr. Morfitt, who visited Texas in 1838. He was a cultured gentleman of education and nice manners. He did not long remain in Texas, but returned to Alabama, where he died a few years since. I met him in 1839, and he related the story of the stirring events of the "Gauchapin war," in which, with Magee, Guttierez, Toledo, Kemper, Ross, Lockett, and Perry, he was an actor.

Extracts from the Diary of General Urrea

"La Bahia, March 26, 1836

"To General Urrea: In compliance with the definite orders of his excellency the general in chief, which I received direct, at four o'clock tomorrow morning the prisoners sent by you to this fortress will be shot. I have not ventured to execute the same sentence on those who surrendered to Colonel Varra at Copano, being unacquainted with the particular circumstances of their surrender; and I trust that you will be pleased to take upon yourself to save my responsibility in this regard by informing me what I am to do with them.

"J. N. De Portilla

"March 24-27—These days were passed in necessary regulations, in refitting the troops, and in the care of the sick and wounded. On the 26th I sent Ward and his companions to La Bahia. On the 27th, between nine and ten o'clock a.m., I received a communication from Lieutenant Colonel Portilla, military commandant at La Bahia, informing me that he had received an order from his excellency the general in chief, directing him to shoot the prisoners, and that he had resolved to comply with the same. The order in question was received by Portilla at seven o'clock on the evening of the 26th, and he communicated it to me the same day; but necessarily it only came to my knowledge after the execution had taken place. Every soldier in my division was confounded at the news; *all was amazement and consternation*. I was no less struck to the heart than my companions in arms, who stood there the witness of my sorrow. Let one of those present at that painful moment deny the fact! More than *one hundred and fifty* of those who fortunately remained with me escaped this catastrophe, comprising those who surrendered at Copano, together with the surgeons and young men whom I had placed to attend in the hospitals, whose services, as well as those of many others of the prisoners, were important to the army.

"The melancholy event of which I here speak has caused a more than ordinary sensation, not only among my own countrymen, but among strangers the most distant from us. Nor have those been wanting who would fix the fearful responsibility on me, although nothing could be more clear and unequivocal than my conduct in relation to this horrid transaction. Nothing could have been more painful to me than the idea of sacrificing so many gallant men, and particularly the amiable spirited and soldier-like Fannin. They certainly surrendered in full confidence that Mexican generosity would not be sterile in their regard; they assuredly did so, or otherwise they would have resisted to the last and sold their lives as dearly as possible.

"March 20—The instant the fire was opened, and the movement which I had ordered was taking place, the enemy, without offering any resistance, raised the white flag. I immediately ordered the firing to cease, and despatched Lieutenant Colonel Holtzinger, and my adjutant, Don José Gonzales, to learn the enemy's intentions. The former soon returned, stating that they proposed to capitulate. I replied that I could accede to nothing less than an unconditional surrender; and Señors Morales and Solas hastened to communicate the same to the enemy's commissioners, who had already come forth from their entrenchments. Some communications passed, but, desiring to terminate the affair as speedily as possible, I repaired to the spot in person, and repeated to the head of the deputation the impossibility of my acceding to any other than those terms already designated.

"The following articles of capitulation were presented by the Texan deputation, and to which I specifically refused to subscribe:

> "Art. 1. The Mexican troops having planted their artillery at a distance of one hundred and seventy paces, and having opened their fire, we raised the white flag, and instantly there came Colonels Morales and Holtzinger, and to them we proposed to surrender at discretion on the terms they should judge suitable.

"Art. 2. That the wounded and the commander, Fannin, be treated with all possible consideration, it being proposed that we should lay down our arms.

"Art. 3. That all the detachment be treated as prisoners of war and placed at the disposal of the supreme government.

> "The Plain on the Coletto River,
> between Victoria and La Bahia,
> March 20, 1836."

The foregoing "articles" evince a haste in the construction and an absence of system but little in accordance with the proceedings of a deliberative commission; but it is no less my province than inclination to sit in judgment at this late day on this question of near a half-century's standing. I give Dr. Barnard's arguments *in extenso* elsewhere in this volume in support of the fact that there was a formal capitulation; and it is but a parity of justice to give General Urrea's specific denial of that alleged fact. The absolute truth will never be known, and the sympathies and inclinations of each individual must be left to influence the judgment in regard to it.

The following account of the expedition of Lieutenant Colonel Ward and Captain King to the mission of Refugio, and which is somewhat at variance with Dr. Barnard's account of the same expedition, was furnished me by the three men who joined me at the mouth of the Garcitas, as heretofore stated. These men left the mission at night and, passing through Victoria just ahead of the Mexican advance guard, were saved by me in the manner elsewhere recorded. Their names were: Jackson Davis, of King's company; H. G. Hudson, and Richard Rutledge, of Ward's battalion. Believing them to have been honorable men, I have no hesitation whatever in subscribing to their voluntary and unbiased statement.

On the receipt of General Houston's order to evacuate La Bahia some little opposition was manifested by the men, who did not wish to leave the place without a fight. At this juncture a request came to Fannin from Refugio, asking assistance to aid some families who desired to remove to Goliad for protection. Among them Mr. Louis Ayres sent a special request. Captain King and his company volunteered to undertake the mission, and set out for Refugio at once. Colonel Fannin gave King strict orders not to delay a minute and to return as soon as possible. King, wholly disregarding the wise injunctions of his commander, straggled off to some ranches below Refugio without a definite object in view, save the hope of impressing a few horses, and consumed in this worse than idle employment two invaluable days. On their return to the mission from the ranches they encountered the advance guard of the Mexican army.

King made a stand in the post oaks some two miles below Refugio, on the west side of the river. King, as if to atone for his previous *laches*, made a heroic resistance, and repulsed the attacks of the Mexicans throughout the day.

Becoming apprehensive of the fate of King, Fannin despatched Lieutenant Colonel Ward with one hundred men to his relief. Ward, by a forced march all night, entered Refugio in the early morning. King had still not returned, nor could Ward obtain any tidings of him since his departure for the ranches.

Ward received intelligence of King's situation in the post oaks early in the forenoon, and was making hasty preparation to march to his succor when a Mexican force was descried advancing on the town. Ward occupied the old church, in the walls of which they improvised portholes, and a spirited engagement commenced. Some of Ward's men took position in the cupola and fired with fatal accuracy and effect at the exposed Mexicans. A Mexican officer, with more temerity than discretion, charged the American position at the head of about fifty dragoons, and lost his own life, together with that of several of his men, as the penalty of his rashness. The Mexican loss was out of all proportion to the numbers engaged. In the afternoon General Urrea placed a gun in position on a slight elevation east of the church, and several shots were sent through the roof, without, however, accomplishing any results. The firing continued until dark, when the Mexicans retired to the west side of the river. Some of King's men, escaping from his position in the post oaks, joined Ward in the church early in the night. At this time it was that Davis, Rutledge, and Hudson left Refugio for Victoria. King, after holding the Mexicans at bay all day, retired deliberately with his command to the church during the night. A difference arose between the two commanders in relation to the command, which seemed to be irreconcilable, as they could not be coerced into a concert of action, even by the perils that threatened them both so imminently.

Colonel Ward commenced his retreat on the road leading to Victoria, and Captain King took that leading to La Bahia, thus causing the fate of their weak commands to be a mere matter of time. King was overtaken in the prairie three miles above Refugio, surrounded, and himself and all his men killed.

Ward proceeded on his way to Victoria, and while on the Coletto heard the firing of Fannin's men at the battle on the prairie. He reached Victoria, but, finding the town occupied by Mexicans, he crossed the river below and surrendered to the Mexicans three miles south of Victoria, was conveyed back to La Bahia, and he and his men were executed with the remainder of Fannin's ill-fated command.

Charles Frazier[16] was the expressman engaged by Fannin to communicate with King and Ward at Refugio. He made three trips safely, and was last seen mounted and en route to La Bahia, bearing Fannin the intelligence of Ward's battle at Refugio. Frazier was a brave man, honest and honorable. He was a native of Nova Scotia. After the burial of the remains of Fannin's men General Rusk returned to Victoria. A great number of his men were newcomers and required the utmost exertion of their general to control them. Their creed was the total extermination of the Mexican race and the appropriation of their property to the individual use of the exterminators. General Rusk repressed such outrages as far as was possible, and in so doing constituted himself

---

[16] Ed. Note: Hugh M. Frazer.

the only law that the outraged citizen could invoke. Such was the antipathy against Fernando de Leon that he was forced to seek an asylum at the headquarters of the commanding general. He accompanied General Rusk to Goliad, and while there accompanied a number of gentlemen to the river for the purpose of enjoying a bath. While in the water he was wounded by a rifle-shot in the hands of a concealed assassin. This was generally believed to have been the deed of a notorious character of the name of Bradley, who was afterwards killed as he was leaving a church, of which he was a member, by a man he had bribed a professional assassin to kill. The "professional" informed the party whose life it was intended to take, and he lay in wait for Bradley at the church door, with the result given.

De Leon, as elsewhere stated, had brought a cargo of supplies, arms, ammunition, etc., to Texas for the use of the patriots, which were taken by the Mexican war vessel *Brazo*, and subsequently recaptured by men from Matagorda and appropriated to their own use, De Leon losing the whole. He was refused even a carriage which he had purchased in New Orleans for the use of his family. He was incarcerated in the jail at Matamoras, but fortunately made good his escape.

A Just Alcalde

Don Silvestre de Leon was alcalde of Victoria in the year 1832. He was a son of the impresario, Don Martin de Leon. Upon one occasion a poor man complained to the alcalde that Don Martin de Leon had wilfully killed his hog. Court was opened in due time and Don Martin summoned. The alcalde stated the case. Don Martin acknowledged killing the hog, but justified his act on the ground that the hog had destroyed his garden.

The alcalde asked if he had a "lawful fence." The old gentleman replied that it was not the best, but asked the alcalde if he would give judgment against his father.

Don Silvestre replied that in his capacity of a public officer the ties that bound him as an individual were inoperative. On the bench he would perform his duty with strict impartiality, but off the bench he became again the dutiful son. With this prelude the alcalde announced that he would assess the damages sustained by the plaintiff in the loss of his hog at twenty dollars. Don Martin promptly paid the amount, with the remark that he was proud of such a son, to the disappointment of a crowd that had collected to see some fun.

Rencontre with an Indian

Some time in the year 1830 a party of Indians visited the settlements below Gonzales and stole a few horses. They were pursued by John Tomlinson, Charles Lockhart, Bird Lockhart, Andrew Lockhart, and William Pettas, who followed the trail to the vicinity of the present town of Seguin, where they lost all trace of it. Descrying a lone Indian on foot on the prairie, they rode up to him and were questioning him in regard to the party they had been pursuing. It was noticed that the Indian regarded Tomlinson with ill-suppressed evidences of hatred, though Tomlinson did not remember having ever seen him before. Tomlinson was cautioned by his friends to be on the alert, and replied that he was so.

Suddenly the Indian whipped out his hunting knife and made a spring at Tomlinson with the agility of a panther. Quick as he was, however, the white man anticipated the onset, and at the distance of half the length of his gun barrel sent a bullet through the Indian's heart. Tomlinson, in stepping back, caught his foot in a vine and threw himself upon the ground. The dying Indian fell upon him, and, nerved to a superhuman degree by the intensity of his thirst for revenge, plunged the knife into the heart of Tomlinson. While Tomlinson was falling Charles Lockhart had sent another bullet through the Indian's body. Just as he plunged the knife into Tomlinson's bosom Bird Lockhart shot him through the body.

They dragged him off the dead body of Tomlinson, and, though his spirit had flown, he still grasped the knife with the hold of a vise. Either of the three wounds would have proved mortal, Mr. Charles Lockhart informed me. Mr. Tomlinson was a respected citizen, and the fortuitous circumstances attending his untimely taking off cast a shade of gloom over the whole circle of his acquaintances.

Chapter 10

San Jacinto

In pursuit of the leading events of the main thread of the narrative, the San Jacinto campaign is next in order. I will give the official report of General Houston, the correctness of which is vouched for, and append to the same the account of the battle of San Jacinto from a Mexican standpoint, written by Colonel Delgado, and which appeared first in the memoirs of General Fillasola in regard to the campaign of 1836 in Texas:

"Headquarters of the Army
San Jacinto, April 25, 1836

"To His Excellency D. G. Burnet,
President of the Republic of Texas:

"Sir: I regret extremely that my situation since the battle of the 21st has been such as to prevent my rendering you my official report of the same previous to this time.

"I have the honor to inform you that on the evening of the 18th inst., after a forced march of fifty-five miles, which was effected in two days and a half, the army arrived opposite Harrisburg. That evening a courier of the enemy was taken, from whom I learned that General Santa Anna, with one division of his choice troops, had marched in the direction of Lynch's Ferry, on the San Jacinto, burning Harrisburg as he passed down. The army was ordered to be in readiness to march early the next morning. The main body effected a crossing over Buffalo Bayou, below Harrisburg, on the morning of the 19th, having left the baggage and sick and a sufficient camp guard in the rear. We continued the march throughout the night, making but one halt in the prairie for a short time, and without refreshment. At daylight we resumed the line of march, and in a short distance our scouts encountered those of the enemy, and we received information that General Santa Anna was at New Washington and would that day take up the line of march for Anahuac, crossing at Lynch's Ferry. The Texan army halted in some timber within a half-mile of the ferry, and were engaged in slaughtering beeves, when the army of Santa Anna was discovered to be approaching in battle array, having been encamped at Clopper's Point, eight miles below. Disposition was immediately made of our forces, and preparation for his reception. He took a position with his infantry and artillery in the centre, occupying an island of timber, his cavalry covering the left flank. The artillery, consisting of one double-fortified medium brass twelve-pounder, then opened on our encampment. The infantry in column advanced with the design of charging our lines, but were repulsed by a discharge of grape and canister from our artillery, consisting of two six-pounders. The enemy had occupied a piece of timber within rifle shot of the left wing of our army, from which an occasional interchange of small arms took place between the troops until the enemy withdrew to a position on the bank of the San Jacinto, about three-quarters of a mile from our encampment, and commenced a fortification. A short time before sunset our mounted men, about eighty-five in number, under the special command of Colonel Sherman, marched out for the purpose of reconnoitring the enemy.

"Whilst advancing they received a volley from the left of the enemy's infantry, and after a sharp *rencontre* with their cavalry, in which ours acted extremely well and performed some feats of daring chivalry, they retired in good order, having had two men severely wounded and several horses killed. In the meantime the infantry, under the command of Lieutenant Colonel Millard, and Colonel Burleson's regiment, with the artillery, had marched out for the purpose of covering the retreat of the cavalry, if necessary. All then fell back in good order to our encampment about sunset, and remained without any ostensible action until the 21st, at half-past three o'clock taking the first refreshment which they had enjoyed in two days. The enemy in the meantime extended the right flank of their infantry so as to occupy the extreme point of a skirt of timber on the banks of the San Jacinto, and secured their left by a fortification about five feet high, constructed of packs and baggage, leaving an opening in the centre of the breastwork, in which their artillery was placed, their cavalry being upon their left wing.

"About nine o'clock on the morning of the 21st the enemy was reinforced by about five hundred choice troops under the command of General Cos, increasing their effective force to upwards of one thousand five hundred men, while our aggregate force for the field numbered seven hundred and eighty-three. At half-past three o'clock in the evening I ordered the officers of the Texan army to parade their respective commands, having in the meantime ordered the bridge on the only road communicating with the Brazos, distant eight miles from our encampment, to be destroyed, thus cutting off all possibility of escape. Our troops paraded with alacrity and spirit and were anxious for the contest. Their conscious disparity in numbers seemed only to increase their enthusiasm and confidence, and heightened their anxiety for the conflict.

"Our situation afforded me an opportunity of making arrangements preparatory to the attack without exposing our designs to the enemy. The First Regiment, commanded by Colonel Burleson, was assigned the centre. The Second Regiment, under command of Colonel Sherman, formed the left wing of the army. The artillery, under the special command of Colonel George W. Hockley, Inspector General, was placed on the right of the First Regiment; and four companies of infantry, under the command of Lieutenant Colonel Henry Millard, sustained the artillery on the right. Our cavalry, some sixty-one in number, commanded by Colonel Mirabeau B. Lamar, whose gallant and daring conduct on the previous day had attracted the admiration of his comrades and called him to that station, were placed on our extreme right, completing our line.

"Our cavalry was first despatched to the front of the enemy's left for the purpose of attracting their notice, whilst an extensive island of timber afforded us an opportunity of concealing our forces and deploying from that point agreeably to the previous design of the troops. Every evolution was performed with alacrity, the whole advancing rapidly in line and through an open prairie without any protection whatever for our men. The artillery advanced and took station within two hundred yards of the enemy's breastworks, and commenced an effective fire of grape and canister.

"Colonel Sherman, with his regiment, having commenced the action upon our left wing, the whole line at the centre and on the right, advancing in double-quick time, rung out the war-cry, 'Remember the Alamo!' received the enemy's fire, and advanced within point-blank shot before a piece was discharged from our lines. Our line advanced without a halt until they were in possession of the woodland and the enemy's breastwork, the right wing of Burleson's and the left of Millard's taking possession of the breastwork; our artillery having gallantly charged up in seventy yards of the enemy's cannon, when it was taken by our troops. The conflict lasted about eighteen minutes from the time of close action until we were in possession of the enemy's encampment, taking one piece of cannon (loaded), four stand of colors, all their camp equipage, stores, and baggage. Our cavalry had charged and routed that of the enemy on the right and given pursuit to the fugitives, which did not cease until they arrived at the bridge which I have mentioned before, Captain Karnes, always the foremost in danger, commanding the pursuers. The conflict in the breastworks lasted but a few minutes. Many of the troops encountered hand to hand, and, not having the advantage of bayonets on our side, our riflemen used their pieces as war clubs, breaking many of them off at the breach. The rout commenced at half-past four, and the pursuit by the main army continued until twilight. A guard was then left in charge of the enemy's encampment, and our army returned with their killed and wounded. In the battle our loss was six killed and twenty-three wounded, six of whom mortally. The enemy's loss was six hundred and thirty killed, among whom were one general officer, four colonels, two lieutenant colonels, five captains, twelve lieutenants; wounded, two hundred and eight, of which were five colonels, three lieutenant colonels, two second lieutenant colonels, seven captains, one cadet; prisoners, seven hundred and thirty. President General Santa Anna, General Cos, four colonels (aides to General Santa Anna), and the colonel of the Guerrero battalion are included in the number. General Santa Anna was not taken until the 22nd, and General Cos on yesterday, very few having escaped. About six hundred muskets, three hundred sabres, and two hundred pistols have been collected since the action. Several hundred mules and horses were taken, and near $12,000 in specie. For several days previous to the action our troops were engaged in forced marches, exposed to excessive rains and the additional inconvenience of extremely bad roads, ill supplied with rations and clothing; yet amid every difficulty they bore up with cheerfulness and fortitude, and performed their long marches with spirit and alacrity. There was no murmuring. Previous to and during the action my staff evinced every disposition to be useful and were actively engaged in their duties. In the conflict I am sure that they demeaned themselves in such a manner as proved them worthy members of the army of San Jacinto. Colonel T. J. Rusk, Secretary of War, was on the field. For weeks his services had been highly beneficial to the army. In battle he was on the left wing, where Colonel Sherman's command first encountered and drove the enemy. He bore himself gallantly and continued his efforts and activity, remaining with the pursuers until resistance ceased.

"I have the honor of transmitting herewith a list of all the officers and men who were engaged in the action, which I respectfully request may be published as an act of justice to the individuals.

"For the commanding general to attempt discrimination as to the conduct of those who commanded in the action, or those who were commanded, would be impossible. Our success in the action is conclusive proof of their daring intrepidity and courage; every officer and man proved himself worthy of the cause in which he battled, while they received a lustre from the humanity which characterized their conduct after victory, and richly entitles them to the admiration and gratitude of their general. Nor should we withhold the tribute of our grateful thanks to that Being who rules the destinies of nations, and has in the time of greatest need enabled us to arrest a powerful invader whilst devastating our country.

"I have the honor to be, with high consideration, your obedient servant,

"Sam Houston
Command*er in Chief*"

Return of Killed and Wounded in the Actions of 20th and 21st of April, A.D. 1836[17]

First Regiment Texas Volunteers

Company A, George Waters, private, slightly wounded on the 21st.

Company B, James County, private, badly wounded on the 21st; William S. Walker, private, badly wounded on the 21st.

Company C, Captain Jesse Billingsly badly wounded on the 21st; Lemuel Blakely, private, killed on the 21st; Logan Vandeveer, private, badly wounded on the 21st; Washington Anderson, private, slightly wounded on the 21st; Calvin Page, private, slightly wounded on the 21st; Martin Walker, private, badly wounded on the 21st.

---

[17] Ed. Note: Even though Houston indicates that "I have the honor of transmitting herewith a list of all the officers and men who were engaged in the action," the format of the original indicates that the list of dead and wounded and the roster of participants were not part of Houston's report. This may be explained by the material from the Department of Insurance, Statistics, and History that follows the rosters and precedes a report by Mexican Colonel Pedro Delgado, in which the commissioner of that department explains the provenance of a version of Houston's report published by his department; apparently, Linn then transcribed that version into his manuscript.

Company D, Captain Mosely Baker slightly wounded on the 21st; C. D. Anderson, private, slightly wounded on the 21st; Allen Ingram, private, badly wounded on the 21st.

Company F, Leroy Wilkinson, private, slightly wounded on the 21st; James Nelson, private, wounded on the 21st; Mitchell Putnam, private, wounded on the 21st.

Company H, A. R. Stevens, private, wounded on the 21st; J. Tom, private, killed on the 21st; J. Cooper, private, badly wounded on the 21st; B. R. Bingham, private, killed on the 21st.

Killed, 3; wounded, 15; total, 18.

Second Regiment Texas Volunteers

Company D, Lieutenant Lamb killed on the 21st; G. W. Robinson, private, severely wounded on the 21st; William Winters, private, severely wounded on the 2lst; Albert Gallatin, first sergeant, slightly wounded on the 21st.

Company E, Washington Lewis, private, severely wounded on the 21st.

Company D, E. G. Rector, private, slightly wounded on the 21st.

Company F, Alfonso Steel, private, severely wounded on the 21st.

Company K, First Lieutenant J. C. Hale killed on the 21st.

Company I, Captain Smith slightly wounded on the 21st; First Sergeant Thomas F. Fowl killed on the 21st; W. F. James, private, severely wounded on the 21st.

Killed, 3; wounded, 8; total, 11.

Dr. William Motley, wounded on the 21st severely, since died; A. R. Stevens, wounded on the 21st severely, since died; Lieutenant Colonel J. C. Neill, artillery, severely wounded on the 20th; William A. Park, artillery, slightly wounded on the 21st; Devereaux J. Woodlief, cavalry, wounded severely on the 21st; Olwyn J. Trask, private, cavalry, wounded severely on the 20th.

"Army Order
Headquarters, San Jacinto
May 5, 1836

"Comrades: Circumstances connected with the battle of the 21st render our separation for the present unavoidable. I need not express to you the many painful sensations which that necessity inflicts upon me. I am solaced, however, by the hope that we will soon be reunited in the great cause of liberty. Brigadier General Rusk is appointed to command the army for the present. I confide in his valor, his patriotism, and his wisdom; his conduct in the battle of San Jacinto was sufficient to insure your confidence and regard.

"The enemy, though retreating, are still within the limits of Texas. Their situation being known to you, you cannot be taken by surprise. Discipline and subordination will render you invincible. Your valor and heroism have proved you unrivalled. Let not contempt for the enemy throw you off your guard. Vigilance is the first duty of a soldier, and glory the proudest reward of his soils.

"You have patiently endured privations, hardships, and difficulties. Unparalleled you have encountered odds, two to one of the enemy against you, and borne yourself in the onset and conflict of battle in a manner "unknown in the annals of warfare.

"While an enemy to our independence remains in Texas the work is incomplete; but when liberty is firmly established by your patience and valor it will be fame enough to say: 'I was a member of the army of San Jacinto.' In taking leave of my brave comrades in arms I cannot suppress the expression of that pride which I so justly feel in having had the honor to command them in person, nor will I withhold the tribute of my warmest admiration and gratitude for the promptness with which my orders were executed and union maintained throughout the army. At parting my heart embraces you with gratitude and affection.

"Sam Houston
Comma*nder in Chief"*

※

<u>A List
Of Officers, Non-Commissioned Officers, and Privates engaged in the
Battle of San Jacinto on the 2lst of April, 1836</u>

Major General Sam Houston Commander in Chief of the Texan Forces

Staff

John A. Wharton, adjutant general; George W. Hockley, inspector general; John Forbes, commissary general; William G. Cooke, assistant inspector general; A. Horton, William H. Patton, James Collingsworth, R. M. Coleman, aides-de-camp; Hon. Thomas J. Rusk, secretary of war; William Motley, M.D.

Medical Staff

Alexander Ewing, surgeon First Regiment Artillery, acting surgeon general; _____ Davidson, surgeon First Regiment Volunteers; _____ Fitzhugh, assistant surgeon First Regiment Volunteers; Anson Jones, surgeon Second Regiment Volunteers; Shields Booker, N. D. Labadie, assistant surgeons Second Regiment Volunteers.

Artillery Corps

J. C. Neill, lieutenant colonel; Isaac N. Moreland, captain; W. Stillwell, first lieutenant; Richardson Scurry, first sergeant; Thomas Plaster, second sergeant. Privates: T. O. Harris, John M. Wade, Hugh M. Swift, William A. Park, Thomas Green, Clark M. Harman, T. J. Robinson, M. Baxter, Ben McCulloch, Joseph White, Thomas N. B. Green, John Ferrill, L. B. Bardwell, T. C. Edwards, Joseph Floyd, Alfred Benton, D. T. Dunham, Willis Collins, assisted by the following regulars from the companies of Captains Teal and Turner: Campbell,

Millerman, Gainer, Cumberland, of Teal's company; Benson, Clayton, Merwin, Legg, of Turner's company.

Cavalry Corps

Mirabeau B. Lamar, commanding; Henry Karnes, captain; W. H. Smith, captain; J. R. Cook, first lieutenant; Wm. Harness, second lieutenant; Lem. Gustine, M.D. Privates: W. Secrest, F. Secrest, A. Allsbury, S. C. Turnage, D. W. Reaves, E. R. Rainwater, J. D. Elliott, J. P. Davis, J. Neil, N. Nixon, G. Deadrick, J. Nash, Isaac W. Burton, Jacob Duncan, A. W. Hill, Young P. Allsbury, D. McKay, W. J. C. Pierce, W. King, Thomas Blackwell, _____ Goodwin, J. Coker, W. B. Sweeney, Benjamin F. Smith, Thomas Robbins, Elisha Clapp, H. Henderson, George Johnson, J. W. Williamson, Wilson C. Brown, J. Thompson, John Robbins, William F. Young, James Douthatt, John Carpenter, William Taylor, Anthony Foster, Z. Y. Beauford, Spencer Townsend, James Shaw, William D. Redd, _____ Clopper, P. H. Bell, J. W. Robinson.

Regulars

Lieutenant Colonel Henry Millard, commanding; Captain John M. Allen, acting major.

Company A. Andrew Briscoe, captain; Martin K. Snell, first lieutenant; Robert McClosky, second lieutenant; Lyman F. Rounds, first sergeant; David S. Nelson, second sergeant; Daniel O. Driscoll, third sergeant; Charles A. Ford, fourth sergeant; _____ Richardson, first corporal; Harry C. Craig, second corporal; _____ Bear, third corporal; _____ Flores, musician. Privates: Bruff, Bebee, Benton, H. P. Brewster, Cassady, Dutcher, Darrl, Elliott, Flynn, Farley, Grieves, Warner, Henderson, Lang, Larbartare, Limski, Mason, Montgomery, Marsh, Morton, O'Neil, Pierce, Patton, Rheinhart, Smith 1st, Smith 2nd, Kainer, Richardson, Sullivan, Saunders, Swain, Tindall 1st, Taylor, Van Vinkle, Wilkerson, Webb.

Volunteers

Company B. Turner, captain; W. Millan, first lieutenant; W. W. Summers, second lieutenant; Charles Stewart, first sergeant; _____ Swearinger, second sergeant; Robert Moore, corporal; Thomas Wilson, corporal; M. Snyder, corporal. Privates: Bernard, Browning, Bissett, Belden, Colton, Callahan, Christie, Clarkson, Dalrymple, Eldridge, Edson, Harper, Hogan, Harvey, Johnson, Keeland, Ludus, Lind, Minnett, Mordoff, Massie, Moore 2nd, Nirlas, Pascal, Phillips, Smith 1st, Smith 2nd, Scheston, Sigman, Tyler, Woods, Wardryski.

Company B.[18] Richard Roman, captain; Nicholas Dawson, second lieutenant; James Wharton, sergeant; A. Mitchell, sergeant; S. L. Wheeler, sergeant; A. Taylor, corporal; J. S. Egbert, corporal; W. Moore, corporal. Privates: _____ Angell, G. Brown, Joseph Barstow, J. B. Bradley, B. Coles, J. S. Conn, J. H. T. Dixon, William Dunbar, H. Homan, J. M. Jett, Stev. Jett, A. S. Jordan, S. W. Lamar, Edward Lewis, J. W. B. McFarlane, A. McStea, H. Miller, W. G. Newman, James Ownby, W. Richardson, D. Tindale, J. Vinaler, C. W. Waldron, W. S. Walker, F. P. Williams, James Wilder.

Company I. W. S. Fisher, captain; R. W. Carter, second lieutenant; _____ Jones, sergeant. Privates: George W. Leek, N. Rudder, J. W. Stroud, Jos. Sovereign, W. Sargeant, R. J. W. Reel, Rufus Wright, Jos. McAllister, B. F. Starkley, _____ Day, John Morgan, _____ Tewister, _____ Slack, Jacob Maybee, _____ Graves, R. Banks, B. F. Fry, E. G. Marie, _____ McNeil, J. M. Shreye, W. Pace, Ch. Stebbins, R. Crittenden, Adam Hosier, J. S. Patterson, Joseph Douane, E. Knoland, A. H. Miles, George W. Mason, Thomas Pratt, _____ Lewellen, Joseph Joslyn, W. S. Armot, M. W. Brigham, P. Burt, H. Bond, George Fennell, W. Gill, Joseph Gillespie, A. J. Harris, D. James.

---

[18] Ed Note: Thus in the original. Two volunteer companies are identified as Company B.

Staff of the Command

Nicholas Lynch, adjutant; W. M. Carper, surgeon; John Smith, sergeant major; Pinkney Caldwell, quartermaster.

First Regiment Texas Volunteers

Edward Burleson, colonel; Alexander Somerville, lieutenant colonel; J. W. Tinsley, adjutant; H. N. Cleveland, sergeant major.

Company A. William Wood, captain; S. B. Raymond, second lieutenant; J. C. Allison, first sergeant; James A. Sylvester, second sergeant; O. T. Brown, third sergeant; Nathaniel Peck, fourth sergeant. Privates: Irwin Armstrong, William H. Berryhill, Uriah Blue, Seymour Blottsford, Luke W. Bust, James Cumbo, Elijah V. Dale, Abner C. Davis, Jacob Eiler, Simon P. Ford, _____ Garner, Giles A. Giddings, James Greenwood, William Griffin, William C. Hays, Thomas C. Haskin, Robert Howell, William Lockridg, Edward Miles, Benjamin Osborne, James R. Pinchback, Joseph Rhodes, John W. Rial, Ralph E. Sevey, Edward W. Taylor, John Viven, George Waters, James Welsh, Ezra Westgate, Walter Winn.

Company C. Jesse Billingsly, captain; Micha Andrews, lieutenant; James A. Craft, second lieutenant; Russel B. Craft, first sergeant; William H. Magill, second sergeant; Campbell Taylor, third sergeant. Privates: L. C. Cunningham, John Herron, Preston Conley, Jackson Berry, Jefferson Barton, Dempsey Pace, Lemuel Blakely, George Self, Thomas Davy, Jacob Standefer, Wayne Barton, Sampson Connell, William Simmons, George Green, George P. Erath, John W. Bunton, William Crisswell, Samuel McClelland, Lewis Goodwin, Joseph Garwood, Willis Avery, Jesse Haldeman, Charles Williams, Aaron Burleson, Garnett E. Brown, Robert M. Cavens, Walker Wilson, Prior Holden, Thomas H. Mays, A. M. Highsmith, James Curtis, Thomas M. Dennis, James R. Pace, John Hobson, V. M. Bain, Robert Hood, Logan Vandeveer, Washington Anderson, William Standefer, Calvin Gage, Martin Walker, Dugald McLean, Thomas A. Graves.

Company D. Mosely Baker, captain; J. P. Borden, first lieutenant; John Pettus, second lieutenant; Joseph Baker, first sergeant; E. O.

Pettus, second sergeant; M. A. Bryan, third sergeant; James Bell, first corporal; James Priel, second corporal; Isaac L. Hill, third corporal. Privates: O. D. Anderson, J. B. Alexander, John Beachom, T. H. Bell, S. R. Bastic, P. P. Borden, J. Carter, Samuel Davis, G. W. Davis, J. R. Foster, A. Greenland, _____ Fowler, Hugh Frazier, William Isbell, R. Kleburg, James Tarleton, Matt. Kuykendall, Robert Moore, Joseph McCrabb, Louis Rorder, Y. W. Swearengen, Joseph Vermilion, J. E. Watkins, A. W. Wolsey, W. R. Williams, Ellison York, Patrick Usher, J. S. Menefee, Paul Scarbrough, John Flick, J. H. Money, Allen Ingraham, _____ Weppler, John Marshall, Philip Stroth, William Hawkins, Thomas Gay, William Mock, T. R. Jackson, William Bernbeck, Andreas Voyel, John Duncan, Joseph Miller, S. H. Isbell, _____ Millett, Nicholas Peck, George Sutherland, G. W. Gardner, McHenry Winburn, D. D. D. Baker.

Company K. R. J. Calder, captain; John Sharpe, first lieutenant; M. A. Bingham, first sergeant. Privates: B. Bingham, T. Cooke, Granville Mills, T. M, Fowler, J. Green, J. W. Hassell, C. Malone, H. Stanfer, S. B. Mitchell, J. Smith, C. Forister, J. Conner, S. Conner, Elias Baker, H. Fields, W. C. Hogg, W. Lambert, J. Plunkett, J. Threadgill, B. F. Fitch, T. D. Owen, W. K. Denham, F. S. Cooke, George J. Johnstone, H. Dibble, B. C. Franklin, J. Hall, B. Mims, W. P. Reese, W. Muir, C. K. Reese, W. P. Scott, W. W. Gant, W. Hale, E. B. Halstead, P. D. McNeil, J. A. Spicer, R. Crawford, J. S. Edgar, A. G. Butts, D. Dedrick.

Company F. William J. E. Heard, captain; William Eastland, first lieutenant; Eli Mercer, first sergeant; Wilson Lightfoot, second sergeant; Alfred Kelso, first corporal; Elijah Mercer; second corporal. Privates: Robert McLaughlin, Leroy Wilkinson, William Lightfoot, Daniel Miller, Jesse Robinson, D. Dunham, William Passe, James S. Lester, Fidelie Breeding, Christian Winner, P. B. O'Conner, Thomas Ryons, John Lewis, Joseph Highland, Leander Beeson, Josiah Hogans, John McCrab, Maxwell Steel, John Bigley, Hugh McKenzie, Joseph Elinger, John Halliet, J. Robinson, James Nelson, John Tumlinson, Francis Brockfield, Charles M. Henry, James Byrd, Nathaniel Reed, Andrew

Sennatt, S. T. Foley, Allen Jones, Thomas Adams, Mitchell Putnam, T. M. Hardiman, Charles Thompson, William Waters.

Company H. William W. Hill, captain (sick, and company commanded by Lieutenant Stevenson); R. Stevenson, lieutenant (commanding company in battle of 21st); H. H. Swisher, first lieutenant; C. Rany, first sergeant; A. R. Stevens, second sergeant; William H. Miller, fourth sergeant. Privates: E. Whitesides, J. S. Stump, J. M. Swisher, Moses Davis, John Lyford, John Tom, Nicholas Crunk, Lewis Clemins, William Hawkins, W. J. Cannon, Jacob Grace, F. B. Gentry, J. G. Wilkinson, A. Dillard, E. Bowen, James Farmer, A. Lesassier, W. R. Dallis, M. B. Gray, James Gray, B. Doolittle, John Graham, James M. Hill, J. Ingraham, F. K. Henderson, Uriah Sanders, John Craddick, John Gafford, N. Mitchell, David Karneky, George Petty, James Evetts, Prosper Hope, J. Powell, Matthew Dunn, J. D. Jennings, John C. Hunt, J. Lawrence, A. Carruthers, Daniel McKay.

Second Regiment Texas Volunteers

Sidney Sherman, colonel; Joseph L. Bennett, lieutenant colonel; Lysander Wells, major; Edward B. Wood, adjutant; Bennett McNeely, sergeant major.

First Company. Hayden Arnold, captain; R. W. Smith, first lieutenant; Isaac Edwards, second lieutenant. Privates: Sam. Leiper, Peter W. Holmes, W. P. Kincannon, Daniel Doulet, John Moss, E. E. Hamilton, David Rusk, W. F. Williams, J. W. McHorse, H. Malena Alexin, John Marvey, M. G. Whitaker, John Taney, S. Tarborough, Thomas G. Box, Nelson Box, G. R. Mercer, William Nabors, William T. Sadler, James Mitchell, James E. Box, Samuel Phillips, John B. Trenay, Levy Perch, Crawford Grigsby, John McCoy, Dickinson Parker, Jesse Walling, J. W. Carpenter, John Box, W. E. Hallmask, Thomas D. Brooks, S. F. Shanks, Howard Bailey, H. M. Brewer, Stephen McLin.

Second Company. William Ware, captain; Job S. Collard, first lieutenant; George A. Lamb, second lieutenant; Albert Gallatin, first sergeant; William C. Winters, second sergeant. Privates: S. F. Winters,

J. W. Winters, C. Edenburg, Lewis Cox, G. W. Robinson, G. W. Laurence, William Cartwright, John Sadler, James Wilson, James Devitt, Matthew Moss, Jesse Thomson.

Third Company. W. M. Logan, captain; Franklin Harden, first lieutenant; B. J. Harper, second lieutenant; Edward T. Branch, first sergeant. Privates: John Biddle, J. M. Maxwell, M. Charencan, E. Bollinger, P. Bollinger, John Slayton, Patrick Carnel, William M. Smith, David Choat, David Cole, L. J. Dyches, David H. McFaddin, Thomas Orr, Luke Bryan, William Kibbe, E. M Tanner, H. R. Williams, Michael Peveto, Lefroy Godree, Joseph Farewell, C. W. Thompson, Cornelius Devore, M. J. Brakey, Thomas Belnap, William Duffee, Joseph Ellender, William Smith, William Robertson, W. A. Smyth, James Cole.

Fourth Company. William H. Patton, captain; David Murphree, first lieutenant; Peter Harper, second lieutenant; John Smith, first sergeant; Pendleton Rector, second sergeant; A. W. Breedlove, third sergeant; G. L. Bledsoe, first corporal. Privates: James Bradley, J. C. Boyd, Robert Barr, A. J. Beard, Alexander Bailey, J. J. Childs, St. Clair Patton, Claiborn Rector, Phineas Ripley, Thomas J. Sweeney, J. B. Taylor, L. Willoughby, G. Wright, M. B. Athison, Colden Denman, Edward Darst, R. B. Darst, J. K. Davis, E. Gallaher, James Hall, S. Phillips, Thomas McGay, J. A. Barklay, Francis Walnut, Hinton Curtis, J. B. Grice, Nathaniel Eager, B. F. Cage, J. M. McCormack, James Hayr, Charles Hicks, A. D. Kenyon, G. W. Lewis, J. Pickering, James Harris, William Brennan, William H. Jack, Doct. Baylor, Thomas F. Coney, A. Lewis, W. P. Lane, E. G. Rector.

Fifth Company. Thomas H. MacIntyre, captain; John P. Gill, first lieutenant; Bazil G. Ijams, second lieutenant; Robert D. Tyler, first sergeant; John Wilkinson, second sergeant; E. G. Coffman, first corporal. Privates: William Boyle, Benjamin Bencroft, George Barker, William Bennett, John Clarke, J. B. Coliant, John Chevis, Thomas Cox, J. Campbell, _____ Cooper, T. Davis, Oscar Parish, Thomas Hopkins, Jack Lowrie, Cyrus Cepton, Ambrose Mayer, Moses Allison,

Placido McCurdy, David Odom, G. W. Penticost, S. W. Peebles, Samuel Sharpe, Isaac Jaques, Isaac Maiden, F. Wilkinson.

[No company stated in original] James Gillaspie, captain; William Finch, first lieutenant; A. L. Harrison, second lieutenant; R. T. Choderick, first sergeant. Privates: John Sayres, P. B. Lassiter, M. R. Goheen, T. H. Webb, John Peterson, J. Montgomery, T. F. Johnson, Hez. Harris, W. T. Ferrill, Samuel Wyley, William Fertilan, A. Montgomery, A. Lolison, E. McMillan, S. Darling, J. W. Scolling, J. Richardson, Jennings O'Bannion, Willis L. Ellis, James Walker, Alphonzo Steel, Benjamin Johnson, F. M. Woodward, William Peterson, J. C. White, Robert Henry, Elijah Votan, G. Crosby, Joel Dedrick, L. Raney.

[No company stated in original] B. Bryant, captain; Jolin C. Hale, first lieutenant; A. S. Lewis, second lieutenant. Privates: William Earle, J. S. P. Irven, Sim. Roberts, Joseph. P. Parks, C. Rockwell, R. B. Russel, L. H. White, A. McKenzie, A. Cobble, John F. Gilbert, D. Roberts, William B. Scates, J. R. Johnson, William Pate, B. Lindsay, James Clarke, Robert Love.

[No company stated in original] William Kimbo, captain; James Rowe, first lieutenant; Jolin Harman, first sergeant; William Fisher, second sergeant; Henry Reed, third sergeant. Privates: D. Brown, William Bateman, J. A. Chaffin, E. O. Legrand, D. Love, D. H. McGary, W. B. Bennett, B. Green, J. Kent, H. Corsine, Joel Crane, R. T. Crane, Josh. Clelens, W. H. Davis, S. Holeman, H. Hill, George Hancock, Thomas Maxwell, A. G. McGowan, J. W. Proctor, Benjamin Thomas, D. Watson, Lewis Wilworth, R. Stevenson, G. W. Jones, _____ Caddell, R. Hotchkiss, Thomas M. Hughes, A. Buffington, James Burch, R. Burch, A. E. Manuel.

[No company stated in original] Juan N. Seguin, captain; Manuel Flores, first sergeant; Antonio Manchaca, second sergeant; Nep. Flores, first corporal; Ambro Rodriges, second corporal. Privates: Antonio Cruz, José Maria Mocha, Euduado Samirer, Lucien Enriquez, Mattias Currer, Antonio Cuevies, Simon Ancola, Manuel Tarin, Pedro Henern, Tom. Maldonart, Cesario Cormona, Jacinto Pena, N. Navarro, A. Varcinas, Manuel Avoca.

List of Texans Killed at the Battle of San Jacinto[19]

Dr. William Motley, aide to the secretary of war; Lieutenant J. C. Hale, Second Regiment; Lieutenant George A. Lamb, Second Regiment; Sergeant Thomas P. Fowl, Second Regiment. Privates: Lemuel Blakely, First Regiment; _____ Cooper, First Regiment; R. A. Stevens, First Regiment; _____ Trask, Second Regiment; _____ Brigham, Second Regiment.

Regarding Houston's Report

"Department of Insurance, Statistics, and History
Austin, Texas, April 21, 1878

"The original official report of the battle of San Jacinto was made by General Houston a few days after the memorable event to which it refers, and was then filed among the records of the republic. After the annexation of Texas it was transferred to the military archives of the new State, from which it has disappeared, having probably been destroyed by the fire that consumed the adjutant general's office in October, 1855.

"A correct copy of this report has, however, been fortunately preserved, for in the same year in which the battle was fought the document was published in pamphlet form at the *Bulletin* office in the city of New Orleans.

"The publication was doubtless made in deference to the request of General Houston, who urged it 'as an act of justice to the individuals' who participated in the engagement. From this pamphlet a

---

[19] The above list of the names of those killed at San Jacinto is deemed to be accurate, though never before in print. Some of them I knew, and have received the names of others from different sources.

written transcript was made under the auspices of the late Adjutant General James Davidson, and by him filed in the records of his office as late at least as 1870.

"The copy now presented to the public is reproduced from the *Bulletin's* print of 1836, and carefully compared with the official manuscript referred to. In its preparation for the press the Hon. E. M. Pease and the Hon. Moses Austin Bryan have been freely consulted in regard to the corrections of manifest errors in the orthography of proper names. With the exception of such emendations, this copy does not vary in any particular from the record now on file in the adjutant general's office. Appended to this report will be found that of Colonel Pedro Delgado, a staff officer in the service of General Santa Anna. The latter was published in General Fillasola's 'Memoirs on the Campaign of 1836 in Texas,' and is presented in this connection in order that the scene may be reviewed from both an American and Mexican standpoint, and that an approach to historical completeness may thus be given to the subject.

"The whole is now republished on the State's anniversary, to commemorate the greatest event in her history, in the hope that the perusal may kindle afresh the homage due to brave men, and inspire in every Texan heart a proud fealty to the principles for which they fought. The glories of Marathon were painted in the porticos of Athens, her heroes were sculptured at Delphi, and a temple to Minerva was built from the spoils taken upon her bloody plains. No memorial perpetuates our Marathon; the deeds of her illustrious dead are destined to live without the monuments of art; and each of her veterans must feel, in the language of his commander, that it is fame enough to say, 'I was a member of the army of San Jacinto!'

"V. O. King
Commissioner"

Mexican Account of the Battle of San Jacinto

By Colonel Pedro Delgado, of General Santa Anna's Staff.

"On the 14th of April, 1836, his excellency the president ordered his staff to prepare to march with only one skiff, and leaving his own and the officers' baggage with General Ramirez y Sesma, who was instructed to remain at the crossing of the Brazos, whither we expected to return in three days. On the 13th the flank companies of the battalions of Matamoras, Aldama, Guerrero, Toluca, Mexico, and, I believe, Guadalajara, had commenced crossing the river with a six-pounder, commanded by Lieutenant Ignacio Arrenal, and fifty mounted men of Tampico and Guanajuato, who formed his excellency's escort. The whole force amounted to six hundred men, more or less.

"About four o'clock p.m. his excellency started for Harrisburg with the force above mentioned.

"The bottom of the Brazos is a dense and lofty timber over three leagues wide. On reaching the prairie we found a small creek which offered only one crossing. The infantry passed it comfortably over a large tree, which had fallen in such a manner as to form a convenient bridge. The ammunition was passed over by hand. But his excellency, to avoid delay, ordered the baggage and the commissary stores to remain packed on the mules. However, the water was soon over the pack saddles, and the opposite bank was steep and slippery. Several mules fell down, interfering with each other, which resulted in a terrible jamming of officers and dragoons, horses and mules. This, together with shouts and curses, completed a scene of wild confusion, which his excellency witnessed with hearty laughter. Several officers and dragoons fell into the water; the stores were damaged, and two mules were drowned. So much for the precipitation of this march. The sun had already set when we resumed the march over a muddy prairie.

"The night was dark, a great many men straggled off, and our piece of artillery bogged at every turn of the wheel. Such was our condition when at about nine o'clock his excellency ordered a halt in a small grove, where we passed the night without water.

"On the 15th, at eight a.m., most of the stragglers joined; we started again. At about noon we reached a plantation abundantly supplied with corn, meal, sheep, and hogs; it had a good garden and fine cotton gin. We halted to refresh men and beasts.

"At three o'clock p.m., after having set fire to the dwelling and gin house, we resumed our march. Here his excellency started ahead with his staff and escort, leaving General Castrillon in command of the infantry. We travelled at a brisk trot for at least ten leagues without halting, until we reached the vicinity of Harrisburg about eleven o'clock at night. His excellency, with an adjutant and fifteen dragoons, went afoot to that town, distant about one mile, entered it, and succeeded in capturing two Americans who stated that Zavala and other members of the so-called government of Texas had left the morning before for Galveston. A part of the infantry joined us on the following morning at daylight.

"On the 16th we remained at Harrisburg to await the arrival of our broken-down stragglers, who kept dropping in until two or three p.m.

"On the opposite side of the bayou we found two or three houses well supplied with wearing apparel, mainly for women's use, fine furniture, an excellent piano, jars of preserves, chocolate, fruit, etc., all of which was appropriated for the use of his excellency and his attendants. I and others obtained only what they could not use. After the houses had been sacked and burned down a party of Americans fired upon our men from the woods. It is wonderful that some of us, camped as we were along the bank of the bayou, were not killed. The quartermaster sergeant of Matamoras was seriously wounded. This incident took place at five o'clock p.m. On the same day Colonel Almonte started from Harrisburg for New Washington with the cavalry.

"On the 17th, at about three p.m., his excellency, after instructing me to burn the town, started for New Washington with the troops. It was nearly dark when we finished crossing the bayou. Then a courier from Colonel Almonte arrived, upon which his excellency ordered Colonel Iberri to start with his adjutant bearing despatches to General Fillasola, on the Brazos. At seven o'clock p.m. we resumed our march. Our piece of artillery bogged at every moment in some hole or ravine. As it was found impossible for the draught mules to cross a narrow bridge, rendered still more dangerous by darkness and rain, his excellency instructed General Castrillon to head the bayou with the cannon three leagues above, with an escort of only one company of infantry.

"Shortly after ten o'clock at night a violent storm set in: darkness caused us to wander from our course, in consequence of which his excellency caused a halt, requiring every man to stand in the ranks without shelter from the rain. On the morning of the 18th we moved on, our cannon still being far away. At noon we reached New Washington, where we found flour, soap, tobacco, and other articles, which were issued to the men. His excellency instructed me to mount one of his horses, and with a small party of dragoons to gather beeves for the use of the troops. In a short time I drove in over one hundred head of cattle, so abundant are they in that country. General Castrillon came in at five o'clock p.m. with the cannon.

"On the 19th his excellency ordered Captain Barragan to start with a detachment of dragoons to reconnoitre Houston's movements. We halted at that place, all being quiet.

"On the 20th, at about eight o'clock a.m., everything was ready for the march. We had burnt a fine warehouse on the wharf and all the houses in the town when Captain Barragan rushed in at full speed, reporting that Houston was close on our rear, and that his troops had captured some of our stragglers and had disarmed and despatched them.

"There is in front of New Washington a dense wood, through which runs a narrow lane about half a league in length, allowing passage to pack mules in single file only, and to mounted men in double file.

This lane was filled with our pickets, the drove of mules, and the remainder of the detachment. His excellency and staff were still in the town. Upon hearing Barragan's report he leaped on his horse and galloped off at full speed for the lane, which, being crowded with men and mules, did not afford him as prompt an exit as he wished. However, knocking down one and riding over another, he overcame the obstacles, shouting at the top of his voice: '*The enemy are coming! The enemy are coming!*'

"The excitement of the general in chief had such a terrifying effect on the men that every face turned pale. Order could no longer be preserved, and every man thought of flight or of finding a hiding place, and gave up all idea of fighting. Upon reaching the prairie a column of attack was formed with trepidation and confusion, amid incoherent movements and contradictory orders. At this moment his excellency did me the honor to place me in command of the artillery and ordnance, giving me his orders verbally, with strict injunctions as to my responsibility.

"Meanwhile the officers having dismounted and taken their stations in front of their commands, we moved in search of the enemy, with flankers on both sides to explore the woods. As the knapsacks might impede the movements of the men, his excellency ordered that they should be dropped on the road, still preserving our formation. The order was obeyed, the knapsacks being left in the keeping of Providence or fortune, and we resumed our march.

"It was two o'clock p.m. when we descried Houston's pickets at the edge of a large wood in which he concealed his main force. Our skirmishers commenced firing, when they were answered by the enemy, who fell back into the wood. His excellency reached the ground with the main body, with the intention, as I understood, of attacking at once; but they kept hidden, which kept him from ascertaining their position.

"He therefore changed his dispositions and ordered the company of Toluca to deploy as skirmishers in the direction of the woods. Our cannon, established on a small elevation, opened its fire. The enemy responded with a discharge of grape, which wounded severely Captain Urrezza and killed his horse. At this moment his excellency came to me and ordered me to unload the ordnance stores and to turn over the twenty mules on which they were packed to Captain Barragan, who was instructed to bring in the knapsacks that had been left on the road. I was cautious enough to part with only eighteen mules, keeping two for an emergency. Then his excellency went to look for a camping ground, and established his whole force along the shore of San Jacinto Bay, at least one mile from the place where I had been left. About one hour later I received orders through Colonel Bringas to come into camp immediately with the ordnance stores and the piece of artillery. That officer was also the bearer of an order to the company of Toluca, the only force that checked the enemy, to fall back likewise. I observed to Colonel Bringas that it would take some time to execute this order, the chests, as his excellency knew, being piled up upon the ground, and I having only two mules upon which to load them; and that, furthermore, if the company of Toluca left me unsupported the enemy would probably pounce upon the stores, all of which would go to the devil. Colonel Bringas advised me to do as best I could, adding that I ought to know that no observations could be made to his excellency, and he had no desire to argue with him in the raving state of mind in which he was. The colonel parted from me, followed by the company of Toluca. It may well be imagined that when the enemy saw our artillery and stores unprotected he paid them special attention. He established his cannon in such a manner as to disable our gun and to support an attack, should it take place. Their first shot shattered the caisson on the limber; another scattered about our ordnance boxes; another, again, killed two fine mules; and they kept annoying us during the two long hours it took me to remove, with only two mules, forty and odd boxes of ammunition. How the general in chief had endangered the whole division!

"I acknowledge that I had never before been in such danger. What would have become of me if in consequence of the general's order the enemy had captured our artillery and ordnance stores, as he might have done, unsupported as it was? I had no resource left but to make the best defence I could with my gun. For this purpose I instructed Lieutenant Arenal to have it loaded with grape, and not to fire until the enemy came in close range, in order both to spare ammunition and to intimidate the assailants.

"At length, at five o'clock p.m., my duty was performed, and as I entered the camp with the last load I was closely followed by the enemy's cavalry. His excellency, noticing it, instructed me to order Captain Aguirre, who commanded our cavalry, to face the enemy without gaining ground. This movement checked the enemy for a few moments; but soon after they dashed upon our dragoons and were close enough to engage them with the sword, without, however, any material result.

"Then his excellency, deploying several companies as skirmishers, forced the enemy back to his camp, on which he retired sluggishly and in disorder. This engagement took place after sundown. At daybreak on the 21st his excellency ordered a breastwork to be erected for the cannon. It was constructed with pack saddles, sacks of hard bread, baggage, etc. A trifling barricade of branches ran along its front and right. The camping ground of his excellency's selection was in all respects against military rules. Any youngster could have done better.

"We had the enemy on our right in a wood at long musket range. Our front, although level, was exposed to the fire of the enemy, who could keep it up with impunity from his sheltered position. Retreat was easy for him on his rear and right, while our own troops had no space for manoeuvring. We had in our rear a small grove, reaching to the bay shore, which extended on our right as far as New Washington. What ground had we to retreat upon in case of a reverse? From sad experience I answer, none!

"A few hours before the engagement I submitted to General Castrillon a few remarks on the subject, suggested by my limited knowledge; but he answered: *'What can I do, my friend? I know it well, but I cannot help it. You know that nothing avails here against the caprice, arbitrary will, and ignorance of that man!'*

"This was said in an impassioned voice and in close proximity to his excellency's tent.

"At nine o'clock a.m. General Cos came in with a reinforcement of about five hundred men. His arrival was greeted by the roll of drums and with joyful shouts. As it was represented to his excellency that these men had not slept the night before, he instructed them to stack their arms, remove their accoutrements, and go to sleep quietly in the adjoining grove.

"No important incident took place until half-past four p.m. At this fatal moment the bugler on the right signalled the enemy's advance upon that wing. His excellency and staff were asleep. The greater number of the men were also sleeping. Of the rest, some were eating, others were scattered in the woods in search of boughs to prepare shelter. Our line was composed of musket stacks. Our cavalry were riding bareback to and from water. I stepped upon some ammunition boxes the better to observe the movements of the enemy. I saw that their formation was a mere line in one rank, and very extended. In their centre was the Texas flag. On both wings they had two light cannon, well manned. Their cavalry was opposite our front, overlapping our left. In this disposition, yelling furiously, with a brisk fire of grape, muskets, and rifles, they advanced resolutely upon our camp. There the utmost confusion prevailed. General Castrillon shouted on one side; on another Colonel Almonte was giving orders; some cried out to commence firing, others to lie down to avoid the grapeshot. Among the latter was his excellency.

"Then already I saw our men flying in small groups, terrified and sheltering themselves behind large trees. I endeavored to force some of them to fight, but all efforts were in vain; the evil was beyond remedy. They were a bewildered, panic-stricken herd.

"The enemy kept up a brisk crossfire of grape on the woods. Presently we heard in close proximity the unpleasant noise of their clamors.

"Meeting no resistance, they dashed lightning-like upon our deserted camp.

"Then I saw his excellency running about in the utmost excitement, wringing his hands and unable to give an order. General Castrillon was stretched upon the ground, wounded in the leg. Colonel Treviño was killed, and Colonel Marcial Aguirre was severely wounded. I saw also the enemy reaching the ordnance train and killing a corporal and two gunners who had been detailed to repair cartridges which had been damaged on the previous evening. Everything was lost. I went, leading my horse—which I could not mount, as the firing had rendered him restless and fractious—to join our men, still hoping that we might be able to defend ourselves or to retire under shelter of the night. This, however, could not be done. It is a known fact that Mexican soldiers, once demoralized, cannot be controlled unless they are thoroughly inured to war. On the left, and about a musket-shot distant from our camp, was a small grove on the bay shore. Our disbanded herd rushed for it to obtain shelter from the horrid slaughter carried on all over the prairie by the bloodthirsty usurpers. Unfortunately we met in our way an obstacle hard to overcome. It was a bayou, not very wide, but rather deep. The men, on reaching it, would hopelessly crowd together, and were shot down by the enemy, who was close enough to not miss his aim. It was there that the greatest carnage took place.

"Upon reaching that spot I saw Colonel Almonte swimming across the bayou with his left hand, and holding up his right, which grasped his sword. I stated before that I was leading my horse, but at this critical situation I vaulted upon him, and with two leaps he landed me on the opposite side of the bayou. To my sorrow I had to leave the noble animal mired in that place, and to part with him probably forever.

"As I dismounted I sank into the mire waist deep, and I had the greatest trouble to get out of it by catching hold of the grass. Both my shoes remained in the bayou. I made an effort to recover them, but I came to the conclusion that did I tarry there a rifleshot would make an outlet for my soul, as had happened to many a poor fellow around me. Thus I made for the grove barefooted.

"There I met a number of other officers, with whom I wandered at random, buried in gloomy thoughts upon our tragic disaster.

"We still entertained a hope of rallying some of the men, but it was impossible.

"The enemy's cavalry surrounded the grove, while his infantry penetrated it, pursuing us with fierce and bloodthirsty feelings.

"There they killed Colonel Batres; and it would have been all over with us had not Providence placed us in the hands of that noble and generous captain of cavalry, Allen, who by great exertion saved us repeatedly from being slaughtered by the drunken and infuriated volunteers.

"Thence they marched us to their camp. I was barefooted; the prairie had recently been burned, and the stubble, hardened by the fire, penetrated like needles the soles of my feet, so that I could scarcely walk. This did not prevent them from striking me with the butt end of their guns because I did not walk as fast as they wished. These savages struck with their bayonets our wounded soldiers lying on the way; others following them consummated the sacrifice by a musket or a pistol shot. I cannot forbear the mention of an incident that affected me deeply, and, I believe, had the same effect on my companions. We were about one hundred and fifty officers and men picked up by Allen's party, who marched us to their camp under a close guard. I have no doubts that the Americans, amidst the hurrahs and exultation of their triumph, were lavish of insults; however, not understanding their language, we did not feel them. But one of our own countrymen, who had joined the enemy's cause, assailed us in our own language with such a volley of threats, insults, and abuse that the tongue of that vile and recreant Mexican seemed to have been wrought in the very caves of hell and set in motion by Lucifer himself. 'Now you shall see,' he said, 'contemptible and faithless assassins, if you do not pay with your vile blood for your murders at the Alamo and La Bahia. The time has come when the just cause that we defend triumphs over you; you shall pay with your heads for the arson, robberies, and depredations that you have committed in our country,' etc., etc. What a welcome to honorable men, who knew in the depths of their hearts that they had acted in accordance with the dictates of duty, when, unfortunate, prostrate, and humble in the extreme, the fate of war had placed their lives in the hands of these brigands, and when they were waiting with resignation the consummation of the sacrifice! Can such wicked men exist?

"At last we reached the camp. We were seated on the ground by twos, as we had marched. On the bay shore our thirst had been quenched by an abundance of water, which Allen and others allowed to pass from hand to hand until all were satisfied. A crowd gathered around us, asking with persistent impertinence: 'General Santa Anna?' 'General Cos?' We knew not the fate of these gentlemen; but to rid ourselves of their repeated questions we answered, 'Dead!' 'Dead!' I still wore my embroidered shoulder straps on my jacket; they attracted their attention, and one after another would say, 'You general?' 'Me no general,' would I answer, until one of the indefatigable questioners tore off my shoulder straps angrily. I was glad of it, as they ceased importuning me with their questions.

After keeping us sitting there about an hour and a half they marched us into the woods, where we saw an immense fire, made up of piles of wood, even whole trees being used.

I and several of my companions were silly enough to believe that we were about to be burnt alive in retaliation for those who had been burnt in the Alamo. We should have considered it an act of mercy to be shot first. Oh! the bitter and cruel moment. However, we felt considerably relieved when they placed us around the fire to warm ourselves and to dry our wet clothes. We were surrounded by twenty-five or thirty sentinels. You should have seen those men, or rather phantoms, converted into moving armories. Some wore two, three, and even four brace of pistols, a cloth bag of very respectable size filled with bullets, a powder horn, a sabre or a Bowie knife, besides a rifle, a musket, or carbine. Every one of them had in his hand a burning candle. I wonder where they obtained so many of them, for the heat and the breeze melted them very fast; and yet that illumination was kept up the whole night. Was this display of light intended to prevent us from attempting to escape? The fools! Where could we go in that vast country, unknown to us, intersected by large rivers and forests, where wild beasts and hunger, and where they themselves, would destroy us?

"Early on the morning of the 22nd our camp was visited by the so-called Secretary of War, Mr. Rusk, who asked us endless questions upon the grand topic of the day—our defeat and their unexpected success. Colonel Juan N. Almonte, the only one of us that spoke English, answered his questions. That gentleman renewed his visits. Once he asked for a list of the names, surnames, and rank of all the captured officers, which list was promptly made up by Almonte, with a pen or a pencil, I do not remember which, and handed over immediately.

"There were not wanting among us officers sufficiently forgetful of duty, and the dignity and decorum of their rank, to mingle with the enlisted men, because it was rumored that from sergeant down would be spared, and from lieutenant up would be shot. What a shame that such contemptible beings, destitute of honor, should still associate with those who have always proudly borne and gloried in their noble badges of office!

"Some Americans would come and tell us in broken Spanish what was going on among their leaders, stating that the officers and the people—that is, the soldiery—were holding a meeting to consider the question whether we should be shot before notifying it to their government, or whether the execution should be postponed until ordered by the superior authority.

"Such was the state of our affairs when the assembly roll, or something else, was beaten. Over a hundred men fell into line. They loaded their guns, and then stood at ease. We felt nervous. I, for one, was as cold as ice, believing that those who were in favor of immediate execution had carried the point, and that the fatal moment had come. Soon, however, our confidence returned when a good man (they are to be found everywhere) told us to cheer up, as Houston, Rusk, Allen, and others, whom I respect for it, had opposed the motion. In fact, the party that had formed near us had gone to relieve the guard.

"At this time they began bringing in on wagons and on our own mules the arms, stores, baggage, clothing, and all the spoils of our camp, which operation took four whole days.

"At two o'clock p.m. his excellency the general in chief, Don Antonio Lopez de Santa Anna, arrived under the charge of a mounted soldier. He wore linen trousers, a blue cotton jacket, a cap, and red worsted slippers. His leader did not know him, but, noticing a movement of curiosity amongst us as he approached, he became satisfied that he was conducting no common officer, and reported at once with him to General Houston. The latter sent two of his adjutants to inquire of us whether Santa Anna had lost any teeth. Some answered that they did not know, but others, with more candor, or perhaps less discretion, said: 'Yes, gentlemen; and you can further say to your general that the person just brought before him is President Santa Anna himself.' The news spread over the whole camp, and the inquisitive fellows who surrounded us ran to strike up an acquaintance with his excellency. Some of them proposed to fire salutes and to make other demonstrations to celebrate the capture of so lofty a personage; but Houston courteously forbade it. From this time we were left alone, his excellency having become the centre of attraction.

"On the 23rd seventy or eighty loads of ordnance stores had been brought in and deposited, together with piles of loaded muskets and cartridge boxes, in close proximity to our camp. We had noticed repeatedly that some of the Americans went about that combustible matter, and even handled it, with their pipes in their mouths. In one of these instances of carelessness some grains of powder scattered on the ground were ignited. The fire reached the cartridge boxes and their contents, and soon extended to the pans of the muskets, which exploded like an infernal machine. The prairie, too, was set on fire, and the covers of the ordnance boxes were already burning. Those nearest to the scene of danger took to flight. We and our sentinels followed, and, although we knew they would be dissatisfied at our race, and might possibly fire at us, we kept running. Then the guard and some of the officers, in view of the increasing danger, chose not to remain hindmost, and kept pace with us, expecting at every moment the fatal explosion. We had run a considerable distance when we turned and looked back, and discovered that the fire had been extinguished. We could not help applauding the resolution and bold determination with which some of these extraordinary men had rushed into the flames and smothered them with their feet and blankets and some water from the bay. We had a narrow escape. I thought at one time that the conquerors of San Jacinto would all be blown up into eternity; not, however, without some regret on my part to have to go the way they went, owing to their stupid carelessness.

"On the 24th several batches of officers and men were brought in by the numerous scouting parties sent out to search the country.

"At five o'clock p.m. a steamboat arrived, having on board the Texan president, Vice President Zavala, and other members of the administration. The artillery on board, consisting of two guns, fired a salute of five rounds. The troops in camp were formed in line, and received their supreme magistrate with hurrahs. Then he was conducted triumphantly to General Houston's tent.

"Among the Yankees who spoke Spanish a little, and came to talk with, or rather to insult, us, was a hunchback, an inveterate talker. The wretch, who did not measure a yard and a half above the ground, took a wicked pleasure in bringing us stirring and unpleasant news. He boasted much of his gallantry, and when reciting his many acts of prowess the little rascal would say: 'Well, did Santa Anna believe that he could trifle with us? Not he! He can, perhaps, fight his own people, because he knows them, and knows also that they are not brave, gallant, and determined as we are. He thought us far away, poor fellow, without noticing that we were on his track, keeping him in sight, counting with our spyglasses, on treetops, his men one by one, and allowing him to come and entrap himself in this corner with no means of escape, as we had burnt the bridge over the bayou behind him and made our preparations to bag every one of you. If he does not at once sign a treaty putting an end to the war, and removing every Mexican soldier from our territory, it will cost not only his life but also the lives of all you prisoners.' Such was the conversation of our bold little hunchback.

"On the 25th General Cos and Captains Bachiler and Iberri were confined with us. The presence of the general had created such a sensation among the conquerors that they crowded and quarrelled for a sight of him. They would even push off the sentinels. The general found it expedient to lie down, wrapping his head in his blanket, to avoid the annoyance of their impertinent curiosity. Scoundrels were not wanting who would have murdered him.

"On the 26th our property was sold at auction. It was hard to see them breaking our trunks open and every one of them loaded with our shirts, trousers, coats, etc., while we remained with what we had on our bodies. I saw my boots going, while my blistered feet were wrapped in pieces of rawhide. To make up for our cloaks, overcoats, and blankets, which belonged to the highest bidder, they favored us with the greatcoats of our own soldiers, which were so lousy that we had the greatest trouble to rid ourselves of the vermin. And still we had nothing else with which to cover ourselves. His excellency the general in chief alone had the good fortune to preserve the most, if not all, of his baggage. The saddles and pack mules belonging to our division were also distributed among the conquering officers and soldiers. It was quite amusing to see these gentlemen putting riding saddles on some fractious and wicked mule which knew nothing beyond the pack. They would adorn them with the green and red cords which our grenadiers and voltigeurs wore on their caps, placing them on their ears, necks, and backs. One did put two pairs of blinds on one mule—one on the headstall, as it should be, and the other on the nose band, stopping the poor animal's nostrils. They would also bedeck their mules with the epaulets of our officers, caring little if the one was white and the other yellow. They glittered—that was enough. They delighted to cover their animals with all sorts of trappings and colors, after the fashion of our bullfight clowns.

"One of these young chevaliers attracted more especially my attention. He had saddled up and adorned his mule, without, however, noticing that the surcingle was loose. He mounted the long-eared steed, which was held fast by some of his friends while he steadied himself in the saddle. They let go, and you should have seen the brute scampering over God's own green fields and scattering about its trappings and ornaments. Lo! our poor Yankee flies on high with his saddle, and drops heavily to the ground, from which he could not rise, his ribs being somewhat damaged.

"This was not the worst, but the mule once in the woods could not be caught again. Trials of horsemanship lasted the whole day, but most of the champions shared the fate of the first one. How strange these men are! Many of them act and feel like the wild Comanche!

"On the 27th and following days no incident took place worth being noticed. I will only say, to the lasting shame of our conquerors, that they kept us starving, sleeping in the mud, and exposed to frequent and heavy showers. Still more intolerable was the stench rising from the corpses on the field of San Jacinto, which they had not the generosity to burn or bury after the time-honored custom, regardless of their own comfort and health and those of the surrounding settlements. On the 3rd of May, at four o'clock p.m., we were sent to another camp, distant a little over one league. There were two or three frame houses, but they were occupied by both the conquering and the conquered generals, lodgings being provided for us under the trees. There again an attempt was made to murder General Cos. Four days passed quietly along. On the 7th, at five o'clock p.m., they marched us on board the steamboat *Yellowstone*, where we found General Santa Anna, the president, Señor Zavala, and other dignitaries of their so-called government.

"Shortly afterwards General Houston was carried on board on his cot, on his way to New Orleans to obtain medical attendance for a wound received in the leg at the battle of San Jacinto. There was also the Mexican general Adrian Woll, who had come from our army under flag of truce. This gallant general, our good friend, was dismissed at sundown, being hardly allowed to embrace two or three of us with a few hurried words, as we were surrounded by very strict and insolent guards. I saw, as he landed, tears of indignation gushing forth from his eyes at the wretched and degraded condition of his brothers in arms. I am sure that he wished he was lightning to smite our oppressors. In parting with us he expressed the deepest sorrow.

"The officer under whose charge we were on board was, if I do not mistake, a physician, and was very harsh and tyrannical. After sunset we were no longer permitted to move, having to sleep on deck, crowded like bars of soap on top of each other. Positive orders had been given the sentinels to blow out the brains of any man who raised his head. Therefore, without obtaining a drink of water or being allowed to attend to the wants of nature, we laid our heads down, motionless until sunrise. Very early on the 8th, after striking a bell three times, as is customary on these vessels, the machine was set in motion and we glided down to Galveston. Not to forget it, I mention a strange incident. As the steamboat passed opposite the battlefield of San Jacinto the troops on board were formed, facing to the field, and presented arms, the drums beating a march. They remained in that position until they had lost sight of the field. What was their object?

"A little after twelve o'clock m. we reached Galveston, remaining in the sun the rest of the day. There we passed another unpleasant moment. The company from Kentucky was composed of the most reckless, drunken, and lawless men in the Texan army, and we prisoners were placed under the charge of these lambs. Some of the men began—I know not why—to fight with their fists, which soon brought about a general melee. They struck at each other indiscriminately, some seizing their rifles and pistols. Officers interfered and were soon mingled in the row, giving and receiving blows. Soldiers knew no longer their officers, and a fierce affray raged for some time. The uproar and stamping of feet on deck arrested the attention of the gentlemen in the cabin below. They came out to ascertain the cause of the difficulty, but the rascals were so hotly engaged in their contest that they did not mind the voice of their president and other chiefs any more than the barking of dogs. Fearful that the disorder might increase, and perhaps end in a tragic manner, we remained motionless. At last, by choking some of them and by the utmost exertion, the brave Captain Allen succeeded in restoring order. Santa Anna was transferred on board the *Independence*, and we were landed at sunset. I was lucky enough to meet Lieutenant Carlos Ocampo, of the battalion of Jimenes, who gave me a bounteous supply of coffee and hard bread, with which I made up for the past two days' fast.

"For several days our philanthropic benefactors had allowed us but one ounce of food. The citizens, Don Ramon Murgo and Don Gil Hernandez, who had been captured on a Mexican vessel boarded by the Texans, shared the captivity of Lieutenant Ocampo. The bad treatment inflicted by these wretches on that officer can scarce be conceived. I saw his shoulders covered with stripes and sores resulting from one hundred lashes laid on him while fastened to a gun. On the 9th we were assigned a camping ground about fifty square feet, where we remained until the middle of August.

"On the 16th the Mexican prisoners were removed to Anahuac, where they remained until the 25th, when they were started, in charge of Judge William Hardin, for Liberty. Colonel Delgado pronounces the highest eulogiums upon the kindness and generosity of this gentleman, and the friendly offices performed by his estimable wife in behalf of the sick Mexicans.

"A ball was given by the citizens of Liberty on the 21st of April, 1837, to which all the neighboring families were invited. The ball was intended to commemorate the bloody 21st of April, 1836, on which day so many illustrious Mexicans were immolated. These people had the effrontery to invite to that criminal entertainment General Cos, who, of course, declined.

"A petition was gotten up, says Colonel Delgado, asking the Texan government to despatch the prisoners at once or release them.

"Hallowed be the hour when this petition was inspired! Its results were that we were set free, which happy news reached us on the memorable 25th day of April, 1837."

Chapter 11

In compliance with General Houston's order directing that the inhabitants of the western counties should remove east, so that they might enjoy the protection of his army, I, as the alcalde of Victoria, notified the people that the enemy would soon be upon us, and counselled a retreat to Cox's Point, on the east side of Lavaca Bay, as affording, with our limited means of transportation, the most feasible mode of escape from the invading armies of Santa Anna. My public duties being thus fulfilled, I next found employment in devising means for the removal of my own family. Don Fernando de Leon, as soon as he had taken his family to his ranch on the Garcitas, placed at my disposal two yoke of oxen; and with these and a cart I commenced the weary exodus. In the vehicle I placed a few articles of prime necessity, my wife with an infant but fifteen days old, and two poor women with two or three children who had no means of leaving the town. My household effects, residence, as well as my store and stock of goods, were left in the almost deserted village and consigned to the care of Providence. My doleful procession, consisting of the ox cart before mentioned and one small wagon, set out on its pilgrimage the 17th day of March, 1836. I intended going by my warehouse on the bay (the location known as "Linnville"), but received information that my boat had gone up the Garcitas, and so I directed my course to that point. We camped in the prairie that night; and a norther, with some rain, coming up, we spent anything but an agreeable night. The next day we reached the mouth of the Garcitas, and I despatched a messenger for the boat. While here three men, Rutledge, Davis, and Hudson, who had escaped from Colonel Ward's ill-fated Georgia battalion, came to us. They had left Ward at the crossing of the Guadalupe River, and had subsisted on wild onions solely for several days, and were consequently weak and emaciated as the result of such unwholesome food. On the arrival of my boat I took them with me to Cox's Point, where I found the people panic-stricken at the startling news that was sweeping the country. All were engaged in preparing for a hasty flight "east"—an ambiguous locality, between which and the legions of his Mexican excellency the safety of space interposed. I procured a barrel of flour of Mr. J. R. Foster, who had in charge all the stores at the "Point," and also engaged a "lighter" and a man to manage it, by which means I purposed landing my family and effects. The fellow, however, deserted me with the "lighter," and I was left to the reliance of my own resources for assistance. Upon landing a family "council of war" was held, and, as the barrel of flour constituted our sole provision, it was deemed best that we should proceed to the De Leon ranch, on the Garcitas, and kill a beef. On the way we met Don Fernando de Leon, who informed me that he had met Colonel Horton at the crossing on the Garcitas, in full retreat; that Horton represented Colonel Fannin as surrounded by the army of Urrea in the prairie, and that he would inevitably be forced to succumb. De Leon advised me to leave my family at his ranch, promising to protect them as his own, and to hasten eastward myself, as the Mexican army would be in Victoria very soon after disposing of Fannin. There being no alternative, I accepted the kind offer of my friend, and, bidding a sorrowful adieu to my wife and sister in the lone prairie, turned the head of my horse and took my solitary way in the direction of the rising sun and General Houston's army. I swam the Garcitas and, lost in solemn thoughts suggested by my separation from my loved ones, journeyed on in silence. My departure was not too early, as I afterwards learned, for my family had reached the ranch of Mr. De Leon but a few minutes when a Mexican officer and five soldiers arrived from Victoria. The officer made minute inquiries of the Texan army and in regard to the antecedents of Mr. De Leon. This officer was a German and spoke English fluently; hence had been selected by General Urrea for this mission. He stated that it was not the purpose of General Urrea to molest the inhabitants of the country who remained at their homes and took no part in the war. This officer was Captain Holtzinger. He informed De Leon of Fannin's surrender and the occupation of Victoria by General Urrea; that the general would depend on the citizens for much subsistence, and that the principals of the various ranches must present themselves at headquarters within three days. Captain Holtzinger took the two boats that were at the ranch and proceeded to Cox's Point to capture the stores; but the *Brutus* landed there, and everything was consigned to the flames, so that Holtzinger found only the charred remains on his arrival.

I will here remark that it was extremely fortunate that I did not send my family to Matagorda, as I at one time thought of doing, as the Carankua Indians were committing depredations on the coast and had killed several persons in the vicinity of where now stands Indianola.

I crossed the Lavaca River at Dr. Wells's crossing, and camped, or rather made my lonely bivouac, in the post oaks near Texana. The norther which had sprung up the previous night continued to blow, and the cold prevented me from sleeping. I passed through Texana at daybreak, and found the village deserted by all its inhabitants. I crossed the Navidad at Frank White's. I found his premises deserted, but in the smoke-house I found a piece of dried beef, which constituted my breakfast.

I arrived at Casey's farm, on the Colorado, just at sundown, and ascertained that all the refugees from the Lavaca and Navidad rivers were congregated on the east bank of this stream. Among all the human race I knew of but one whom I had any reasons to regard in the light of a personal enemy; and this one was Mr. Ira Ingram, a person of a very forbidding nature, who would scruple not to justify any means for the attainment of a desired end. Him I met at the ferry, and recognized in the dark scowl of his dissembling countenance the evil elements that were prompting his vengeful heart to action. At his instance I was speedily arrested as a spy—solely at his instigation, I repeat, and without the shadow of a single specific charge. I was perfectly aware of the illegality of the arrest, and, indeed, there was not an intelligent man who knew the circumstances but regarded it in the light of an outrage. I was left to pursue the even tenor of my way, and proceeded to Matagorda, intending, however, at the first convenient season to demand an investigation of Ingram's charges. The inhabitants had left this place apparently in the greatest haste. At the mouth of the bayou I saw a piano and much other furniture that had been left, or thrown from the boats to allow the lighters to pass the bar.

I proceeded to the domicile of my old friend S. R. Fisher. I turned my horse loose to graze, and, contrary to his invariable custom, he did not come up the next morning. In vain I searched for my horse the whole forenoon, feeling as much vexed as did the Highland huntsman when he gazed for the last time, in pensive mood, upon

"Thy fleet limbs, my matchless steed."

Finally I went up the road about a mile, and saw a man leading a horse which distance presented to the view with all of the outlines of my own. The image of the individual leading him was presented to the camera of my mind's eye as the enemy before alluded to. I was fully determined now to give the miscreant a sound thrashing, and so announced my purpose in language more vigorous than polite as I made for him; but the cowardly poltroon absolutely disarmed me by the profusion of his servile supplications for mercy. Taking my horse, I returned to the house of my friend, intending to set out again in the afternoon, when I was arrested once more at the instance of Ingram.

I endeavored to have some specifications in substantiation of the charge, but in vain. Mr. Fisher, who was a justice of the peace, would not investigate the matter, alleging want of jurisdiction. He (Ingram) had made application for the arrest, and Mr. Fisher refused to have anything to do with it. But I wished to free myself in some manner of the sleuth hound, who I knew would dog my trail throughout the land, and so requested Mr. Fisher that he should send me to General

Houston in charge of a nominal guard. This my friend consented to do; and with Mr. Diggs, my *soi-disant* guard, I set out for the Brazos. The army was finally reached, in camp near "Groce's Retreat," and I proceeded immediately to the tent of General Houston. General Houston expressed astonishment at the story of my persecution, and said that he never entertained a doubt of my patriotism and the rectitude of my intentions. The general also did me the honor to ask an expression of my opinions in regard to the political and military situation. He presented to me an outline of his "Fabian policy," and stated his belief that the Mexican dictator would meet with a defeat as crushing and disastrous to his unholy cause as that which befell the great Napoleon in Russia, could he once be seduced sufficiently far east.

The result of the glorious battle of San Jacinto was a thorough verification of General Houston's acuteness and sagacity as expressed in this interview. But I dissented very respectfully from his views at the time, believing that the army, which was composed of the best of our population, and rendered desperate by the inhuman atrocity of the butchers of the Alamo and La Bahia, would prove itself more than a match for the "ragged Indians" of the "Napoleon of the west" at any time, in whatever latitude, and under whatever circumstances they should be permitted to encounter them. I urged the peculiar desirableness of the Brazos upon which to make the trial of strength and valor on whose issue the fate of an empire depended. The general said that he had given this point much consideration, and that he had the steamboat *Yellowstone*, with which he could throw troops to either side with speed and facility.

Though rumors of Fannin's tragic fate had spread over the land, no authoritative announcement had been received. Confirmation, however, of an indisputable correctness now came to the general's knowledge. The loss of this disastrous battle seemed for a while to cast a gloom over the countenances of the men, but it was succeeded by a fixed resolution of terrible earnestness, and henceforth the wish most dear to the hearts of the men of that army was to meet the Mexicans in battle.

I was here a witness of some of the trials to which the commander in chief was subjected in his efforts to discipline a turbulent body of citizen soldiery. Two men had been tried and condemned to death for mutiny. One, and the leader in the crime, was an elderly person. The other was a young man. Sentence had been passed, the coffins arranged, and the doomed men placed in position to receive the leaden messengers of fate. The general in chief had given instructions to the officer of the day that he should be apprised five minutes before the hour designated for the execution. The last notes of the "Dead March" were still lingering like sepulchral echoes upon the air; the doomed men were kneeling beside the yawning "six-foot headright" that destiny seemed according them instead of the princely domain of their anticipations, when the majestic form of the general in chief appeared upon the scene, accompanied by his adjutant, John A. Wharton.

The general addressed the kneeling figures upon the magnitude of their crime in lofty and touching terms, and concluded by offering them a pardon. The men, especially the younger, seemed touched by the general's magnanimity and returned thanks for his clemency.

General Houston, knowing that I had a vessel plying between New Orleans and the ports of Texas, advised me to go to Harrisburg and see the president relative to the removal of families in exposed localities to Galveston. I did so, and was accorded interviews with President Burnet and Vice President Zavala, both of whom expressed astonishment and mortification at the persecutions to which I had been subjected by Ingram, and advised me to pay no further attention to the fellow. Upon learning that I was expecting the arrival of a vessel from New Orleans with a cargo of goods, Mr. Burnet proposed to purchase for the use of the army all groceries and such clothing and material as would be serviceable; that Colonel Triplett, late of Kentucky, was appointed a financial agent of Texas, and would be able to pay me for the same speedily. While I was here a man arrived who represented himself as one who had escaped the "Fannin massacre." Some doubted the correctness of his story, and I was called upon to see if I could recognize him. I did. He was one Hobson (if I now have the name correctly), and formerly, I think, of Captain Collingsworth's company. He said that he was of the party who were shot near the river; that at the first fire he broke and ran to the river, in which he submerged himself, with only his nose out of the water, until all danger had passed, when he made his way to the east. During his first night after the massacre he passed over the identical spot of the late battle and the sadder *noche trieste* that succeeded it. The bodies of many of the slain yet remained on the field—ghastly monuments to the inhumanity of the victors. His tale was only too true!

Being in New Orleans in May 1837, a friend of mine, William McMasters, one day inquired respecting my difficulties with Ingram, and expressed surprise that a man who was a total moral wreck, as Ingram was, could have attained to any prominence in Texas. McMasters stated that while he was teaching school in Utica, New York, Ingram was convicted and sentenced to the penitentiary for uttering a forged note for the paltry sum of twenty dollars.

After ascertaining these facts I caused to be published in the Louisiana *Advertiser* the following letter, and sent copies to various friends in Texas, among whom were Dr. Archer and Judge Franklin. Dr. Archer, on reading the letter, went to Ingram and informed him of the same, and stated that were he Ingram, and the statements were untrue, he would slay the author. "Supposing they were true?" asked mine enemy.

"Then," replied Archer, "I would forsake society and retire to the solitudes of the forest." The miserable wretch did this, and died not a great while afterwards in his hermit's hut on the peninsula.

From the Louisiana Advertiser, May 6, 1837

(Communicated.)

"In your paper of the 5th ultimo there was a paragraph, headed 'Vicissitudes of Fortune,' which goes on to state how one Ira Ingram was convicted in 1813 or 1814, in the town of Utica, New York, for forgery, and that one Ira Ingram is now Speaker of the Texas House of

Representatives. This is the identical Ira Ingram, who has imposed himself on the good people of Matagorda, and to the disgrace of Texas, with many others—such men as M_____ B_____, etc.—who now cut such conspicuous figures before the world. I have no particular objection to the men in question, but I think it is a republican principle that each man should be treated according to his real merits, and should always appear in his proper garb, particularly public men. It would better suit, and be more in place and character, for the first-named demagogue to put on his robes of membership while in the New York State prison, and for the other to have a label on his back with a reward of five thousand dollars as an absconding felon; then we could judge accordingly, and the public would know how to appreciate their real worth. Such is and has been the audacity of villains of all times and ages that we hope, for the honor of our sister republic, that the people will, by their own inherent love of justice, drive such villanous scoundrels from among their councils. They have honest and good men enough among them, and equally as capable of filling their stations, and not to have themselves derided with the oft-repeated insult that none but swindlers and outlaws go to Texas. Let them, I say again, attend to this. If any one feels aggravated at the above statement let him call at this office, and he can be fully satisfied as to its correctness and the author's name.

"A Friend to Texas"

A meeting of the citizens of Jackson County, to take into consideration the political aspect of affairs, was held at Navidad as early as July 19, 1835, of which body James Kerr was chairman and Samuel Rodgers secretary. The organization formulated their opinions in a series of resolutions, in which Santa Anna was pronounced an enemy to the constitution of 1824 and to local State government. Opposition to any force that might be introduced into Texas by the dictator was advised, unless it was evident that the presence of such troops was designed to conserve some useful and constitutional purpose. And as it was reported that a body of troops was then en route from La Bahia to San Antonio, it was the sentiment of the meeting that such troops ought to be intercepted by the authorities of the State, and that the city of San Antonio de Bexar should be taken and occupied by State militia.

A report of the proceedings of this spirited meeting was sent to San Felipe de Austin, but no official action was predicated thereupon.

Mr. Lewis, of Matagorda, addressed the citizens of San Felipe in favor of subscribing to the Navidad resolutions in a speech replete with arguments, but to no purpose. I was present at the Navidad meeting. The people of that vicinity always maintained a high standard of patriotism and public enterprise, and they were well represented in the battles about Bexar by a company composed of their best citizens.

I will in this connection mention briefly a matter somewhat personal, which, in reality, is unworthy of any notice whatever. Yokum, page 494, reproduces a letter *alleged* to have been written by General Houston to David Thomas, acting Secretary of War, from his camp on the Brazos, April 11, 1836, in which is suggested the propriety of "watching" "Lynn" and "Kerr."

That General Houston ever wrote this letter in relation to the Hon. James Kerr and myself I cannot believe. I had slept in the tent of the commander in chief on the nights of April 12, 13, and 14, and, as before stated, was invited by him for an expression of my views in regard to the situation of affairs. General Houston was not a hypocrite, and in the plenitude of his power had nothing to gain from dissimulation. He met me with the affable and courteous friendship that had previously characterized his bearing toward me. He expressed his disgust at Ingram, and the absurdity of his malicious charges, and invited me to a confidential interchange of views with himself. Can any man who knew the lofty nature of Houston imagine that he would thus have met me, and the ink yet not dry in which he had written Thomas to "watch" me? Houston's manhood was incapable of sinking to such despicable depths. Again, at the instance of the commander in chief I went to his excellency the president of Texas, who, reposing full confidence in my fidelity and fealty to the Texan government, hastened to engage my services in a field where absolute probity was an indispensable requisite. Certainly, had I the power to have timed coming events, I would have charged with my countrymen on the field of the ever-memorable 21st. But, however great my services in the field could have been, they could not have subserved so materially and effectually the cause of my country as those did which, under Providence, I was enabled to render. But General Houston was well acquainted with me long prior to this time, and as familiar with the orthography of my name as with that of his own. He never addressed me as "Mr. Lynn." Major James Kerr, if indeed he was the individual intended, was among the earliest and the most honorable of Texan immigrants. He performed much labor in the field as a surveyor before and after "annexation." He was a member of the Consultation, and subsequently a member of the Third Congress, well known and esteemed for his intelligence, integrity, and patriotism throughout Texas.

If, perchance, "Peter Kerr" was the suspected one, and not the Hon. James Kerr, a brief mention of him would seem no less appropriate than just.

Peter Kerr, then, was an "old Texan," who traded extensively in livestock. He drove a *caballado* of horses to Louisiana in 1835, as did Fernando de Leon and Jesus J. M. Carbajal immediately after Ugartechea's order for the latter's arrest. After disposing of their animals they chartered a schooner in New Orleans, the *Elizabeth*, and loaded her with goods suitable for the Texas trade, including a quantity of arms and ammunition intended for the use of the patriot Texans. In returning the *Elizabeth* was sighted by the Mexican man-of-war the *Bravo*, and in attempting the east pass of Pass Cavallo was run ashore and seized by the *Bravo*. A prize crew was placed on board the *Elizabeth*, and Carbajal and De Leon removed to the *Bravo* as prisoners. Kerr was left in the custody of the prize crew. A norther springing up that night, the *Bravo* was driven to sea, and ultimately made the port of Matamoras, where Carbajal and De Leon were imprisoned. Fortunately, however, through the assistance of friends, they soon perfected an escape, and ere long arrived at home. A party of enterprising citizens of Matagorda, learning of the situation of affairs at Pass Cavallo, came down in the *William Bobbins* and retook the *Elizabeth*, cargo, prize crew, and all. The captors appropriated the cargo to themselves, offering to allow Peter Kerr to redeem his goods upon the payment of one-half their value. As he was unable to do this, he lost the whole. But that the actions of Peter Kerr ever gave the authorities of Texas ground for suspicion I can not believe. He ultimately settled on the Colorado below Austin, where he died, esteemed by all who knew him as a good citizen. Fernando de Leon was subsequently persecuted by the presentation of unjust claims against him, and, owing to the prejudice then existing against the Mexicans, many illegal and unfair judgments were rendered against him. Thus was a princely landed estate dissipated, and its owner died in comparative poverty.

Many years after its publication Hon. John Henry Brown called my attention to the *alleged* letter of General Houston, just adverted to, for the first time. The lapse of time had rendered its contents of as little moment as the question of its authenticity, and *knowing* my own rectitude, and disbelieving that General Houston was its author, I can say truthfully that it caused me not a moment's anxiety whatever.

And now briefly in regard to the duties that were engaging my attention at the time that *Lieutenant* Yoakum alleges I was an object of suspicion to the government.

My schooner arrived at Galveston with her cargo, and, in conformity to my agreement with President Burnet, I delivered groceries suitable for the army to the amount of thirty-six hundred dollars to the quartermaster, Patrick Jack, receiving in payment therefor a draft on Colonel Triplett, payable in sixty days. Colonel Morgan, who was in command at Galveston, despatched the steamboat *Cayuga* with a portion of these supplies to the army at once.

As we were engaged in loading the *Cayuga* the steamboat *Flash* arrived from New Washington with the president and his suite on board. The enemy had surprised them at the mouth of the San Jacinto, and so close were they pressed that a Mexican soldier actually touched

President Burnet with his gun as the chief executive was stepping into a "flat" that was to bear him to the steamboat. The island was at this time a scene of the utmost confusion. It was the ultimate haven of all refugees from the rapacious soldiery of Santa Anna. The idea of house-room for their accommodation was entirely out of the question, and consequently shelters of every description were improvised, the materials principally entering into their construction being blankets, bed quilts, old pieces of sail, etc.

Quite a fatal accident occurred during the passage of the *Cayuga* to the island. A gun or pistol was carelessly discharged by some negligent person, and the ball entered the leg of Mr. David Thomas, the attorney general, of which wound he died three days after.

The steamboat *Yellowstone* succeeded in running the gauntlet at Fort Bend, where the Mexican army was preparing to cross the Brazos, and brought another cargo of refugees to the "last ditch" of Texan endeavor. These were citizens from the Navidad, the Colorado, and other points. The Mexicans perforated the smokestacks with bullets, but Captain Rose had taken the precaution to protect the pilot with cotton bales; and a full head of steam soon bore her beyond the range of their missiles. The Mexicans attempted time and again to lasso the boat, but fortunately their ropes were not sufficiently long. These were the soldiers who in two or three days afterwards encountered destiny on the plain of San Jacinto. The *Yellowstone* brought us the intelligence that the Texan army had taken the road to Harrisburg. I accidentally discovered a plan which had for its object the seizure of the small boats (as many as would serve their purposes) by a number of restless adventurers who purposed to go that night to Bolivar Point. I lost no time in communicating these facts to Colonel Morgan, and he to the higher authorities. A meeting of patriots was convened on the beach, the president, vice president, and other dignitaries attending. President Burnet made a stirring and patriotic appeal in behalf of the duties of the hour. He appealed to all able-bodied men to go at once to the army; that a decisive battle was imminent. He stated that he had two steamboats loaded with supplies for the army, which he would forward without delay.

Colonel Robert M. Potter, the Secretary of the Navy, who was a cultured gentleman and an elegant orator, followed the president in an eloquent appeal to duty. He pointed to the sad and dejected women who lined the beach, bereft of all the comforts of life by the cruel invader. The eloquent orator concluded by expressing the hope that no man would prove to be a coward in this supreme crisis, and invited all who desired to leave Texas to step to the front. Not one responded!

The next morning two schooners entered the bay, one from New Orleans, and having on board Captain Logan's company of volunteers, some thirty in number; and the other came from Matagorda and had Captain Dimmitt on board. From Dimmitt I received the welcome intelligence that my family were safe at the ranch of De Leon.

After much difficulty in procuring wood for the steamer we finally departed, having some fifty or sixty men on board, in quest of the army, wherever it might be. This was April 21. We also had on board the boat two pieces of cannon, with several rounds of grape and shot. I was placed in charge of the guns, with sufficient men to manage them.

At New Washington—which town had been destroyed by the Mexicans—we received the first intelligence of the battle of San Jacinto. At Lynch's Ferry I met General Rusk, who familiarly greeted me with the exclamation, "Linn, we've got him now!"—meaning Santa Anna. We steamed up Buffalo Bayou, and were soon at the camp of the army. Our arrival with the much-needed supplies was the signal for general rejoicing, as the men had subsisted for several days on a diet of fresh beef without salt. I delivered to "Old Bennett," so well known to all Texans, an abundance of flour, coffee, sugar, soap, powder, lead, etc.

T. F. McKinney and myself, at San Jacinto, went to visit the field of battle. The ghastly spectacle of six hundred Mexican corpses festering in the sun met our gaze. The pockets of every one had been turned in the search for plunder. In passing the breastworks I noticed a man who was extracting the teeth of the dead Mexicans. He was a dentist from the United States, and was supplying himself with these valuable adjuncts of his trade. We stood uncovered at the grave of our seven slain heroes; and I could but recognize in this unparalleled result the immediate interposition of Divine Providence. Three days after the battle a detail was made from each company to bury the dead; to this the men objected. I suggested to General Houston that some two or more hundred prisoners, under a strong guard, should perform this duty, which ought to be as agreeable to the one as disgusting to the other. Houston communicated the suggestion to Santa Anna, who replied that he was wholly indifferent and cared not what disposition was made of the bodies. He also volunteered the information that where fuel was abundant and convenient he generally found incremation a ready solution for similar problems. Here the matter ended. The stench became intolerable, and citizens living in the vicinity of the field were compelled to remove from their houses for some time.

Mrs. McCormick, on whose estate the principal portion of the slain lay, called at the headquarters of the commander in chief and requested him to cause "*them* stinking Mexicans" to be removed from her land. "Old Sam" replied with mock seriousness: "Madam, your land will be famed in history as the classic spot upon which the glorious victory of San Jacinto was gained! Here was born, in the throes of revolution, and amid the strife of contending legions, the infant of Texan independence! Here that latest scourge of mankind, the arrogantly self-styled 'Napoleon of the West,' met his fate!" "To the *devil* with your glorious history!" madam replied. "Take off your stinking Mexicans."

The spoils taken in the battle were considerable. The cannon, muskets, ammunition, and mules were retained as property pertaining to the State. The baggage and other stores, as well as the treasure of the military chest, was divided among the men. It was stated that the money of the military chest had been counted several times, and that it fell short a few dollars at each counting. But when everything had been sold at auction, and the funds of the chest ascertained, the pro rata of each man actually engaged in the fight was nine dollars and seventy-five cents, which would establish the aggregate value of the property taken, exclusive of that reserved to the State, at about seven thousand dollars—not a large amount to appertain to the number of Mexicans engaged, with the large proportion of officers that were present. Among the saddles captured was that owned by Santa Anna, a silver-mounted and otherwise highly ornamented one. It was originally the property of the Spanish General Bradas, who brought it to Tampico in 1829. This was purchased and presented to General Houston. Mr. Joseph Kuykendall, who resided on the Brazos below San Felipe, advertised for a lost pocketbook containing valuable papers; but no money except a counterfeit New Orleans banknote for fifty dollars. One day, as Tom McKinney and myself were walking along, I thoughtlessly kicked a Mexican knapsack which was lying on the ground, when a pocketbook fell from it. From the description I immediately became satisfied that this was Kuykendall's. But in addition to the advertised contents it now contained three or four doubloons, some half-quarters and eights—in all amounting to some one hundred and eighty or two hundred dollars. In obedience to General Houston's order governing the disposition of spoils, I turned the pocketbook, together with its contents, over to the officer placed in charge of such things. In a few days Kuykendall visited me for the purpose of reclaiming his property. I went with him to the officer in question, who readily produced the pocketbook, as well as the papers, but the gold, like a departing dream, had vanished.

The president and cabinet had now arrived, and it was purposed to hold a meeting to decide upon the action that should be adopted in regard to Santa Anna. President Burnet requested me to interview the captive "Napoleon," and I was presented to him by Colonel Juan Almonte, who immediately retired.

Santa Anna inquired my name, and, as immediately he heard it pronounced, said:

"You live in Guadalupe Victoria?"

He was posted minutely and generally accurately in regard to Texan affairs.

His ex-excellency was quite communicative, and did not hesitate to go over the late campaign for my edification. He said that his rapid and unsupported march on Harrisburg was prompted by his wish to capture the Texan president and cabinet, and that he was greatly disappointed in not being able to do so, as they had left the town. He stated that he gave the order to burn the steam mill at Harrisburg with reluctance. He said that ever since he crossed the Colorado he had experienced strange sensations at seeing the country absolutely deserted by the inhabitants; that he disliked personally to be a witness of the devastations caused by war, but as a Mexican, and the chief executive of Mexico, it was his duty to preserve the eminent domain of his state intact; he only wished to save Texas to Mexico. He was anxious to ascertain the feeling of the people in regard to himself.

I replied that the people of Texas were at first devoted to the constitution of 1824, and never meditated severing their relations with Mexico until he had subverted the organic law of the republic and centralized the powers of government in his own person; and that, independent of the bad faith that had been shown Coahuila and Texas, we considered his usurpation as freeing us from pre-existing obligations and leaving us to set up for ourselves; that his slaughter of the Alamo and atrocious butchery of Fannin's men had created a sentiment of horror and detestation at the very thought of his name.

He quickly replied that Mexican law left him no alternative, the Congress having decreed that all Texans taken in arms should be summarily shot as pirates. To this I rejoined that his arbitrary will had heretofore paused at no legal obstacle; and that he, in assuming the role of Caesar, had constituted his will a law unto himself. I reminded him that Antonio Lopez de Santa Anna and the supreme government of Mexico were synonymous terms, of which the will of the first meant the will of the whole.

"Ah! well," he replied, with a shade of sadness overspreading his countenance, "what is done cannot be undone. We must condone misfortunes. Ah! what a misfortune to me is this disastrous campaign in Texas. It was our misfortune that we dwelt so far apart we did not know each other; we are now better acquainted. I will act differently to you in the future, and you will regard me with more charity of opinion." The expression of these better sentiments imparted to his countenance a glow of hopeful animation. Was the captive "Napoleon" dreaming a noonday dream of the salvage of his wicked fortunes? But soon the sinister shade reappeared, and he continued in a tone of lowered sadness: "I will make the Rio Grande the boundary line between Texas and Mexico; it is a natural boundary. I am willing to negotiate on the basis of Texan independence from Mexico, and if I am liberated before my presidential term expires I can give executive force to the treaty.

"Of course obligations assumed in duress are not binding; this is the spirit of universal law. But I will take a peculiar pride, in this instance, in vindicating my aspersed honor to the civilized world. If I am retained a captive until my term of office expires I would be powerless to do you good. . . ." Such was the substance of my interview with General Antonio Lopez de Santa Anna. The president general tendered me some flattery, which I appreciated at its true value—nothing!

A few days after the battle of San Jacinto General Fillasola, anxious in regard to the fate of his captive chief, sent General Adrian Woll, a native of Belgium, accompanied by one lieutenant and a servant, under flag of truce to the American camp. Very unwisely on the part of the Texan authorities, there were no restrictions placed upon General Woll's movements within our lines at all, and, unless he was wilfully blind, must have posted himself pretty accurately in regard to our strength, situation, and all else worth knowing. He visited General Houston, General Santa Anna, and the prisoners, and when ready to set out on his return the idea forced itself on the mind of General Houston that as the Mexican force yet in Texas amounted to about three thousand men, he had best detain General Woll for a few days. Woll was indignant at his detention, but under the circumstances General Houston would have been justified in no other course. Woll was detained about eight days. General Rusk had assumed the command of the army and marched for the west. The feelings of the soldiers were generally very hostile to General Woll, and had I not exposed a conspiracy to General Rusk he had inevitably been assassinated on his return to the Mexican army.

General Woll appreciated the service that I had rendered him, and on the eve of his departure called to thank me and say adieu.

General Woll informed me that Urrea's division was composed of the very rabble of the Mexican population, and that many of them were forced conscripts; that the Yucatan battalion could not speak Spanish, and were, as a matter of course, inefficient troops. He unhesitatingly gave as his opinion that had Fannin resolutely attacked Urrea he would indubitably have routed him.

General Woll had a poor opinion of Horton, who, he said, witnessed the first day's fight and could easily have rejoined Fannin at any time during the day.

I append two letters written to my New Orleans correspondents, as serving to elucidate somewhat that now far-distant time, and exhibit the motives, the hopes, the fears, and the resolution of the citizens in general:

"Galveston Bay, April 15, 1836
Messrs. Perks and Hall:

"Gentlemen: You will no doubt be surprised somewhat to hear from me at this place, but such are the fortunes of war. It would be quite unnecessary to detail all the reasons that influenced us to desert our section of the country. Suffice to say the enemy made some rapid movements, cut off some of our ports, etc., and our people took up a panic instead of taking up arms, and many left home so precipitately that they had no thought of even a change of clothing, and so left everything behind. The panic has now subsided, and the men are rallying. The enemy is on the Brazos, and the general opinion is that he—or what remnant shall be left of him—will soon be marching back with a gait considerably more accelerated than he came. If not we will be a 'poor lot of fellows' indeed. But if we beat him on the Brazos, or beyond, our 'Lone Star' will be high in the ascendant. Of one thing certain—we will have to fight for whatever we gain.

"But now to business. . . . I turned over my goods to the government, and will send you a draft drawn on the new agent, Colonel Triplett, at sixty days, etc. Hoping to visit your city soon,

"I am, yours very truly,

J. J. Linn"

"Galveston Bay, April 28, 1836
Messrs. Perks and Hall:

"Since my last to you our political situation has materially changed for the better.

"Our army, under the immediate command of General Houston, attacked a division of the Mexican army commanded by Santa Anna in person. The Mexicans were routed and destroyed as an organization, leaving about five hundred killed on the field, and about the same number of prisoners in the hands of the victors. Among the latter is Santa Anna himself, Almonte, and many of his principal officers. Our loss was but six killed and fifteen wounded (one of whom has since died).

"This sounds impossible, but it is nevertheless true.

"Santa Anna offers to acknowledge our independence, with western boundary of Texas on the Rio Grande. This I had from his own mouth in a conversation with him.

"He is rather uneasy in his present situation, and will make any promises to get off; but we will hold him fast until we are secure. We purpose 'giving another knock on the head' to the other division of his army in a few days, and you may look for another victory as decisive as this last has been, as we now have more men than we had then. We had only seven hundred and eighty men at San Jacinto, but such a slaughter I never wish to see again.

"Our riflemen charged the artillery, and killed every man that was serving the guns.

"We captured several mule-loads of money and great quantities of arms, stores, baggage, etc. Some members of the cabinet were in the fight. . . . With due respect, I remain,

"Yours, etc.,
John J. Linn."

❦

When this letter appeared in the morning papers it created quite a sensation in New Orleans. The house of Lazardie, etc., who were the agents of Santa Anna, offered to bet one hundred thousand dollars that the letter was a canard. But many of my friends accepted wagers on the correctness of my statements, and won, in some instances, amounts of value.

Among the chivalric spirits who came to tender their swords to the service of Texas was Captain Quitman, of Mississippi, who in the "Mexican war" figured conspicuously as major general of United States volunteers. He arrived from Natchez, Miss., at the head of a company, a few days after the battle of San Jacinto. The company consisted of twenty-five men, and they had marched the entire distance on foot. There being no prospect of immediate active service in the field, Captain Quitman resigned the command to his first lieutenant, Isard, and returned home. This was a well-organized and thoroughly equipped body of excellent young men; and upon the advance of the army west, in command of General Rusk, I accompanied the Mississippians in the quasi capacity of guide until the Lavaca River was reached. I here bid them adieu and hastened to rejoin my long-deserted family, which, thanks to a beneficent Providence, I was permitted to do; and my joy at finding them preserved safe in the midst of such strife and turmoil more than compensated for the heart pangs at parting with them on that lone prairie. Fernando de Leon had been true to the trust reposed in him in every particular; and this illustration of his loyal friendship will never fail to command my gratitude so long as I shall live.

Chapter 12

     Pending the election of delegates to the Convention that was called to meet at Washington on the 1st of March, 1836, General Houston, being present at Refugio on the day of election, was chosen a delegate from the municipality of Refugio. General Houston was a most influential member of that body, having seen much of public life and enjoyed the acquaintance of many of the leading men of the United States. He was by no means a classical scholar, nor even a fair grammarian; but he had a remarkable memory and was a good judge of human nature. His personal appearance was grand; standing over six feet in height, his body and limbs were well proportioned. His voice was excellent; and, altogether, a more commanding figure and effective speaker would be difficult to find. He never failed to command attention from his audience. His was of a kindly and generous disposition when pursuing the even tenor of its flow, but harsh and vindictive when thwarted or opposed. Especially did those who had the temerity to cross his political pathway become the objects of his scathing invective. His memory was equally as tenacious of the acts of an opponent as of the kindly offices of friendship; he never forgot either, and he seldom failed to repay his enemies in kind and with the addition of usurious interest. While president, Houston appointed W. H. Wharton as charge d'affaires at Washington. Wharton, presumably expecting something better, remarked to a friend that the president was sending him into honorable exile to get him out of someone else's way. Wharton's remark did not come to Houston's ears until some months afterwards. At this time three commissioners were to be named by the president whose duties were the purchase of a navy for the infant republic. Among the names of the candidates recommended by their friends to the president was that of John A. Wharton, brother of W. H. Wharton. To the surprise of many Houston did not name John A. Wharton one of the commissioners, notwithstanding the fact that President Burnet had called him "the keenest blade of San Jacinto." No reason was assigned for the omission. But the president, casually meeting W. H. Wharton one day, could not resist the temptation of inflicting a home thrust: "I did not appoint John A. Wharton one of the three naval commissioners," explained his excellency, with a smile that was "childlike and bland," "because I did not wish to drive any more of the Wharton family into exile." This was extortion on the part of "Old Sam," and the refinement of cruelty.

While the "Mier prisoners" were incarcerated in the dungeon of Perote the Texas Congress appropriated three thousand dollars for their benefit. But unfortunately at that period the great expectations of Texas had never redounded to a plethora of the treasury, and the written appropriations were always greatly in excess of the tangible evidences of ability to meet the same. General T. J. Green, one of the prisoners aforesaid, sighed for the green pastures and balmy airs of Texas, and longed to sport in the senatorial toga that awaited his coming. He was languishing in a foreign prison, and, like the dying gladiator, his thoughts were with his heart, and that was far away. But he managed to concentrate his truant thoughts long enough to dwell upon this appropriation, in connection with the wealthy house of Hargos, a German merchant of the city of Mexico. Mr. Hargos was a good friend of Texas, and did not know that we called them "appropriations" in Texas presumably because nothing was appropriated. General Green represented to Mr. Hargos that he was authorized to draw for one thousand dollars out of the appropriation of three thousand dollars; and in the scarcely problematical event that an abundance of golden doubloons were not resting in the Texas treasury, he gave as additional security his brother, John Green, a wealthy commission merchant of New Orleans. General Green obtained the ducats, through which "open sesame" he so wrought upon the incorruptible officials of the prisons that they shut their eyes as General Green walked out and proceeded to Texas in quest of the senatorial toga. Mr. Hargos, in due time, forwarded to President Houston the draft of General Green on the treasury of Texas for one thousand dollars. Mr. Hargos was informed that there was no grist at the mill, and furthermore that General Green had no more authority to draw on the so-called appropriation than any other of the Mier prisoners. He also volunteered the cheering information to Mr. Hargos that John Green was not worth a "continental cent."

General Green was elected a member of Congress, and appeared at the next session, habited in the toga aforesaid. Impelled by some inscrutable cause, and not having the fear of "Old Sam" before him, General Green proceeded from the first to antagonize the president, and at times suffered his invective to degenerate into personal abuse.

During the last days of the session some member introduced a resolution calling on the president for any and all papers or other information that he might have relative to the Perote prisoners. The resolution was unanimously adopted, and in cheerful compliance the president hastened to submit every paper in his possession bearing, however remotely, upon the subject of the resolution. Of course he included the letters of Hargos, the draft of Green, and a copy of his own reply. When these papers were reached by the Congress efforts were made to lay the matter on the table, or, in fact, any course that would avoid their being read. But read they were, and to the complete discomfiture of General Green and to the grim and silent satisfaction of "Old Sam." The foregoing incident is not reproduced in attempted disparagement of General Green, who was as brave, true, and honorable a man as ever lived, but as tending to illustrate the means employed by Houston in getting even with his detractors.

Sam Houston as president of Texas was irrefragably "the right man in the right place." No other hand like his could have steered the frail ship of state through the tortuous channels and frowning dangers of the times into the haven of peace and safety. He was the Jupiter Tonans of the most rigid economy in our straitened financial circumstances, and looked upon a national debt as the nucleus of a concentrating incubus far more potent for destruction than the legions of the Mexican invader. He came into office without a cent in the treasury. The customs duties amounted to nothing; the impoverished people had nothing with which to pay direct taxes; and the public domain alone remained upon which to predicate a financial basis, and the rich leagues and labors of Texas lands had only a nominal value. Texas credit abroad, and at home for that matter, was an unknown quantity, to the cultivation of which the bluff old soldier-president gave his most assiduous care. By the greatest care, prudence, and sagacity on his part, magnanimously aided by a few noble and liberal spirits at home and abroad, was Houston enabled to rescue Texas from dangers as fell and far more perplexing than those over which he triumphed with the shout and tread of victory at San Jacinto. Sam Houston appears far grander in the cabinet at this period of our country's history, environed as he was by harassing difficulties more interminable than the woes of the "Iliad," than as the spurred and belted knight of Texan independence. Grand old man! To him Texas was his alter ego, and with the instinct of self-preservation which man in common with all animals possesses, he read with the ken of a seer the evils that were destined to burst above our devoted heads when Texas joined the frenzied saturnalia of secession. His warning voice was raised in his tent to stay her precipitation. His warning voice was drowned in the clangor of fratricidal strife; and he turned from the scene, lay down, and died ere the sovereignty of Texas became a thing contemned and despised.

An incident that occurred at Columbia in 1837 illustrates what was expected of the impecunious president by some of the "sovereign people," and the stratagems that he employed to rid himself of annoyances. Houston was sitting on a log one day, engaged in earnest conversation with a friend, when a ragged volunteer of San Jacinto came up and brusquely demanded of the president a coat. In vain did Houston inform his importunate comrade that he had but the one which now covered his back. "Give me an order, then, on the stores," demanded the citizen-soldier. "My comrade," said the old hero kindly, "the order of your general in chief and president will not be accepted by the tradespeople." The soldier was still importunate, and the general, pulling off his own coat, sadly said: "Take my coat, my comrade; the defenders of Texas shall be clothed. Take my coat!" This was too much for the soldier, who hastily fled.

Houston's first inaugural address

It was on the 3rd of October, 1836, when the delegates assembled at Columbia, and then the first Congress of the republic of Texas was organized. On the morning of the 22nd the president ad interim tendered his resignation, and a resolution was immediately introduced that the inauguration take place at four o'clock this day. A committee from both houses waited upon the president-elect, and at four o'clock he was introduced within the bar of the House of Representatives. The speaker administered to him the oath of office, and then proclaimed Sam Houston President of the Republic of Texas.

The following is his inaugural address delivered on this occasion:

"Mr. Speaker and Gentlemen:
"Deeply impressed with a sense of the responsibility devolving on me, I cannot in justice to myself repress the emotion of my heart, or restrain the feelings which my sense of obligation to my fellow citizens has inspired. Their suffrage was gratuitously bestowed. Preferred to others not unlikely superior in merit to myself, called to the most important station among mankind by the voice of a free people, it is utterly impossible not to feel impressed with the deepest sensations of delicacy in my present position before the world. It is not here alone, but our present attitude before all nations has rendered my position and that of my country one of peculiar interest.

"A spot of earth almost unknown to the geography of the age, destitute of all available resources, few in numbers, we remonstrated against oppression; and when invaded by a numerous host we dared to proclaim our independence and to strike for freedom on the breast of the oppressor. As yet our course is onward. We are only in the outset of the campaign of liberty. Futurity has locked up the destiny which awaits our people. Who can contemplate with apathy a situation so imposing in the moral and physical world?

"The relations among ourselves are peculiarly delicate and important; for no matter what zeal or fidelity I may possess in the discharge of my official duties, if I do not obtain cooperation and an honest support from the co-ordinate departments of the government, wreck and ruin must be the inevitable consequences of my administration. If, then, in the discharge of my duty my competency should fail in the attainment of the end in view, it would become your sacred duty to correct my errors and sustain me by your superior wisdom. This much I anticipate—this much I demand.

"I am perfectly aware of the difficulties that surround me and the convulsive throes through which our country must pass. I have never been emulous of the civic wreath; when merited it crowns a happy destiny. A country situated like ours is environed with difficulties; its administration is fraught with perplexities. Had it been my destiny I would infinitely have preferred the toils, privations, and perils of a soldier to the duties of my present station. Nothing but zeal, stimulated by the holy spirit of patriotism and guided by philosophy and reason, can give that impetus to our energies necessary to surmount the difficulties that obstruct our political progress. By the aid of your intelligence I trust all impediments to our advancement will be removed; that all wounds in the body politic will be healed, and the constitution of the republic derive strength and vigor equal to any emergency. I shall confidently anticipate the consolidation of constitutional liberty. In the attainment of this object we must regard our relative situation to other countries.

"A subject of no small importance is the situation of an extensive frontier, bordered by Indians and open to their depredations. Treaties of peace and amity, and the maintenance of good faith with the

Indians, seem to me the most rational means for winning their friendship. Let us abstain from aggression, establish commerce with the different tribes, supply their useful and necessary wants, maintain even-handed justice with them, and natural reason will teach them the utility of our friendship.

"Admonished by the past, we cannot in justice disregard our national enemies. Vigilance will apprise us of their approach; a disciplined and valiant army will insure their discomfiture. Without discrimination and system how unavailing would all the resources of an old and overflowing treasury prove to us! It would be as unprofitable to us in our present situation as the rich diamond locked in the bosom of the adamant. We cannot hope that the bosom of our beautiful prairies will soon be visited by the healing breezes of peace. We may again look for the day when their verdure will be converted into dyes of crimson. We must keep all our energies alive, our army organized, disciplined, and increased to our present emergencies. This is the attitude we must at present regard as our own. We are battling for human liberty; reason and firmness must characterize our acts.

"The course our enemies have pursued has been opposed to every principle of civilized warfare; bad faith, inhumanity, and devastation marked their path of invasion. We were a little band, contending for liberty; they were thousands, well appointed, munitioned, and provisioned, seeking to rivet chains upon us or to extirpate us from the earth. Their cruelties have incurred the universal denunciation of Christendom. They will not pass from their nation during the present generation. The contrast of our conduct is manifest; we were hunted down as the felon wolf, our little band driven from fastness to fastness, exasperated to the last extreme. While the blood of our kindred and our friends, invoking the vengeance of an offended God, was smoking to heaven, we met our enemy and vanquished them. They fell in battle or suppliantly kneeled and were spared. We offered up our vengeance at the shrine of humanity, while Christianity rejoiced at the act and looked with pride at the sacrifice. The civilized world contemplated with proud emotions conduct which reflected so much glory on the Anglo-Saxon race. The moral effect has done more toward our liberation than the defeat of the army of veterans. Where our cause has been presented to our friends in the laud of our origin, they have embraced it with their warmest sympathies. They have rendered us manly and efficient aids. They have rallied to our standard, they have fought side by side with our warriors. They have bled, and their dust is mingling with the ashes of our heroes. At this moment I discern numbers around me who battled in the field of San Jacinto, and whose chivalry and valor have identified them with the glory of the country, its name, its soil, and its liberty. There sits a gentleman within my view whose personal and political services to Texas have been invaluable. He was the first in the United States to respond to our cause. His purse was ever open to our necessities. His hand was extended in our aid. His presence among us, and his return to the embraces of our friends, will inspire new efforts in behalf of our cause."

[The attention of the speaker and that of Congress was directed to Wm. Christy, Esq., of New Orleans, who sat by invitation within the bar.]

"A circumstance of the highest import will claim the attention of the court at Washington. In our recent election the important subject of annexation to the United States of America was submitted to the consideration of the people. They have expressed their feelings and wishes on that momentous subject. They have, with a unanimity unparalleled, declared that they will be reunited to the great republican family of the north. The appeal is made by a willing people. Will our friends disregard it? They have already bestowed upon us their warmest sympathies. Their manly and generous feelings have been enlisted on our behalf. We are cheered by the hope that they will receive us to participate in their civil, political, and religious rights, and hail us welcome into the great family of freemen. Our misfortunes have been their misfortunes; our sorrows, too, have been theirs, and their joy at our success has been irrepressible.

"A thousand considerations press upon me; each claims my attention. But the shortness of the notice of this emergency will not enable me to do justice to those subjects, and will necessarily induce their postponement for the present."

[Here the president, says the reporter, paused for a few seconds and disengaged his sword.]

"It now, sir, becomes my duty to make a presentation of this sword—this emblem of my past office . . ."

[The president was unable to proceed further; but having firmly clenched it with both hands, as if with a farewell grasp, a tide of varied associations rushed upon him in a moment; his countenance bespoke the workings of the strongest emotions, his soul seemed to dwell momentarily on the glistening blade, and the greater part of the auditory gave outward proof of their congeniality of feeling. It was, in reality, a moment of deep and painful interest. After this pause, more eloquent and impressive than the deepest pathos conveyed in language, the president proceeded.]

"I have worn it with some humble pretensions in defence of my country; and should the danger of my country again call for my services, I expect to resume it, and to respond to that call, if needful, with my blood and my life."

In regard to religious toleration under the Mexican government I deem a few words not inappropriate. Not one in ten of the colonists introduced into Texas were Catholics; and to my certain knowledge no efforts were made to secure forcible subscription to the tenets of that church. Every man was free to follow the bent of his own inclinations in this respect. A Protestant Sunday school was organized in San Felipe as early as 1835.

We had a member of the Consultation, Daniel Parker, who was a Baptist preacher, and who frequently preached as publicly as it was possible to do, without let or hindrance. Richard Ellis and Collin McKinney, both members of the Convention, exhorted at religious meetings frequently. The candid Texan reader, whatever may be his religious bias or prejudice, will agree with me that upon this subject, as with all else that appertains to history, the high old Roman maxim, "Let the truth be told, though the heavens dissolve," should always be kept in view. Mr. Daniel Parker, in a speech delivered on the floor of the Consultation, declared that the liberality of Mexico in her dealings with the colonists was unparalleled in the annals of time. To the head of each family a league of land was given; exemption from all taxes, customs, duties, etc., for ten years. To what land could they have turned for a more liberal tender?

We can render the Mexican justice in all that he deserves it, and condemn him whenever he merits censure—which unfortunately is too often the case.

During the latter portion of March 1836, two families living on Clark's Creek, in Lavaca County, were murdered by the Toncahua Indians. The first was Mr. John Douglas, wife, son, and daughter. The second was Mr. Bernard O'Dougherty, wife, and two daughters aged twelve and fourteen years, and a boy of ten years. Two boys of the Douglas family, Augustus and Thaddeus, left the camp early in the morning for the purpose of killing a deer, leaving their father making a slide, on which they purposed removing their effects east as soon as it was completed. The boys returned home in the afternoon, and, to their astonishment and horror, found their cabin a heap of smouldering embers and their people ruthlessly butchered. A few moments' survey of the ruin wrought by the savages sufficed, and they turned their faces towards the east. They came to the camp of the Mexican General Woll on the Colorado, who treated them kindly and relieved their necessities. Woll sent them to a camp up the river a short distance, occupied by a Frenchman and some runaway Negroes. Here they remained until the news came of the disaster at San Jacinto, when General Woll dismissed them, giving them a horse and some money, and telling them to go down the river until they met some of their own countrymen. A Mexican officer, who spoke English, was desirous that they should accompany him to Mexico, but General Woll dissuaded him, saying it was best that they should remain with their own countrymen.

The effects of the murdered families were subsequently found among the Indians before named, which fact was sufficient to fix the guilt at their doors.

Manuel Escalera (still living), a brother in law of Fernando de Leon, was impressed into the service by order of General Urrea, and, being acquainted with the principal roads through the country, he was sent as a courier with special despatches from Urrea to Santa Anna. Upon arriving at the camp of General Fillasola on the Brazos he found that Santa Anna had gone on to Harrisburg.

Escalera was present on the day after the battle when Captain Barragan arrived at the quarters of General Sesma. All were satisfied from his manner that something extraordinary had occurred. To Sesma's inquiry, "What of his excellency and the army?" Barragan replied: "All gone to the devil!" (*Lleve el diablo todos.*) He gave a vivid narrative of the exciting scenes that he had witnessed. He stated that the Texans were incarnate devils, and that nothing could stop them.

It seemed that the Mexicans fell dead before them, without even the formality of being fired at.

In about an hour some more stragglers came up, and among them a woman who was wounded in the thigh. As soon as the news reached General Fillasola he ordered that no more troops be posted on the Brazos. The stragglers, some forty in all, related most marvellous stories of escapes by field and flood, and all agreed concerning the diabolism of the Texan soldiers. Each one regarded his escape as a miracle. The army was thoroughly panic-stricken and demoralized by the excited tales of these refugees.

During that day the army was withdrawn from the river, and guards posted so as to prevent a surprise. Before authentic reports of the disaster reached them General Sesma, thoroughly frightened, could stand the strain no longer and set out for Mexico to bear the tidings as he had received them from the fugitives.

Munson, formerly a resident of San Felipe, and a watchmaker by trade, was a prisoner in the hands of the Mexicans, and was forced to take charge of the ferry at Richmond, which post he filled several days under guard; and his statements coincide with those of Escalera, just related. Upon the withdrawal of the Mexican forces he was set at liberty.

If General Sesma was a fair sample of the Mexican officers—and it is probable that he was—the result of the battle of San Jacinto is less surprising and more readily accounted for.

General T. J. Rusk, commanding the army of Texas, arrived at La Bahia (Goliad) about the last of May, and performed the last sad offices for the charred remains of Fannin and his men. The following letter, written from the spot, describes the performance of that melancholy duty:

"La Bahia, June 4, 1836

"On arriving at this place we found no difficulty in discovering the ground upon which Fannin and his gallant men were shot by order of Santa Anna. Most of their bodies were burned, while there were many bones and some entire skeletons scattered over the plain for some distance. It had long been determined that as soon as practicable after the arrival of the army here, these remains should be collected and a day set apart for their burial with all the honors of war. Accordingly on the 1st instant General Rusk issued the following order:

'As a token of respect, as well to the men who fell a sacrifice to the treachery and bad faith of our enemy as a duty that we owe to the relatives of the unfortunate deceased and ourselves, it is ordered that the skeletons and bones of our murdered countrymen be collected into one place in front of the fort, and buried with all the honors of war.

'Thomas J. Rusk,
Brigadier-General Commanding'

"On the afternoon of the ensuing day, the bones having been collected, the following order was given:

'A general parade of the army will take place tomorrow at half-past eight o'clock. The funeral will take place at nine a.m. Colonel Sidney Sherman will take command and conduct the procession in the following order:

'First, artillery.

'Second, music.

'Third, Major Morehouse's command.

'Fourth, six commissioned officers; the corpses; six commissioned officers.

'Fifth, five mourners. Those of Colonel Fannin's command who are with the army, and who so miraculously escaped, will attend as mourners.

'Sixth, commanding general and staff.

'Seventh, medical staff.

'Eighth, Second Regiment.

'Ninth, First Regiment.

'Tenth, regulars.

'Major Poe will cause a minute-gun to be fired from the fort, commencing at the time the procession moves and continuing until it arrives at the grave.

'Thos. J. Rusk,
Brigadier-General Commanding'

"The following morning, being Friday, June 3, the army was paraded within the walls of the fort at the hour appointed; and at nine o'clock, with arms reversed, moved slowly toward the place of burial, on reaching which General Rusk pronounced a brief but feeling and eloquent address:

'Fellow-soldiers: In the order of Providence we are this day called upon to pay the last sad offices of respect to the remains of the noble and heroic band who, battling for our sacred rights, have fallen beneath the ruthless hand of a tyrant. Their chivalrous conduct entitles them to the heartfelt gratitude of the people of Texas. Without any further interest in the country than all noble hearts feel at the bare mention of liberty, they rallied to our standard. Relinquishing the peace, the ease, the comforts of home; leaving behind them all they held dear—their mothers, sisters, daughters, and wives—they subjected themselves to fatigue and privation, and nobly threw themselves between the people of Texas and the legions of Santa Anna. There, unaided by reinforcements, and far from hope and help, they battled bravely with the minions of the tyrant, ten to one. Surrounded in the open prairie by this fearful odds, cut off from provision and even water, they were induced, under the sacred promise of receiving the treatment usual to prisoners of war, to surrender. They were marched back, and for a week treated with the utmost inhumanity and barbarity. They were marched out of yonder fort under the pretence of getting provisions, and it was not until the firing of musketry and the shrieks of the dying were heard that they were satisfied of their approaching fate. Some endeavored to make their escape, but they were pursued by the ruthless cavalry, and most of them cut down with their swords. A small number of them now stand by the grave—a bare remnant of the noble band. Our tribute of respect is due to them and to the mothers, sisters, and wives who weep their untimely end, that we should mingle our tears with theirs. In that mass of remains and fragments of bones many a mother might see her son, many a sister her brother, and many a wife her own beloved and affectionate husband. But we have a consolation yet to offer them. Their murderers sank into death on the prairies of San Jacinto under the appalling cries: "Remember La Bahia!" We have another consolation to offer. While liberty has a habitation and a name their tragic fate will be handed down to remotest posterity on the brightest pages of history. Santa Anna, the black-hearted murderer, the mock hero, is within our grasp. There he must remain, tortured by the aching pain of a corroding conscience. He must sometimes reflect on the tragedy of La Bahia! While the names of those whom he murdered shall soar to the highest pinnacle of fame, his shall sink down to the deepest depths of infamy and disgrace.'

"During the delivery of this address the general had the attention of the whole army. When he spoke of the sufferings of these martyrs in the cause of liberty I saw tears flow from the eyes of more than one brave man. At its conclusion I observed many compress their lips and involuntarily grasp their weapons more firmly, as if they felt that the holocaust of San Jacinto had not compensated them for the brutal murder of their comrades at La Bahia. The army marched back to their quarters.

"Sam'l Dexter
Aide-de-camp"

General Andrade, whom we left in a former chapter evacuating San Antonio, appeared with his army at the "upper crossing" on the San Antonio River, a few miles from La Bahia, while Rusk and his comrades were performing the sad duties just narrated. He sent in a message to the Texan commander, complaining that he had not complied with the stipulations of the treaty of San Jacinto, in that the "Texan army should not approach within less than five leagues of the retreating Mexicans."

This clause of the treaty had unintentionally been violated by both Rusk and Andrade, as they were each in ignorance of the movements of the other. Possibly Rusk manifested too much zeal in pushing so rapidly westward, and Andrade could have found a much nearer route to the Rio Grande than by way of La Bahia. He wished to visit this scene of Mexican treachery, however, presumably on the principle that where the carcass is, there will the eagles be gathered also. General Rusk informed Andrade that he had better push on in conformity to other stipulations of the same treaty, as the Texans were exasperated by the scene of demoniacal barbarism which they had just witnessed, and if the Mexican army came in sight he could not answer for the acts of his men. General Andrade was one of the bravest and most efficient of the Mexican general officers. He was now at the head of seven hundred and fifty fresh troops, well armed, and supplied with a full park of artillery. We thought another battle was inevitable; but Andrade, perhaps thinking discretion the better part of valor, turned the head of his columns towards the Rio Grande.

The internal dissensions of Mexico proved ultimately to be the best friend Texas had, for the doughty warriors had been home but a little time when the chronic entertainment of slitting one another's throats commenced. According to the statements of Captain Barragan the industry could be pursued in Mexico with less hazard than in Texas. Barragan said "*los Tejanos* were devils, and that no troops could stand up before them."

A false alarm

One night, _____, 1836, Captain White's company was stationed in Victoria, and, as the Mexicans were expected at almost any time, he had issued orders that his men should sleep on their arms and for the guards to exercise unusual vigilance. Affairs wore on, however, with wonted peace and silence until far into the night. Soldiers and citizens were alike wrapped in slumber, when suddenly a sentinel posted on the outskirts of the town fired off his gun, and fled to town with the alarming report that Victoria was surrounded by Mexicans. Confusion reigned supreme for a while throughout the camp and town. Citizens were running about half clad, making anxious inquiries, and Captain White was disposing of men to anticipate the threatened cavalry charge. A scouting party was despatched to ascertain something more definite in regard to the position of the enemy, and soon returned with the assuring report that there was no enemy present. The over-vigilant guard had mistaken a cavallado of horses for the cavalry of the Mexicans.

The Red Rovers

While I was alcalde of Victoria, in the year 1836, it was my pleasure as well as duty, being a quartermaster in the Texan army, to prepare a reception for the "Red Rovers"—Captain Shackleford's company from North Alabama. The company landed at Dimmitt's Point and marched to Victoria. Having notice of their approach, I prepared them comfortable quarters and had a supply of hot coffee and other refreshments gotten ready for them. The boys enjoyed the collation, and found in their reception much to lessen the sad thoughts of dear ones at home and the fatigue of the toilsome march which they had just made.

Among the men was an ex-dancing-master, Anderson, who, procuring a violin, regaled us with music after the repast had been concluded. They were very appreciative of the attention shown them, and were profuse in their thanks. Alas! they little recked of the sad and miserable fate that was so soon to befall them in consequence of Santa Anna's cruel fiat.

The members of the company had much paper money about their persons, principally New Orleans bank notes, which passed current at par. Many purposed purchasing lands with a view to locating. After the massacre the Mexican soldiers exhibited quantities of these notes, which they would dispose of upon almost any terms, not knowing their value. Colonel William P. Miller informed me that he had but little silver with him; but he purchased some of the paper, giving five dollars for one hundred, and others bought at the same rates.

The "Red Rovers" were composed of many of the best young men of Alabama, and their fate was peculiarly hard.

Episodes in Indian life

In the year 1838 a party of some twenty-five Lipan Indians visited Victoria, as was their custom, to barter dressed deer pelts, buffalo robes, etc. Among them was a Dr. Hanam, formerly a practising physician of Matagorda, where he had a wife, who was an intelligent and accomplished lady. He had deserted his wife, however, under the siren blandishments of a pretty Lipan squaw, with whom he lived.

The Indians visited my store, and I purchased much of their peltry. Dr. Hanam bought a jar of preserves, and he and his *bonne amie*, the pretty squaw, sat down on the doorsteps to partake of the same. Being well acquainted with Hanam, I could not refrain from asking him how it was possible that he could gain his own consent to desert the haunts of his civilized species and adopt this mode of life, so radically different from all that he had heretofore been accustomed to.

He wished me to believe that he was doing so in a quest for scientific knowledge in regard to medicinal roots and herbs, and stated that he was acquiring a vast repertory of such knowledge. I made no reply to all this, but was satisfied that in the balances of his desires the squaw would vastly outweigh his thirst for knowledge. After disposing of their skins, which the Lipans "dressed" much better than any other tribe of Indians, they departed for another hunting expedition. Near the present site of the town of Cuero they encountered a party of Comanches, when a fight ensued, in which the Lipans were the victors. One Comanche warrior was slain. The squaw of Hanam cut off one of the hands of the defunct brave, and brought it to her Æesculapian Adonis with the suggestion that they should prepare it for their evening repast, stating that it was a delicious morsel. Cannibalism the doctor could not subscribe to, and he left the Indians at Gonzales, and ultimately returned to Alabama.

Antonio Vasquez, who was alcalde of La Bahia in 1830, received information that a party of Comanches, camped three or four miles north of town, were preparing to sacrifice a Lipan prisoner. Vasquez, determining to prevent the barbarity, summoned twenty well-armed men and proceeded to the Comanche village. There they found the doomed Lipan securely fastened to a tree, and the Comanches were engaged in piling dry wood about him. A most horrible scene was in contemplation.

Vasquez notified the Comanches that they must desist. The Comanche chief insisted that as this was a matter entirely between Indians, the Mexican authorities had nothing to say. Vasquez informed him that his jurisdiction as alcalde extended over all people within the limits of his somewhat vague and undefined territory.

But the armed men of Vasquez, who were standing in readiness for the word of command, presented a reason more potent in securing the Lipan's release than all the arguments of the Mexican commander.

"Go, mean Lipan," said the proud Comanche. "You have no fat buffalo-meat among your poor tribe, as we have; no fat bear-meat. You are lean, we are fat, and you are not fit to eat, as are we; go!" Such was life among the American aborigines. Yet there are some sentimental human geese who sigh for those "good old times!"

"Old Sam" saves the people of Bexar

Early in January 1837, General Felix Huston, as commanding general of the Texan army, forwarded to Colonel J. N. Seguin, commander of the post at San Antonio, an order directing that the inhabitants of the town should vacate the place and retire into the interior. Colonel Seguin, being reluctant to enforce the harsh and cruel provisions of this autocratic ukase, immediately forwarded a copy to President Sam Houston at Columbia. "Old Sam" promptly countermanded the order, and by so doing spared the people of San Antonio great suffering; for to have been driven from their home to the bleak prairies at the most inclement season of the year would have resulted in fatal consequences to many and suffering to all. If ever any official explanation was deigned of this proposed exercise of arbitrary power, I failed to see or hear it. But I had an acquaintance on the Lavaca River, Mr. B. F. Perkins, who had a store and had accumulated five or six thousand dollars in ready money, who informed me that certain men of prominence proposed to him that they would each contribute five thousand dollars, and, taking advantage of the certain depreciation of city property in consequence of the enforcement of the order, purchase the whole city, or as much as was possible, at all events.

Perkins solemnly asseverated on his honor that such was the project, and that he actually prepared his stock of goods on hand for transportation to San Antonio, and was only prevented from setting out himself for that place by the early publication of President Houston's countermand of Felix Huston's ukase.

In justice to Mr. Perkins I will say that, after mature reflection, he declared that he was far more gratified by the turn the affair had taken than that he should have accumulated property unjustly extorted from others. I merely give the unvarnished facts in the case, which, it would appear, admit of two hypotheses in accounting for the cause of the proposed measure:

1st. That Felix Huston was privy to the machinations of the conspirators, and had consented to degrade his military rank for a paltry monetary consideration; which seems improbable, if not impossible.

2nd. That Felix Huston issued the order in good faith, predicating its necessity upon some imaginary cause, and that the conspirators resolved to reap a harvest from its ruinous effects to the inhabitants of San Antonio, without the connivance of Huston. Perkins enjoined secrecy upon me, very naturally, for it would have been a most atrocious wholesale robbery of defenceless people.

General Dunlap's race for life

In the fall of the year 1838 a party of gentlemen started from Houston to make a tour of western Texas, all being strangers from the United States, with one or two exceptions. I made the acquaintance of the most of them during their short sojourn in Victoria, and among the number that of "General" Dunlap from Mississippi, and afterwards a member of Lamar's cabinet. General Dunlap's horse became lame and unfit for travel, and in his dilemma he applied to me for a steed. I had a magnificent animal that I had lately bought of a Lipan Indian, who had captured him in a fight with the Comanches. The horse had the ear mark of the Tinaconay tribe, and had probably been originally taken from them. My Lipan was profuse in his praises of the horse, whose "good points" confirmed the statements of the Indian. The boys about town, who often borrowed my horse to run races on, declared that he was the swiftest horse for any distance in the country. I informed Mr.

Dunlap that I would not part with my horse for any monetary consideration; but that I would loan him the animal, and that he should return him to me when I visited Houston in attendance on the Congress, of which I was a member.

Dunlap's party reached San Antonio, and while there a Mexican was pursued into town by a band of Comanches, and presented the indubitable evidence of the close pursuit in an arrow that was still piercing his saddle. Quickly a party of fifteen or twenty men sallied forth to engage the enemy. The Comanches succeeded in ambushing them, killing and wounding several. In the pursuit by the Comanches there were many narrow escapes, but none more remarkable than that of General Dunlap, who was closely pursued; but the noble animal that he rode cleared at a bound an almost impassable gulch, at which the horses of his pursuers stopped, and bore his rider into town unscathed. I met General Dunlap in Houston, and he informed me that I could make a selection of all the horses in the city, but that he could not part with the noble animal that had saved his life. I selected a horse belonging to a Red River man. The Comanches captured this one when they burned Linnville; but after an absence of four days he returned home with a lariat made of buffalo hide about his neck.

The capture of Miss Harriet Matilda Lockhart and others

Miss Lockhart, together with four children of the Putnam family—Miss Rhoda Putnam, aged seventeen; James, aged ten; Bertha, seven; and a younger child aged four years. Miss Lockhart was thirteen at the time of her capture.

The little party were picking pecans in the woods when the Comanches came upon them unawares and bore them off into captivity.

James was restored to his friends in about seven months, and two months later Bertha was brought back. The Indians reported that the youngest child had so annoyed them by crying that they had to be rid of it, dashed its brains out against a tree. The capture of the children occurred on the 9th day of December, 1838.

Mr. Lockhart, the father of Harriet, made many efforts to redeem his daughter, and for this purpose deposited sums of money at the various trading posts, to be employed in her ransom. He organized a company of one hundred men, and attacked the Comanches on the San Saba one hundred miles beyond the most advanced settlement, losing one man killed and having two wounded. The Texans lost most of their horses in this engagement, as the Indians greatly outnumbered them, and they marched back to the settlements on foot, bearing their two wounded comrades.

Finally, in June 1840, Miss Lockhart was brought to San Antonio by a party of Comanches. Colonel McLeod was in command of the post, and caused the house in which the council was being held to be surrounded by a company of soldiers commanded by Captain Thomas B. Howard. Colonel McLeod then informed the interpreter that he should say to the Indians that they would be held as prisoners until all the captives in their tribe were surrendered. The interpreter told Colonel McLeod that he dared not so inform the Indians, as he feared they would kill him instantly. McLeod insisted, and the interpreter cautiously placed himself within easy access of the door and communicated to the amazed Indians the resolution of the "pale-face" chief. Simultaneously with the announcement they uttered the fierce war whoop and let fly their arrows. A desperate melee ensued, in which eight whites were killed. Among the killed was the sheriff of Bexar and Mr. Thomas, private secretary of Mr. Lamar.

Of the Indians *thirty-two* braves were killed and three women and two children. Twenty-seven women and children were taken prisoners and placed in the Alamo for safekeeping. Among these was found the scalp of a white woman, supposed to be that of Miss Putnam. The Indian women were enlarged after a brief detention.

An Indian who was in a room adjoining the one in which the council was being held got into a corner that rendered an attack impossible without incurring great danger. A ball of cotton saturated with turpentine was ignited and dropped from the roof upon him.

This brought him out, and he attempted to flee, but soon met his fate at the hands of the vigilant whites without.

This was a most unfortunate affair, as it entailed an unnecessary loss of life, and probably caused the Comanches to desist in the humane line of surrendering up their captives, of which they still held more.

Chapter 13

The fate of Major Morris, Dr. Grant, and others

Major Morris was the commander of the "New Orleans Grays," a splendid organization of gallant and brave young men, who were among the first to respond to "Old Ben Milam's" call for volunteers to drive General Cos out of Bexar. After Cos's surrender time hung heavy on the hands of the volunteers, and many expeditions were planned, the most popular of which seemed to be a descent on Matamoras and the carrying of the "war into Africa." Dr. Grant, who doubtless sighed for the possession of his princely estates near Parras, was the soul of these schemes, albeit he had ready listeners, and not a few who were ready to embark in any enterprise that possessed the elements of adventure, notoriety, and booty. Failing to secure the services of a sufficient number of volunteers to justify the purposed descent on Matamoras, Major Morris, Dr. Grant, Placido Benevides, and others went west of the Nueces River to procure a supply of horses, possibly as a preliminary measure to some more extensive expedition. They proceeded to the ranches near the Rio Grande, and obtained some fifty or sixty good horses, and were returning home when they were surprised by a body of Mexican cavalry near Agua Dulce, some thirty miles west of San Patricio, and the entire party killed, with the exception of Benevides and one Brown. Benevides was in the act of roping a horse for one of the party when the enemy fired from ambush, with the result given. A Mexican soldier charged upon Benevides with a musket in hand. Being an athlete, Benevides seized the musket and wrenched it from the soldier's hand, and, putting spurs to his horse, made good his escape.

In Morphis's caricature of Texas history, page 196, he has a lot of "balderdash" about Dr. Grant being strapped to a mustang, *à la* Mazeppa, and thus horribly tortured and killed. Hundreds of people, among the most respectable, too, of this section, knew Placido Benevides, and have heard him relate the fate of Major Morris and Dr. Grant substantially as I have here presented it. History should not abound in rumors. Dr. Grant was a Scotchman by birth and a physician by profession. He was a gentleman of a thorough education, elegant manners, and at his home in Coahuila he lived like a lord and entertained like a prince. He was the resident agent of an English mining company, and had charge of a number of extensive haciendas. He was a member of the Legislature of Coahuila and Texas in 1835, which was ejected by the orders of Santa Anna, and all its members imprisoned upon whom his minions could lay their hands. Grant escaped with the Texas delegation, which was composed of Joseph Durst, of Nacogdoches; Oliver Jones, of Brazoria; and José Maria J. Carbajal, of Bexar.

Dr. Grant had nothing particularly in common with Texas. He was actuated by a desire for the reclamation of his magnificent estates, and not by patriotism, as some others were. He was brave, liberal, and generous, and deserved a better fate.

I cannot refrain in this connection from remarking on the disastrous results that attended most of the expeditions led in early Texan times by ambitious adventurers. Those who came to Texas primarily for notoriety, adventure pure and simple, and booty were sadly disappointed. It seems that Providence drew the line of demarcation between emprises of this nature and the less pretentious one of patriotic endeavor; while the former all failed, the latter was supreme in the splendor of its final triumph.

With the ill-fated expeditions of Fannin, Ward, King, Morris, and the adventurers who preceded them, should be added the quixotic, the farcical, the disastrous expedition to Santa Fé; and its twin sister in folly and misery, "the Mier expedition," should not be forgotten. I was well acquainted with a brother of Dr. Grant, an educated and refined gentleman, who held a situation in 1836 in New Orleans. I bore him the first correct intelligence of his brother's death.

How a wedding was prevented

Some time in the year 1832 a couple came to San Felipe for the purpose of getting married. Under the Mexican laws no one but a Catholic priest could solemnize the rite of matrimony. There being no priest in Austin's colony, an arrangement *de convenance*, as the French would say, but in Texas called "constitutional marriage," was adopted. The ceremony consisted merely in the appearance of the high contracting parties before the alcalde, and the signification of their purpose to assume the relation of man and wife until an opportunity was had of having the religious rite properly celebrated by a priest. The couple in this instance who were hymeneally inclined was a country lass from "the Cole Settlement" and a "minister of the gospel" from the mountain district of Arkansas. They put up at the house of Mrs. Payton. Fortunately for the prospective bride, James Bowie was also a guest of the same landlady. Bowie recognized the bogus preacher as a scamp who had made too free with his neighbors' stables after dark, and who had fled the country, leaving behind a disconsolate wife and several small children.

Of course high-toned, chivalrous Jim Bowie was not the man to sit down and see a lecherous old villain accomplish his aims.

Bowie got Joe Powell to personate a priest, which, with the proper disguise, he did well. The alcalde, Mr. Christnan, was let into the secret, which he heartily approved of when Bowie had made him somewhat acquainted with the antecedents of the prospective bridegroom. This gentleman was informed that a priest had arrived rather unexpectedly in San Felipe, and that under the law the matter would have to go to him, and not to the alcalde; but he was offered the consoling reflection that it would be a *de jure* marriage, such as civilized people indulge in, and not a mere "constitutional" cohabitation.

The candidate signified the pleasure that this unexpected turn of good fortune gave him with profuse smiles. The priest announced that he was ready to catechise the bridegroom *expectant*. The *padre* spoke no English; bridegroom *presumptive* knew no more of Spanish than he did of Sanscrit. Happy accomplishment of Bowie: he was master of both languages! Bowie would, then, interpret! The females of the house were separated from this interesting coterie only by a thin board partition, through which sound passed unobstructed. Women have curiosity, and they have a right to possess it; it is a commendable quality sometimes. The catechising progressed; and if the gentle reader imagines that Bowie interpreted in a voice too low to pass beyond the partition, then he's wrong, that's all. The bridegroom *doubtful* soon imagined that this padre was a searcher of the hearts of men, and that nothing could be hidden from his ken. His wife and children were each inquired of by name, as was his equine "crookedness." The poor fellow groaned in agony of spirit. The reader may safely imagine that there were some deeply interested "women folk" on the other side of the partition. The padre now announced that he would confess the lady in the case, and give the gentleman another "sitting," as his was a rather tough case. But Mrs. Payton put a stop to further proceedings by incontinently ordering the old scoundrel off the premises. He left, and did not "stand on the order of his going." And when a committee of admiring friends came to present him with an elegant suit of *tar and feathers*, the haunts that had so lately known him knew him now no more forever.

Expulsion of Senator Wilson

Robert Wilson, senator from Houston in 1839-40, was, for disrespect shown the president, expelled the Senate of Texas. Wilson returned home, and in the ensuing election was returned to the Senate. He was accompanied to the capital by a number of his admiring friends, who bore him in triumph through the Senate chamber while that body was sitting, and to the balcony above, where he was called upon for a speech. Bob Wilson was not an orator under the most favorable circumstances, and under the present circumstances he totally failed. On the very scene of his recent expulsion the ovation of his friends could not drown the memory of that public disgrace; and doubtless the words of

Vice President Burnet, in announcing to him the judgment of his peers that he was adjudged unworthy to consort with them, still vibrated on the tympanum of his ears: "By the act of this Senate the senatorial chair from Houston is declared vacant. Robert Wilson, you will go hence; and in the future I trust that you will endeavor to be a better man!" Upon presenting his credentials he was admitted to a seat, and took care to conduct himself with propriety afterwards. Wilson was a partner of William P. Harris, for whom the town of Harrisburg was named. They were the owners of the steam mill which General Santa Anna caused to be burned three days before the battle of San Jacinto.

Campbell hanged

In the year 1838 Michael Campbell, a native of the State of New York, killed a man in Victoria of the name of Lindsay. Sheriff *"Snake" Johnson* arrested the murderer. Campbell got a change of venue to Jackson County, where, in the absence of a jail, he was chained to the sill of a house. During the session of court the jury retired to the shade of a live oak in close proximity to where Campbell was confined, to arrive at a verdict in the case at issue. Campbell heard the jurors order a bottle of whiskey, and saw the sheriff deliver the same; when two of the jurors lay down to sleep, stating that they would subscribe to any verdict that the others should find. Campbell sent for his counsel, Mr. Blow, and instructed him to obtain another change of venue, as he could not trust his life in the hands of such jurors. He was therefore brought back to Victoria. His trial came on in due course, John D. Morris prosecuting attorney, and Mr. Blow counsel for defendant. The jury brought in a verdict of murder in the first degree; and immediately upon the rendition of which Judge J. W. Robinson proceeded to pass sentence: "Michael Campbell, you have been tried in accordance with the laws of this country, and the jury has pronounced you guilty of murder in the first degree. Now, therefore, this day, before the setting of the sun, you must die. Mr. Sheriff, take the prisoner and see that this sentence is executed by his being hanged by the neck until he is dead; and may the Lord have mercy on his soul."

"Judge, you've taken snap judgment on me!" the prisoner exclaimed.

"Not more so than you took on poor Lindsay," was his honor's reply.

Old "Snake" Johnson executed the sentence of the court by hanging Campbell from the limb of a post oak tree on "Diamond Hill." The good people of Victoria have not witnessed a judicial execution since, and may the necessity for one never again arise among the people I have loved so well!

Insubordination of General Green

General T. J. Green landed at Velasco, after the battle of San Jacinto, with about two hundred volunteers for the Texan service, the day before the purposed departure of the vessel that was to bear Santa Anna and the Texan commissioners to Vera Cruz to complete the treaty of peace, under whose preliminary armistice the Mexican army was already evacuating Texan territory.

The question admits of but little doubt that at the time the mission of the commissioners would have been successful, and any act calculated to put a stop to their proceedings would have been a grievous injury to the cause of Texas.

General Green, who had not inhaled the fumes of villanous gunpowder in the service of Texas, *ordered the detention of Santa Anna*; caused him to disembark, and a guard to be placed over him, with the avowed purpose of having him tried by a military court and shot. This was not only mutinous insubordination on the part of General Green, but it was a high-handed usurpation of the highest functions of the Texan government, which, although it had beaten its enemies on the field of battle, was too weak to vindicate its majesty at home, and was in need of help to be saved from its *friends (?)*.

General Green placed the captive president of Mexico, and the generalissimo of her armies, in charge of H. A. Hubbell, an officer of his immediate command. General Green was, however, speedily apprised by unequivocal evidences that his illegal acts, so utterly in disregard of plighted faith, did not meet with the approbation of the public, and his sanguinary programme was never carried into effect; and thus an indelible stain on the escutcheon of Texas was prevented. Santa Anna was, however, detained a prisoner until President Houston's election, October 22, 1836, when he was sent to the United States, and from there to Mexico by President Jackson.

Of course, since General Green had nullified the pending treaty, the matter came to naught.

Santa Anna, on his departure from Texas, issued the following "adios" to the Texan army:

"To the Army of Texas:

"My Friends: I have been a witness of your courage on the field of battle, and know you to be generous. Rely with confidence on my sincerity, and you shall never have cause to regret the kindness shown me. In returning to my native land I beg of you to receive the thanks of your grateful friend.

"Farewell.
Antonio Lopez de Santa Anna
Velasco, June 1, 1836"

The following letter from President Burnet to General Green has reference to the high-handed measures of the latter in seizing the person of Santa Anna and other prisoners from the custody of the government, and assigning them to the charge of his friend, Captain Hubbell. This act of General Green can never be defended on any grounds of good reason and justice, and Mr. Burnet evidently felt the insult thus wantonly offered to the impotent majesty of the new republic. But to the letter:

"Executive Department, Velasco
"July 1, 1836

"To Brigadier General Thomas J. Green:

"Sir: I enclose you a copy of a letter found in *El Correo Atlantico*, and published originally in the New Orleans *Bulletin.*

This redoubtable 'leader' is, I presume, the same you introduced to me as a *confidential* officer, to whom the custody of the prisoners might be committed with perfect safety. If he had then been known as the author of the letter enclosed (in which it is difficult to determine whether impudence or falsehood predominates), he certainly would never have borne a commission in the service of Texas with the approbation of this government. You will please to signify this to Captain Hubbell, whose speedy resignation would be very cheerfully accepted, and would save me the trouble of a more peremptory suggestion.

"Your obedient servant
David G. Burnet"

Letters to General Houston from Generals Gaines and Andrew Jackson

General Gaines wrote, under date of August 3, 1836:

"No inconsiderable portion of your fame resulting from your late campaign, the great victory of San Jacinto, will be found in the magnanimity and moral courage displayed in your preservation of the lives of your prisoners, and more especially of that of the president, Santa Anna, when taken in connection with the great provocation given in his previous conduct at the Alamo and at Goliad. You will derive imperishable fame in consequence of your forbearance in this matter. All civilized and enlightened men, without regard to geographical boundaries, will unite in filling the measure of honor and glory due such magnanimous forbearance and humanity."

General Jackson wrote, under date of September 14, 1836:

"I take the liberty of offering a remark or two upon a report which is current here to the effect that Santa Anna is to be brought before a military court, tried, and shot. Nothing now could tarnish the character of Texas more than such an act as that. Sound policy as well as humanity approves the counsels that spared his life. It gave you possession of Goliad and the Alamo without the loss of any portion of your army. His person is still of much consequence to you. He is the pride of the Mexican soldiers and a favorite of the priesthood. While he is in your power the difficulties of your enemy in raising another army will continue to be great. The soldiers of Mexico will not willingly march into Texas when they know that their advance may cost their favorite general his life. Let not his blood be shed unless imperious necessity demands it as a retaliation for future Mexican massacres. Both wisdom and humanity enjoin this course in relation to Santa Anna."

Depredations on the Rio Grande

In consequence of the troublous times after the battle of San Jacinto, on the Rio Grande border many ranches were abandoned. The restless spirits of the adventurers by which Texas was flooded induced them to enter into competition with the savage Comanche in appropriating the livestock left grazing on the prairies. Anything that belonged to a Mexican was legitimate game. Immense numbers of cattle and horses were so seized and driven east for sale by these remorseless Gaels of the nineteenth century. It was by far the most remunerative industry of the day, but was discountenanced by the respectable class of citizens. Innumerable instances could be given in illustration of this subject; but, to let "bygones be forgotten," and disliking to "open old sores," I will desist, giving one instance only, because of the notoriety it obtained by being dragged into the courts. A Captain Baker, of Goliad, with three or four men, proceeded to the Rio Grande and seized one hundred and twenty head of horses. Having driven them very hard on the return home, he discovered when he reached Goliad that they would require rest and grazing before they would be suitable for market. He therefore drove them down the San Antonio River some fifteen miles and left them to recruit. Some enterprising "hangers-on" stole the stolen horses and drove them to the Guadalupe River. Baker soon discovered this and sued out a writ of attachment, and the cause came on for trial before Justice Vickry, of Victoria County.

Lawyer Tarpley, for the defendant, and Lawyer Thomas Newcomb, for the plaintiff, maintained an animated legal engagement for several days, to the complete bewilderment of Squire Vickry.

The matter was finally compromised by each party paying one-half the costs and dividing the horses equally between them.

Thus was the court appealed to for the justification of theft!

Chapter 14

Not aspiring to the higher *rôle* of historian, the most prominent military operations between Texas and Mexico until "annexation" will only be mentioned *en passant*, as not coming strictly within the purview of my own personal reminiscences; and this rule will be relaxed only in instances where the actors speak for themselves—as in Dr. Bernard's account of the "Fannin Massacre"—in conformity to which rule exact truth will have been attained, and in a manner, it is hoped, that will not fail to command the reader's attention.

A Mexican "raid," led by General Vasquez, penetrated the country as far as San Antonio in the year 1842. They held possession of the city, however, but two days, when they retired to the Rio Grande.

Again in September of the same year General Adrian Woll captured the devoted town while the district court was in session. In this latter expedition Captain Dawson's company of Texans was annihilated.[20] Colonel Caldwell gave the Mexicans battle on the Salado, and succeeded in inflicting a heavy loss on them subsequently, when General Woll retired from the country.

In consequence of the raid of Vasquez, President Houston determined to remove the seat of government from Austin to Houston, as affording greater security. This action of the president was resisted by the Austinians, and the burlesque "War of the Archives" was the consequence.

---

[20] They carried back to Mexico Judge Hutchinson, Lawyer A. Niel, Sam Maverick, John Twohig, and some others.

The invasion of General Woll was resented by the Texan government, and General Alexander Somerville marched to the Rio Grande at the head of some seven hundred and fifty men. General Somerville was restrained by prudential motives from passing this stream; but about two hundred and seventy restless and daring spirits, who would brook no delay, organized, and under the lead of Colonel Fisher passed from the aegis of the "Lone Star's" protecting rays into Mexico proper.

Thus was inaugurated the unfortunate "Mier Expedition," in which Texan heroism received high illustration, and Texan counsels the same lamentable want of foresight that had too often before signalized the want of decision, to the entire nullification of individual gallantry and bravery. The account of the battle of Mier, as published by Mr. George Lord, of De Witt County, himself an actor, is reproduced in this connection.

Battle of Mier

By George Lord

"the Rio Alcantara is a small but rapid stream, about sixty yards in width, which forms a semicircle upon the east side of Mier. The city being built in the curve, the position which our troops occupied was a high hill. Here it was necessary to feel our way with great caution and profound silence. The night being dark and drizzling with rain, the troops were ordered to sit and protect their arms from the damp until more could be learned of the position of the enemy. While in this position Captain C. H. Reese and F. Berry were despatched from the left wing to fire into a picket guard some two hundred yards to their left, for the purpose of extracting their fire and exposing the situation of their different pickets, while T. F. Green felt his way down the bluff in the direction of the lower ford. Here was stationed a strong force of their cavalry to defend this crossing, which he ascertained by the rattling of the cavalry gear when the horses would shake themselves. He returned to the position of our men upon the hill, and obtained of Colonel Fisher to take Captain Baker's spy company and some of the boatmen and thus open a scattering fire upon the cavalry below, while he could hunt out a crossing into the city between the two fords, selecting a position for these men protected by an embankment about three feet high immediately opposite the cavalry, with the river only between them. The signal to commence the action was to be nine shots from his repeating rifle. T. F. Green stepped to the water's edge and fired the nine shots in rapid succession into the enemy, which created some confusion in their lines, but was promptly returned, none of theirs taking effect. The spy company and boatmen kept up the fire, which completely deluded the enemy, for they thought it was our main body, which intended to force that passage. While this fire was kept up with galling effect upon the enemy, T. F. Green passed up the river to hunt out an intermediate crossing. Feeling his way along the almost perpendicular bluff of the river, he found a place which could be descended with difficulty; here he hung up a pocket-handkerchief upon a bush to designate the spot, while he returned to lead the army down. When he returned to the line some delay was occasioned by the following unfortunate circumstances. Reese and Berry, after riding into the picket upon our left, in attempting to retreat the latter fell down a precipice about thirty feet and broke his thigh. Dr. Sinnickson and a guard of several men were detailed for his assistance and placed him in a house nearby. I shall have occasion to speak of this small guard in detailing one of the most desperate and bloody conflicts which they had the next day with the enemy, and which the history of war can hardly parallel.

"After this detail was made the army followed T. F. Green in the most profound silence to where the handkerchief was left, and then in single file down the bluff about forty feet to the water's edge, it being too perpendicular to walk down. We then passed up the river some hundred yards; the cavalry below, being at this time severely galled by our spies and boatmen, were firing at random. We had two men wounded. Fisher and Green headed the line, and effected the crossing with the same silence which had been previously preserved. Green had been appointed to the command of the right wing, and by the time the extreme left was across the river the right was in immediate contact with a picket of the enemy about fifteen or twenty strong. The constant fire below which had been kept up between our spies and their cavalry had so diverted the attention of this picket that they did not discover us until we were almost touching, when the whole of them, in the greatest possible alarm, simultaneously hailed, as they received for answer to their *Quien vive*, 'Let them have it, boys,' when about one hundred shots were poured into them. They never returned the fire, or even kicked, that we know of, and the only thing now to break the silence, save the firing down the river, was the thundering voice of old Colonel Ramires, some few hundred yards off, commanding the cavalry to charge us; but this order was given in vain. We were now fairly in the suburbs of the city, and marching in the direction of the military square, which we had little doubt was the stronghold of the enemy. About fifty yards from the picket we entered a street at right angles, down which an officer, mounted and in full gallop, was passing. As he passed the head of our line some dozen shots were fired at him. The head of the line was wheeled to the right, up the street from whence this officer came, and, proceeding about one hundred yards further, it was necessary to reconnoitre the position of the enemy. Here a halt was ordered. When Green passed the next corner upon our left—which opened upon a street which led directly to the square, and in which was placed their artillery, around which a bustling preparation was making—returning to the line he informed Colonel Fisher of the exact position of the enemy, and obtained his permission to advance with the head of the right wing until it covered the street in which the artillery was placed, when we fired suddenly into them, passed the corner in quick time to make room for the grape and canister, and repeated the fire alternately with them. This was done several times with deadly effect upon the enemy, while twice per minute their grape and canister shot would pour down the street from whence our fire, passing the corner to await theirs, and then returning to re-occupy the firing position again. By this manœuvre, while their artillery was playing upon a vacant street our fire was sure and destructive.

"While the right wing was thus occupied the left unfortunately exposed their situation by returning some random shot, fired from the housetops. This brought upon them a well-directed fire, which killed J. E. Jones. The night continued to drizzle rain, which made it more important that our troops should effect a lodgment in some strong stone houses, as well to protect their arms as to refix those already out of order, some of the men having fallen in the water while crossing the river. The right wing was ordered to take possession of a row of stone houses upon one side of the street leading in the direction of the artillery, which they did by beating down the corner doors, and then, with the aid of an iron crowbar which they found inside, opened breaches through the dividing walls to within fifty yards of the artillery. A breach was ordered to be made in the upper end of this building so as to command the artillery, and no sooner was it commenced on the inside than the artillery was directed against that point on the outside. The wall was thick and strong, and the twelve-pound shots driving against it in rapid succession tended greatly to facilitate our work by loosening the stones for us. No sooner was the opening made than it was filled with our rifles, which were unerringly destructive. Upon the left wing was Captains Reese and Pearson's company. They had been ordered to occupy a row of stone buildings upon the opposite side of the street, and had almost completed their portholes, where the cross-fire from their position was equally destructive. After daylight three times was the artillery manned and as often silenced, the last time sixteen out of seventeen falling, Captain Castro being the only survivor. Our troops had now effected a strong lodgment nearly in the centre of the city, and beaten all opposition, with only one killed and two wounded. The same thing could not have been done in daylight against such odds with one hundred times the loss. In less than one hour after daylight opened upon us their artillery was silenced and deserted and the enemy had recourse to the housetops, from whence they ventured to pour down upon the houses we occupied volleys of musketry. In the many thousand cartridges discharged at us an occasional one would take effect, and we had some valuable men killed and several wounded. In their situation none but our best rifles and surest shots were brought into play.

"The guard which had been left with Berry the night previous, upon the east side of the Alcantara, occupied a small adobe house about six hundred yards distant. Here they had been impatient and anxious spectators of the battle for some seventeen hours, when a troop of cavalry, about sixty in number, passed near their house. Their rifles and double-barrelled guns were brought to bear upon them with most deadly effect, killing their commander and eight or ten others, when the survivors fled in every direction. In a very few minutes afterwards several hundred cavalry and a field piece were brought up. Berry's guard, well knowing that their adobe house could not withstand the force of the cannon shot, determined at once to leave it and charge through the lines of the enemy to our position. They accordingly charged and broke the enemy's lines with the most dauntless bravery, each one killing his man, and some two, for several of them had double-barrelled guns. It was now three hundred yards to the river, to gain which point they would be safe, for the enemy would not venture closer than that to our fire. Finding now their guns empty and no time to reload, the enemy pursuing in overwhelming numbers, their only defence was the butts of their pieces. The multitude prevailed, killing J. Austin, J. Berry, W. Hopson, and F. Jackson; taken prisoners, Dr. T. J. Sinnickson, E. Hean, and D. H. E. Beasley; while Bate Berry and Tom Davis succeeded in reaching our houses with empty guns and hatless. To see the unequal odds which these brave men encountered, without the power to succor them, was painful and exciting beyond anything we had experienced. Poor Berry was bayoneted in his bed. After their cavalry had prevailed over these eight men they manifested their joy by the most antic capers. About this time a column of the enemy charged down a street upon the north side of the building we occupied. Colonel Fisher, being at that point, threw himself with some twenty men suddenly into the street, received their fire, which severely wounded several of his men and, cutting off the ball of his right thumb; they effectually returned their fire, when the party fled.

"Up to this time, for the last six hours, the artillery nearest us had been silenced, and not one of the enemy dared approach. It had already, as we were afterwards told, proved the death of fifty-five out of their sixty choice artillery company. To get it out of our reach they had recourse to throwing a lasso over it from behind a corner and dragging it off. About that time they were blowing a charge in different directions. The lamented Captain Cameron and his gallant company had occupied during the battle a yard in the rear of our buildings. This yard had a low stone wall around it, which they had bravely defended, and from which they had done effectual execution. Here Cameron had seven men wounded and three killed, who had been brought inside the buildings. During this time, when the expected charge was looked for, Cameron came in under much excitement and asked for a reinforcement to defend his position. The white flag, Dr. Sinnickson, was ordered by General Ampudia to say to the Texan commander that he had seventeen hundred regular troops in the city and three hundred fresh troops nearby from Monterey, which would be up in a few minutes, and that it was useless for him to contend longer against such odds, and that if he would surrender his forces they would be treated with all the honors and consideration of prisoners of war; that the Santa Fé prisoners should be treated likewise, and that our men should not be sent to Mexico, but kept upon the frontier until an exchange or pacification was effected, and that if these terms were not acceded to we should be allowed no quarter. Before any communication with the white flag a column of the enemy made a charge within a few feet of the building, which was promptly met and driven back. About the same time General De la Verge, Colonel Carasco Blanco, and the priest of Camargo, Padre De Liver, obtruded themselves into our lines without our permission. The hour was about to close when Colonel Fisher went to see General Ampudia at his headquarters. He was gone some fifteen minutes. Colonel Fisher formed the different companies in the street to communicate the result of his interview with the Mexican commander, which was a reiteration of his former promises, and he concluded by saying: 'I have known General Ampudia for years—know him to be an honorable man—and will vouch for his carrying them out. If you are willing to accept these terms you will march into the public square and give up your arms; or prepare for battle in five minutes. In any view of the case your situation is a gloomy one, for you cannot fight your way out of this place to the Rio Grande short of a loss of two-thirds or perhaps the whole; but if you are determined to fight I will be with you and sell my life as dear as possible.' This speech was a death-blow to all farther prospect of fighting, for it at once determined half of the men to surrender. This closed the battle of Mier, fought December 25 and 26, 1842."

"Camp of the Army of the North
First Division

"Agreeable to the conference I had with William S. Fisher, I have decided to grant—first, that all who will give up their arms will be treated with the consideration which is in accordance with the magnanimous Mexican nation; second, that, conformable to the petition which the said General Fisher has made to me, all persons belonging to the Santa Fé expedition will receive the same treatment and guarantees as the rest; third, all who desire to avail themselves of these terms will enter the square and there deliver up their arms.
"Pedro D. Ampudia"

The aggregate number of Texans engaged in the battle was two hundred and sixty-one, our loss being ten killed, twenty-three badly and several slightly wounded. The aggregate number of the Mexican forces engaged was two thousand three hundred and forty. Their loss was between seven hundred and eight hundred killed and wounded. The Mexican report of their loss on the evening of the surrender was four hundred and thirty killed and two hundred and thirty wounded. Canales in his official despatch, in evading the truth, says: "As every great good costs dear, the streets and gutters of Mier overflowed with valiant Mexican blood."

We repeat that the battle of Mier, in its moral and political consequences to our country, was a glorious triumph. It was there that the people of Texas demonstrated the entire practicability of conquering and holding that rich valley against immense odds. It was there that the people of Texas pursued and fought them nine to one, killing treble their own numbers and proving themselves invincible to everything but duplicity and treachery; and it was there that the Texan made the name of the rifle and death synonymous terms throughout Mexico. Although the survivors of the Mier men have suffered all the horrors of multiplied deaths, and many of the brave companions have gone to their eternal homes in all the agonies of human suffering, yet it was a tribute they freely rendered to their country's honor and liberty. It is for that country to say whether it shall prove a burnt offering or a positive good.

Following the surrender of the Texans came their desperate attempt to escape by seizing the guns of the guard; the hand-to-hand grapple of frenzied men for liberty and life; their hopeless wanderings among the mountain passes, where hunger and thirst seemed to vie in enmity with the Mexicans against them; then their ultimate recapture and decimation—each man drawing a bean from a store similar in number with themselves, one-tenth of which were "black beans " and doomed the drawer to death.

A horrible massacre

During the year 1842 seven Mexicans came from Camargo, on the Rio Grande, to the mission of Refugio, from which place they despatched a messenger to the mayor of Victoria, Wigington, asking permission to visit Mr. Ysidore Benavides at his ranch on the Chocolate. The mayor readily complying with their wishes, the party proceeded to their destination. One of the number was a brother of Mrs. Benavides, and he brought her some money to which she was entitled from her father's estate. They had also some fine "Mexican blankets" and other articles of Mexican manufacture, which they purposed bartering for tobacco and other articles of necessity in their families. In Victoria at that time was a company of organized bandits and cutthroats called "the Cow-Boys," whose leader was one Wells. Among the number was that cold-blooded assassin, Mabry Gray, whose fiendish atrocities furnished the imagination of Hon. Jere Clements, of Alabama, the material for the mock-heroic fiction known once, but now happily scarce, as "Mustang Gray."

The party of seven Mexicans completed the period of their visit, and departed with some bales of tobacco, dry goods, etc., for their homes. The "Cow-Boys," or more properly "Men-Slayers," followed them, instigated by the craving of a consuming cupidity, to their camp a few miles beyond the town of Goliad, where they accepted the hospitalities of their intended victims and ate at their campfire. "Mustang Gray," that moral monstrosity, announced their fate to the doomed men. Doubtless Mustang felt an exquisite thrill of pleasure pervade his brutal soul at this refinement of demoniacal cruelty, as the cat does in torturing the terrorized mouse before feasting upon it. The "doomed seven" were tied together, and (was it in mockery or through respect for the Deity?) informed that they would be allowed a few minutes in which to offer up their prayers. This last sad duty performed, the victims announced with heroic resignation that they were prepared to receive the messengers of death. Whereupon the "Cow-Boys" emptied the contents of their guns into their persons, and the paltry plunder was all their own. To the victors belong the spoils!

The "victors" divided the spoils. The tobacco was hidden in the vicinity, the pirates intending to return at a more convenient season and apportion it among themselves. The horses and their equipments were sent east by two of the number for sale. These two never returned to divide the blood money, thus demonstrating the fact that these degraded beings in the form of men had not that instinct of "honesty among thieves" in common with the felons of other lands. When the buccaneers returned for the tobacco it was not to be found. An enterprising thief had anticipated his "pards," and that was all there was of it.

One of the Mexicans, as if Providence specially interposed to save him, was not hit, though the handkerchief with which his eyes were bandaged was perforated by buckshot and rifle balls. He fell, however, and feigned death. The ghouls stripped him and the others to the drawers and undershirt, and departed, their hearts elated by victory and proud of their prowess at arms!

The survivor found friends to administer to his wants, and eventually came to Victoria. The officers heard his narrative of the horrible affair, myself acting as the interpreter. Good people were horror-stricken at the outrage, but no attempt was made to bring the criminals to justice.[21]

In the year 1843 the "War of the Regulators and Moderators" commenced, and was waged with about equal success by each side for three years. Happily it was confined to a rather circumscribed section in the county of Shelby and others adjacent thereto. Mat Morsman and

---

[21] Manuel Escoban, the sole survivor of this massacre, was a cousin of Mr. Benavides. When Gray announced to the victims their impending fate, they, knowing that robbery was the incentive, offered Captain Wells all they possessed on condition that their lives were spared. Escoban, who was the only unmarried man in the party, offered himself as a vicarious sacrifice for the others. "Kill me, but spare these to their wives and little ones!" he pleaded in vain. The summary execution proceeded as above, and with the fatal volley Escoban fell under the body of the victim who was tied to him, and thus was he miraculously saved.

When the assassins had left his first care was to disengage himself from the corpse, which was accomplished with difficulty.

The scene that met his eyes was heartrending in the extreme. There lay the bodies of his kinsmen, stark and stiff in death. His only article of apparel was his drawers. He picked up a crownless hat from the ground, and, with the evening star for a guide, bent his footsteps towards the west. He met Mr. O'Boyle the next day, near the St. Nicholas Lake, and received the succor he so much needed. After some little time he made his way to Victoria, where his evidence was given.

Bradley were the leaders. The *emeute* was suppressed by the militia being ordered out by President Houston. Bradley, after joining the Methodist Church, hired a man to kill an enemy; the man informed on him, and his would-be victim slew Bradley as he was coming out of a church after preaching.

The first house was built in Seguin in 1842 by Mr. William King, an old follower of those earliest of Texan adventurers, Magee, Kemper, Perry, Ross, and Lockett. This was in De Witt's colony. Mr. King, upon the conclusion of their labors in building the house, made a speech to the workmen, neighbors, and lookers-on. He predicted for the embryo town a magnificent future, situated as it was at the foot of the mountains and at the head of navigation. He long kept an excellent house of entertainment for man and beast, and his hostelry was known, like the fame of Solomon, afar off. Mr. King fought at the disastrous battle of the Medina in 1813, under General Toledo, and escaped the pursuing royalist cavalry to return to his native Tennessee, obtain a wife, and return to Texas. During General Woll's raid to San Antonio Mr. King had so many calls upon his larder from the volunteers who went flocking to San Antonio that it threatened to become exhausted. Immediately after Woll's defeat on the Salado some three or four men, Mr. Ewing being among the number, stopped at Mr. King's and demanded refreshment. The old gentleman was sorry he could not entertain them, but to such an extent had the demands upon his resources extended that he was thinking of removing east in order to be able to provide for his own family. Ewing remarked that they were almost famished, having had nothing to eat since the battle. "The battle!" exclaimed the old man; "has there been a battle?" Ewing assured him that General Woll had been driven from Texas. The old gentleman remarked that possibly his son was in the fight, as he had gone to the front. "I know he was," quickly replied Ewing; "he stood by my side throughout the battle, and a braver boy I never saw!" "It runs in the King blood to be brave," the old man remarked, and straightway he instructed the "boys" to unsaddle and stay a week. "Take the hosses, Jack," he said to his boy, "and feed 'em good. Scare up something for the boys to eat, old woman." Thus by a successful *ruse de guerre* did the strategist Ewing accomplish his object, for he had never seen young King in the battle or elsewhere. Ewing was a merchant at Port Lavaca, and was one of the principal losers at the burning of Linnville by the Comanches. He was genial and witty, as the foregoing incident shows.

Mr. John Twohig's escape

General Woll captured San Antonio on the 11th day of September, 1842. So unexpected was his approach that the citizens had no apprehensions of danger—in fact, did not imagine that there was a Mexican army nearer than the Rio Grande until the column entered the town. District court was in session, Judge Hutchinson presiding. "The court," lawyers and some of the prominent citizens—Mr. John Twohig and Mr. Maverick among the number—were taken prisoners by General Woll and carried to the prison of Perote, in the interior of Mexico, where they remained in durance vile about two years. Mr. Twohig soon tired of the prison, and determined to free himself, if possible. He commenced a tunnel, and by the most assiduous labor succeeded in effecting communication with the outside world. He effected his escape and arrived home in safety. But so did not Mr. Wright, of De Witt County, who, being a large man, stuck in the tunnel about midway its length, and could neither advance nor retire. He had well-nigh despaired of ever seeing his family again on the blue, winding Guadalupe when, by superhuman efforts, he succeeded in "craw-fishing" into the prison again. Mr. Twohig resides in San Antonio, engaged in the banking and exchange business, and is noted for his sterling qualities of mind and heart, honesty, probity, hospitality, etc. He deserves to live long and to prosper yet much more.

Victoria's first jail

In the year 1843 or 1844 it was concluded that Victoria had attained to that degree of enlightenment that demanded a jail in which evil-doers could be confined. It was constructed of hewn logs, about a foot square, and pinned together by wooden pins. Between the door and one corner a log four and a half feet long was fastened to the jamb of the door by an iron spike. The building was soon occupied by two evil-doers, who readily observed that the wooden pins constituted the key of the position. These being cut, a log could very easily be displaced, and through the crevice thus made they could easily effect an escape. Friends on the outside supplied the necessary tools, and the work of liberation was short and easy. The cunning fellows replaced the log so exactly in its original position that its removal could not be detected after the most careful investigation. The honest blacksmith who made the lock was arrested on suspicion that he had made a duplicate key and given it to the prisoners. He was compelled to give bail to await the action of a grand jury. Soon, however, a Mexican was incarcerated for some trivial misdemeanor. The *quid nuncs* let him into the secret, and of course the don kicked out the log and walked forth a free man again. But, as he did not take the trouble to replace the log, the wonder was unravelled with the dawn, much to the gratification of the blacksmith. Victoria now has an "elegant" brick jail; but it is far more pleasant to reflect on the time when no jail whatever was needed in our community, nor even locks to insure the security of valuables. Such, alas! are some of the inevitable concomitants of vaunted progress.

Morphis, the historian

This gentleman grows facetious at the mention of the voluntary mission of the Count Farnese to Texas in an effort to free Texas from the ecclesiastical jurisdiction of the Bishop of Monterey by the acceptance of an archbishop for the new republic, which would have placed Texas in no closer political relationship with Rome than she now maintains with three bishops and the certainty of receiving an archbishop whenever such an appointment shall be judged in the interest of Christianity by the authorities of the Catholic Church. So diverting was this subject to the "learned historian" that he actually gives it more space than the Mier expedition, the advance of General Somerville, the raids of Vasquez and Woll combined; but he reveals his animus when he lets loose the sluice of puritanical bigotry, that always makes use of the phrases stereotyped two hundred years ago by the "Praise-God Barebones" of England, and the Cotton Mathers of New England. He must be allowed originality, however, in manufacturing the expression "lazzaroni-macaroni" Italians, though at the expense of good taste and grammar. The man who disgraces the tolerance of this enlightened age by reciting the religious persecutions that resulted in the death of Latimer, Ridley, and others on the one hand, and of Sir Thomas More, Bishop Fisher, and others on the other hand, only opens old sores to disgust the present generation, who have nothing, happily, to do with those controversies and deeds, that will never redound to the honor of Christianity. Intolerance is the characteristic of semi-civilized people, and persecution is always the work of zealots. Catholicism, as the catacombs of Rome alone attest, was subjected to fiercer and more vindictive persecutions than more modern religion has ever encountered. That Catholicism is less tolerant than Protestantism I deny. That Catholicism has—taking numbers and opportunity into consideration—been guilty of more persecutions than Protestantism, I deny. What a contrast between the intolerant proscriptions of the canting hypocrites of Plymouth Rock, who drove the noble Roger Williams into the wilderness to perish simply because he would not subscribe to their demoniacal exorcisms against witches, and the liberal conduct of the Catholic planters of Maryland, who raised the cross in the wilds of nature, and when they had caused it to blossom as a garden, lo! the persecuted Quakers and Nonconformists of inhospitable New England—yea, the Puritans themselves—came under the aegis of their protecting arms to worship God in conformity to the dictates of conscience.

By extending the parallel a little farther we would discover that ere long the Puritans came to outnumber the Catholics, and that their first act in recognition of the magnanimous hospitality that had been accorded them was to disfranchise their benefactors!

In substantiation of these assertions Mr. Morphis is referred to profane history alone.

I used the expression "hypocrite" in connection with the Puritanism of two hundred years ago. I did so advisedly, and would not mitigate the harshness of the expression, for these canting prayer-mongers were engaged in the African slave-trade *ab initio*, and what Indians they could not enslave at home or trade to the planters of Jamaica they exterminated—not in manly battle, but by and through the cunning artifices of the coward. I call them hypocrites because when the sanctimonious Cotton Mather proposed to capture William Penn and his Quakers on mid-ocean, confiscate their effects, and *sell the men, women, and children as slaves for the glory of God!* he was a blasphemous hypocrite.

Mr. Morphis rather sneers at the claim of Spain to the title to the eminent domain of Texas, and with rare sarcasm intimates that the Comanches had some claim—and he an apologist of that Puritan civilization that has not left even a remnant of the large aboriginal population that once covered New England!

The Catholic Church points with just pride to the millions of Indians of Mexico and the South American republics reclaimed by the arduous labors of her missionaries and priests from savage barbarism.

But "priest-ridden" will hardly apply to the State of Texas during its American colonization, as Almonte's report speaks of but *one priest* in all the vast region east of the Rio Grande. The tyranny of this surpliced servant of God could hardly have borne very grievously on the heroes who broke the power of Santa Anna at San Jacinto. Mr. Morphis forgets that Catholics bore as conspicuous a part in securing the autonomy of Texas as did the Protestants.

Now, the truth in regard to the Count Farnese was this: As a member of some charitable Catholic society he desired to introduce a colony of poor people from France and Germany into Texas, that they might acquire homes; and, being Catholics, he desired that they should recognize not even a nominal ecclesiastical fealty to the Bishop of Monterey, who, as a Mexican, was an enemy of Texas, but that their spiritual concerns should be directed by an archbishop of a purely Texan diocese in conformity to the doctrines of the Catholic Church, in which they had all been reared. Was there in all this anything contrary to the toleration and spirit of enlightenment of the nineteenth century? The flourishing colonies of Fisher, Miller, Castro, Powers, and others were peopled by Catholics, to which faith their prosperous descendants in Medina County, Comal County, Refugio and San Patricio counties are still subscribers, and will always be. Louis Philippe, late king of the French, not long before his abdication, sent the Abbé Martina to make a tour of Texas and report to him concerning the climate, soil, etc., with a special view to the suitableness of the country for the cultivation of the grape, olive, and cereals, as the king had some intention of investing a portion of his capital in the new and prosperous State. I formed the acquaintance of the Abbé Martina in Victoria, and found him to be a gentleman of great and varied information. He was a member of several learned societies in France. The downfall of the Orleans dynasty, of course, put an end to the enterprise.

But the archetype of "historian Morphis" was one Barnett, who so successfully concealed his asinine ignorance that he prevailed upon the people of some district to elect him to the Senate of the republic, where in due course of time he was recognized as the longest-eared animal that brayed beneath the "Lone Star" of Texas.

During the presidency of Louis Bonaparte, or perhaps in the first years of the empire, an effort was made to introduce a colony of the better class of French into Texas, and whose estimated capital exceeded one million of dollars. The bill asking a suitable land-grant passed the House, and failed in the Senate by one vote. Barnett, the brilliant genius and sagacious political economist, had the casting vote, and assigned as a reason for his ignorant action the imbecile declaration that he feared the French would settle up the country too fast and soon "outvote the rest of the people"! If Mr. Morphis discovers any congeniality of sentiment between himself and this illustrious statesman of early Texas I shall not oppose their resolving themselves into a mutual admiration society, with all the puritanical, pope-hating, witch-burning adjuncts that may be deemed necessary as a bulwark against the *armed* Catholic clergy of the world.

Chapter 15

The "missions" and the aborigines

One day a Toncahua Indian, familiarly known as "Joe," came to my store in Victoria, and after a long silence asked me where I came from. I told him Louisiana. He then wished to know of whom I had purchased my land. When I informed him he remarked that the white people were buying and selling the lands of the Indians without any regard to their claim whatever. God had given this country to the Indians who originally peopled it. But they would soon be dispossessed of their inheritance. If I wish to buy something from your store I must do so with your consent, and pay you whatever amount you ask for the article; but if the white man wants a piece of the Indian's land he goes to another white man, and the trade is made. Such were the ideas of Toncahua "Joe" in regard to the title to property. I confess that when he asked if I thought the course pursued by my countrymen was honest, that I would fain have made some ethical defence, but could only say that I had paid for all I possessed, but, alas, *to a white man!*

The Toncahuas were for many years the wards of the Franciscan fathers, and had developed a high degree of civilization and had partially embraced the Christian religion. They spoke the Spanish tongue very readily. They manufactured blankets of a very good quality, and cloth used in their own apparel. They had been instructed some in agriculture, and cultivated corn and vegetables sufficient for their own consumption. They also owned cattle and horses. The Toncahuas were located at or near Victoria, their field being above the site of the present town. They had a church, which was erected on what is now known as "the Toncahua Bank," the foundation of which is still visible, as it was built of masonry. But a remnant of the Toncahua tribe is now left.

The Carankua Indians were situated at the mission of Refugio. They had a substantial stone church, with a chime of bells, one of which is yet at Refugio and bears the date "1737." Another one was in use in Victoria. It bore the date "1751."

Father Diaz, who was the last of the missionaries, gave me quite a history of the different Texas missions. He stated that in the year 1808 the mission of Refugio possessed fully five thousand head of livestock of various kinds; the "flat" in front of the church was their cultivated field. Up to this period they had all necessaries and many comforts of life in abundance, and were making rapid progress in the path of civilization, when the war of Mexican independence came on and destroyed with one fatal breath the work and the fruits of many years of arduous toils and anxieties. It was fatal indeed to the poor Indians, who speedily relapsed into barbarism when associated with the licentious soldiery, and too soon forgot the precepts of Christianity taught them by the good fathers, and when these were forced to abandon their labors the Indian was again the savage that he was at first.

The Carankua women, too, learned the use of the spinning wheel, and manufactured a very good article of cotton cloth, and also blankets of a superior quality, which they rendered quite pleasing to the eye by the skilful combination of colors. The Carankuas were tall, athletic specimens of physical manhood, many of them exceeding six feet in height. Each warrior carried a bow, made of cedar, the length of his own body; their arrows measured about four feet. "Prudencia," the chief, was a tall, well-formed man, and spoke Spanish fluently. The second chief, "Antonio," I thought was the handsomest specimen of physical manhood I ever saw.

These Indians are now probably extinct. Their last visit to Victoria County was in the year 1842, when they killed Mr. Kemper at his ranch, which was situated where the village of "Kemper City" now stands. From Mr. Gus Black, who was then a small boy, I learned the following particulars. The Carankuas had their camp on the east side of the Guadalupe River, on the outskirts of the timber, and near the residence of Mr. Black, to whose family they never offered any violence. Mr. Kemper had a number of cattle in a pen, for what purpose is not known. The Carankuas were out on a hunting frolic, and came to the pen of cattle. They seated themselves upon the rail pen, and occasionally would aim an arrow at a cow in the pen, without, however, letting it fly. Kemper came out of the house and ordered them away in an angry manner; and upon their refusing to comply he returned with a double-barrelled shotgun, but no sooner had he brought it to his shoulder with the intention of shooting than the Indians let fly a cloud of arrows at him. One pierced a vital part, and he fell in the doorway of his house, a corpse.

The Carankuas were frightened at the consequences certain to follow this rash act, and anticipated the vengeance of the whites by seeking safety in flight. They returned to the camp in the neighborhood of Mr. Black's house, and, taking only the most portable objects, started, it is believed, for the Rio Grande.

"Their lodges," says Mr. Gus Black, "long stood just as they left them." The sole survivor of Mr. Kemper is Mrs. David F. Williams, of Anaqua, Victoria County.

The Aranames were located on the north side of the San Antonio River, and opposite the town of La Bahia (old Goliad). They had a large and substantial church, now transformed into "Aranama College," which was enclosed within a stone wall. They had the bend of the river enclosed by a fence, and cultivated the ground. They owned much livestock, and were really a civilized tribe of Indians. Their women manufactured cloth, and also water jars used by themselves. The Aranames were a temperate class of aborigines, and did not indulge in the use of ardent spirits at all.

The young men and women of this tribe were very fond of painting their faces and bodies profusely, and nothing contributed more to their pleasure than to view themselves in a looking glass when so arrayed. When their "numerous familiarity" would force the information that their company was not desirable, they would reply with dignity, "Me gentleman! Me no Toncahua dog!"

Mission valley

This celebrated valley is so called from the mission that stood about one half-mile from the residence of Mr. Patricio De Leon, on the west bank of the Guadalupe River, and about ten miles north of Victoria. The foundations of the mission are yet in a tolerable state of preservation.

A dam, of "concrete" work, was made across a creek some two miles from the valley, for the purpose of filling a reservoir with water. An artfully contrived *ascequia*, or waterway, wound around the hills like the folds of a serpent, seeking the cultivated field in the valley below. This field comprised about sixty acres of land. The ascequia was composed of a bed of durable cement, and can yet be traced for a considerable distance. A "gate" in the dam was opened when the growing crops required irrigation, and the water from the reservoir flowed down the ascequia to the field below. These ruins, the mission, the dam, and the ascequia, remain no less eloquent though silent testimonials to the zeal of the missionaries than monuments to the engineering skill displayed in their erection and government.

The Franciscans commenced the stupendous work of damming the Guadalupe River at the northern extremity of the valley for the construction of a vast reservoir that would have the capacity of holding sufficient water to irrigate the whole valley. Some portions of this work, which the hostile Comanches did not suffer the missionaries to complete, yet stand. These Bedouins of the plains came down from their mountain haunts in such numbers, and were so rapacious and hostile, that the civilized population of the mission were forced to seek refuge at La Bahia; and the fruit of long years of arduous toil was dissipated in a day by the ruthless destruction of the savages.

On these periodical incursions the Comanches often numbered one thousand souls. At first they travelled on foot, but finally came to know the value of the horse as a medium of locomotion, and they speedily developed into the most fearless horsemen of the world.

These forays became so frequent that all the ranches on the border were broken up.

Don Felipe Partilleas (the father of Mrs. Colonel James Powers) owned a ranch on the San Marcos, eight miles above the town of Gonzales, which he finally abandoned, as the Indians became intolerable. In removing his cattle he left some which he failed to find, and these had multiplied to such a degree that when the Anglo-American settlers penetrated that country in 1833-5 they found the section stocked with wild cattle entirely free of all marks or other indices of ownership. But so wild were they that only the most expert hunters might hope to come up with them.

The Comanche raid, and burning of Linnville

On the 4th day of August, 1840, we of Victoria were startled by the apparition presented by the sudden appearance of six hundred mounted Comanches in the immediate outskirts of the village. The first supposition was that they were Lipans, who occasionally paid us friendly visits, but soon the intelligence came that the Indians had killed Mr. McNuner a mile north of town, and Dr. Gray, and also had wounded a boy. By these unmistakable tokens we were made aware of the fact that we were about surrounded by overwhelming numbers of these implacable enemies of the human race.

The men of Victoria, some fifty in number, collected such arms as they could, but the folly of attempting anything against such numbers, and on foot, was apparent to all. The Indians were engaged in gathering up horses, as we could plainly see. Some Mexican traders were in Victoria at the time, and had about five hundred head of horses on the prairie in the immediate vicinity of town. All these the Comanches captured, besides a great many belonging to the citizens of the place.

A Mr. Crosby, who lived a mile below town, had come in in the morning, leaving his wife and little child at home. The Indians took Mrs. Crosby and the child prisoners. It was thought, according to their custom, that, having satisfied themselves with plunder, the Indians would retire toward their usual haunts before a force could be assembled to attack them. With this object in view about fifty of the best men of Victoria were mounted and despatched to the settlement near Cuero Creek, in De Witt County, to get reinforcements and meet the Indians on their return. The Indians retired to Spring Creek, three miles above Victoria, and camped about opposite the site of the present residence of Mr. Thomas Sterne. The men of Victoria crossed Spring Creek near the mouth, in the timber, and so passed the Comanche encampment unobserved and proceeded on their way. The Indians killed a white man on Spring Creek, named Vartland Richardson, and two Negro men, and took a Negro girl prisoner. Contrary to all expectation, and at variance with their usual custom, the Indians did not retreat, but threatened the town again the next day. They dispersed themselves over the whole country and almost surrounded the town. Four men returning from Jackson County encountered the savages a mile or two out of town. Pinkney Caldwell, who was riding a mule, made no effort to escape and was lanced to death on the spot.

Another of the four, a Mexican, was overhauled and killed. Joseph Rodgers and the late Jesse O. Wheeler put spurs to their horses and won the race for life by the veriest good fortune; so close was Captain Wheeler pursued that his enemy did not draw rein until he had entered the streets of the town. The Indians burned a house in the outskirts of the town. The panic-stricken citizens all collected at the public square, and all were speculating with agonizing suspense upon the fate that would probably befall us. But fortunately for us, as it was fatal for others, the Indians passed Victoria and proceeded toward the bay, literally sweeping the whole country of horse stock as they went. They camped for the night on the Benavides Ranch, on the Placido Creek, distance twelve miles from Linnville. They intercepted two wagoners here, one of whom concealed himself in the high grass and saved his life by fleeing to Victoria under cover of the darkness. The other was killed, and in such close proximity to his hidden friend that he could hear him begging for his life. One of the wagons was loaded with two hogsheads of bacon. These the Comanches opened, but not fancying the contents, where fresh meat was so plentiful, unfastened the oxen that were attached to the wagon, and left it and the cargo untouched. Mr. W. G. Ewing, a merchant of Linnville, en route to Victoria, passed these wagons on the roadside and saw the campfires of the Comanches on the creek close at hand, not dreaming of the gauntlet that he was unconsciously running. He imagined the Indian camp was some large Mexican train of wagons going to Linnville for goods. On reaching Victoria the next morning he was much surprised at the revelations that greeted his ears, and considerably troubled at the thought that six hundred hostile Indians interposed between himself and his home. His sister, Mrs. Watts, was in Linnville. In three miles of Linnville the Comanches killed two Negro men whom they found cutting hay. They immediately proceeded to surround the town and to pillage the stores and houses. The people took refuge on a lighter in the bay, and were soon aboard a schooner lying at anchor and safe from the Indians. Major Watts and Mr. O'Neill were killed and Mrs. Watts taken a prisoner. While the Indians were cutting up fantastic antics before high heaven, in Linnville, the refugees on the schooner were the spectators, and witnessed with whatever feelings they could command the wanton destruction of their property. Judge John Hays, however, became so exasperated that he vowed he would have one shot at the "red devils" anyway. So, grabbing a gun, the judge jumped overboard—the water was not over three or four feet deep—and waded to the shore, where, gun in hand, he stood upon the beach anxiously waiting for a Comanche to come within range of his gun. But the Indians imagined the judge was a "big medicine," or something of the sort, and so steered clear of the awful fate in store for him who should invite the judge's fire. Finally the earnest petitions of his friends on the boat availed and the judge returned to them. Now, upon examining the old "fusee" which threatened so lately to consummate such slaughter, it was discovered that *the piece was not loaded!*

In my warehouse were several cases of hats and umbrellas belonging to Mr. James Robinson, a merchant of San Antonio. These the

Indians made free with, and went dashing about the blazing village, amid their screeching squaws and "little Injuns," like demons in a drunken saturnalia, with Robinson's hats on their heads and Robinson's umbrellas bobbing about on every side like tipsy young balloons. In the afternoon the Comanches began to retire. They crossed the bayou near the old road, and there encamped for the night. The Victoria men had now returned with some reinforcement from the Cuero settlement. On the morning of the 7th these fell in with a company of one hundred and twenty men, commanded by Captain Zumaldt, of Lavaca County, and the whole encountered the Indians twelve miles east of Victoria, on a creek called the Marcado, where some skirmishing was indulged in, the whites losing one man, Mordeci. A few of the Indians used guns, the primitive bow and arrow being the arm mainly relied on. It is thought some of the Indians were killed and thrown into the creek to conceal the bodies. Some of Captain Zumaldt's men were anxious to charge them; and, when the disparity of arms is considered, the result must have been the rout of the Indians and their subsequent capture or annihilation. While this skirmish was in progress Indians had scouts out in all directions; some of these crossed the Arenoso and killed Mr. Bell, taking his horse and equipments. In the afternoon the Indians called in their scouting parties by making a black smoke, and proceeded to the Casa Blanca, a branch of the Garcitas, where they encamped for the night. Zumaldt's men also went into camp, not far distant from the Indians, and despatched runners to Victoria for ammunition and provisions.

    The wily Indians silently folded their tents in the night and stole away. Zumaldt saw no more of them until he ran into their rear as they were crossing Plum Creek, and taking position in the post oak point beyond, on what was destined to be a fatal battleground for them. Felix Huston, Ben McCulloch, and others had gathered a force of near four hundred volunteers, and the Indians should have been annihilated. Ewing came up with his sister, Mrs. Watts, just as an Indian boy had discharged, as he imagined, an arrow into her body. Fortunately she wore a steel corset, and the arrow, striking one of the broad bands of this, did her but little injury. Less fortunate was Mr. Crosby, who reached the side of his wife just in time to soothe with endearing offices her last moments. Despairing of effecting an escape with the prisoners, these inhuman monsters had resolved to kill them. The infant of Mrs. Crosby had been killed near Linnville and thrown on the roadside. The Indians were defeated in the engagement that ensued, and left some twenty-five dead on the field. But encumbered with plunder as they were, and principally armed with bows and arrows, they should have been entirely destroyed.

Several hundred head of horses and mules were recaptured, as were also immense quantities of dry goods. "To the victors belong the spoils," and the "Colorado men" appropriated everything to themselves. Ewing recognized many of his goods in the captured property, but identification did him no good. Captain J. O. Wheeler, though one hundred and fifty of the recaptured horses bore his brand, obtained with the greatest difficulty a horse to ride home. Mrs. Watts—late Mrs. Fretwell—states that she was taken under the protection of an old chief who placed her in charge of an ancient squaw. She relates that the Indians brought her a book from which to read to them the "laws of Texas," and upon her prompt compliance they laughed immoderately. When they started from Linnville they strapped her securely upon the back of a mule to prevent her falling off or attempting an escape. Such was the battle of Plum Creek.

Captain Krantz is several times killed already!

Captain Krantz, who had won his spurs, or his title at least, in command of a company in the Texas line during the years 1838-39, was out on the Texana road, some four miles from Victoria, when he encountered the Indians. It is supposed that Captain Krantz dutifully rode right into them, as no account of any attempt on his part to escape was ever announced. They met the captain by a lance-thrust, which unhorsed him. Several more lance-thrusts into his prone body were made, and the Comanches, thinking all was over with Captain Krantz, left him for dead. After a short time he resumed control of his bewildered faculties, and, after convincing himself that he was not dead, made an effort to assume a soldier's position—solid on the bottom, and eyes square to the front; but the effort was an entire failure. But the captain discovered an Indian approaching him. Captain Krantz now "laid close" and "possumed" with all his might. The Indian rode up and jabbed his spear through the prostrate body. The poor fellow, who had already lost gallons of blood, and was sick and faint, nerved himself for this supreme crisis, and did not suffer a groan to escape his lips when the cruel steel went slashing through his flesh and crunching against bones. The Indian dismounted, and, upon turning the body over, discovered a large gold ring upon Krantz's finger. He made several ineffectual attempts to pull it off, and finally jerked out his knife with the too apparent intention of cutting off the finger.

"Gott in Himmel!" ejaculated Captain Krantz, as he jerked off the ring himself, and handed it to the Comanche, "it vas yours, my frent!"

The ungrateful demon took the ring, and, in the language of Captain Krantz, "He youst sticks my body mit de spear through, und kills me another time!"

Poor Captain Krantz had now been "killed" so many times that it was with the greatest difficulty that he managed to crawl to the roadside, though only a few yards distant. Here he could indulge the almost vain hope that some Good Samaritan would come along and relieve his suffering. He remained in this inhospitable place all day and all night, and far into the forenoon of the next day ere succor reached him. The doctors who dressed the captain's many wounds declared that he must die; but Captain Krantz declared that he would not die, and die he did not at that time. It was amusing to hear Krantz tell of his miraculous escape.

A fatal affray

There was a "Major" Tinsley, who fought at San Jacinto, and afterwards went to San Antonio to reside. He had the reputation of being a gentleman and a gallant and brave fellow. Soon after his arrival in San Antonio some malicious person shaved the tail of his horse: Without cause Tinsley accused Navarro, a respectable merchant of the city and a brother of Antonio Navarro, of the misdemeanor.

Navarro promptly and unequivocally denied the accusation, and Tinsley departed apparently satisfied, but soon returned and renewed the charge in more emphatic terms, and volunteered a little gratuitous abuse in addition thereto.

Navarro stated that he had done all that a gentleman could offer in the premises, denied the accusation, and concluded by ordering Tinsley off his premises. Tinsley drew a knife and stabbed at Navarro, who, avoiding the stroke, seized a knife that lay on the counter and plunged it into Tinsley, who, though mortally wounded, with a determination evincing a willpower truly wonderful, drew a pistol and fired upon Navarro, who fell and died in a few moments. Tinsley was borne to his room, but died before reaching it.

The death of Navarro was mourned by the best citizens of the place, and a large concourse followed his remains to the tomb, while there was in attendance on the funeral obsequies of his cruel and unjust assailant but barely enough to perform the necessary offices.

Wounded "honnoh"!

General Sam Houston and ex-President Burnet had an acrimonious newspaper controversy, in which each abused the other without stint. Mr. Burnet condescended to call the hero of San Jacinto "Big Drunk," "Half Indian," etc., and "Old Sam" accused his ex-excellency of being an ex-*hog-thief!*

This was the straw that broke the camel's back, and Mr. Burnet despatched Dr. Archer with a "note."[22]

"What does he predicate this demand upon?" "Old Sam" asked. Archer replied that he had abused Mr. Burnet to such a degree that forbearance had ceased to be a virtue.

---

[22] Ed. Note: Challenging Houston to a duel.

"Hasn't he abused me to an equal degree? He has done so publicly and privately until I am constrained to believe that the people are thoroughly disgusted with both of us."

The stately dignity with which the old hero said this was far more impressive than the words employed. Dr. Archer took the challenge back unopened; and, to the credit of both these her honored sons and the fame of Texas, the matter was suffered to drop.

A fatal duel

Two of the heroes of San Jacinto—Howard, a man of a good reputation, and one "Red," a protégé of General Lamar—fought a duel at "Seguin's Ranch," a few miles below San Antonio, in June 1840. The difficulty was occasioned by some unimportant dispute, and the fiery spirits adjourned the matter to the "code of honor"—a relic of barbarism and most improperly called. At the first fire, which was simultaneous from both pistols, "Red" was shot through the heart, and his bullet went crashing through the brain of Howard.

And this—though so contrary to the experience of the heroes who figure on the dramatic boards of Haverly and the Olympic—was the last of Howard and "Red."

General Albert Sidney Johnston, the great Confederate chief of after-days, and General Felix Huston met in mortal combat on the Lavaca River in the year 1837, which originated about some question in relation to the command of the Texan army. Huston was a most expert marksman, and General Johnston made no pretensions at all in that line. After three exchanges General Johnston was seriously wounded by a ball passing through his hips, but fortunately he recovered after months of suffering.

German colony

The Prince de Solms arrived at Indianola, Texas, with a German colony in the year 1845, and the majority, after suffering much from sickness, and after many had died by the way, finally located in Comal County, on the Guadalupe River, where they have, from the humble beginning, come to rank among the most prosperous citizens of Texas. New Braunfels, their county capital, is a flourishing town of some three thousand inhabitants. The manufacture of cloth has received more attention from this people than elsewhere in Texas; and they now produce from their mills, from both wool and cotton fabrics, goods unsurpassed in appearance and durability.

Many of them have accumulated fortunes, and are classed among the most extensive and enterprising of the business men of Texas; while, by the exercise of the proverbial German thrift and economy, all are earning a comfortable livelihood, educating their children, beautifying their places, and "laying by a little against a rainy day."

There are no better citizens than the Germans, who believe in attending to their own business, and thus always have ample time in which to do it well.

The "Babe of the Alamo"

It will be remembered that Lieutenant Dickinson, of the artillery, with his eldest child perished in the desperate leap made by the frantic father for liberty and life when all the heroic defenders of the Alamo had been cut down. His wife, Mrs. Dickinson, and a babe; Mrs. Alsbury, and a Negro servant of Colonel Travis were sent to Gonzales after the fall of the Alamo. When the "Babe of the Alamo" was about ten years of age, her mother being dependent upon her manual labor for support, some friends interested themselves in the child, and a bill was introduced asking aid from the State for the proper support and education of the little orphan, who should, indeed, have been the adopted child of Texas, rocked as she was in that tempestuous cradle that was baptized by the martyr blood which was destined to be the seeds of Texan liberty forever.

The bill was opposed because some captious persons cast certain unwarrantable imputations upon the character of the mother. It finally passed the House, but was lost in the Senate. I dwell upon the subject now because it has an interest of peculiar charm to every patriotic Texan heart, and called forth two of the most tender heartbursts of eloquence ever uttered by Texan lips.

What a sweet consolation it would have been to us all if the efforts of Mr. Guy M. Bryan and Mr. Wilson had been crowned by success, and the storm-rocked, tempest-tossed "Babe of the Alamo" had been adopted as the "child of Texas" and her education secured! But it was defeated.

But she, too, has gone, "sole daughter of the house and heart" of heroic Dickinson! He gave his life for Texas; and Texas beheld his widow eking out a meagre existence by menial toil, and his daughter—reared in penury and educated in vice.

It should not have been so; it would not have been so, had Texas performed her duty!

Hon. Guy M. Bryan said:

"I had intended to be silent on this occasion; but silence would now be a reproach when to speak is a duty. No one has raised a voice in behalf of the orphan child, while several have spoken against her claim. I rise, sir, in behalf of no common cause; liberty was its foundation, heroism and martyrdom consecrated it. I speak for the orphan child of the Alamo. None save her can say: 'I am the child of the Alamo!'

"Well do I remember the consternation that spread throughout the land in the wake of the sad tidings that the Alamo had fallen!

"It was there that a gallant few, the 'bravest of the brave,' threw themselves between the settlements and the enemy, and swore never to surrender nor retreat. They redeemed their pledges with the forfeit of their lives, and fell the self-chosen sacrifice upon the virgin altar of Texan freedom. Texas, unapprised of the advance of the Mexican invader, was sleeping and dreaming in fancied security, when the alarm-gun of the Alamo first announced that the Attila of the South was drawing near. Infuriated at the resistance of Travis and his noble band, he marshaled his hosts beneath the wall, and rolled wave after wave of his charging legions against those battlements of freedom. In vain he strove; the flag of liberty, the 'Lone Star' of Texas, still streamed out upon the breeze in bold defiance from the outer wall. Maddened and persistent, he planted his batteries, and, after days of bombardment and repeated assaults, he took a blackened and ruined mass, the blood-stained walls of the Alamo. The noble spirits of its heroic defenders had plumed their flight to another fortress, not made with hands.

"But for the stand made at the Alamo Texas would have been desolated to the Sabine. Sir, I ask the pittance, and for whom? For the only living witness —save the mother—of this awful tragedy, this 'bloodiest picture in the book of time,' the bravest deed that ever glowed upon the annals of any land. Grant the boon! She claims it as the Christian child of the Alamo, baptized in the blood of a Travis, a Bowie, a Bonham, a Crockett! To turn her away would be shame. Grant her what she asks, that she may be educated and become a worthy child of the state; that she may take that position in society to which she is entitled by the illustrious services of her father—illustrious because he fell at the Alamo!"

Hon. J. C. Wilson said:

"The student of Grecian history in every age, in every land, has felt his bosom glow with noble fire while reading of Leonidas and the three hundred who fell with him at Thermopylae; but when the Alamo fell a nobler than Leonidas, a more devoted band than the Spartans, sank amid its ruins. They shed their blood for us, they poured out their lives as water for the liberties of Texas, and they have left us of that bloody but glorious conflict one sole memento, one frail, perishable keepsake—the child whose petition for assistance is now before us. Shall we say: 'Though your father served the State in his life; though he fell in the ranks of those men whose names history shall chronicle and nations shall delight to honor; though you alone of all the children of Texas witnessed that direful scene whose bare contemplation makes stout hearts quail; and though the credit and honor of Texas are alike concerned in taking care of your childhood and in watching over your youth, in providing for your happiness and respectability; though you, "the Babe of the Alamo!" will be an object of interest to all who may visit our State in after-years, when the pen of the historian shall have recorded your connection with the early glories and sufferings of our now happy land—yet for all this we will suffer you to grow up in uncultured wildness, in baneful ignorance, perhaps in vice, rather than make this pitiful appropriation to enable you to render yourself capable of occupying that position in society to which you are in a peculiar degree entitled by the strange and thrilling circumstances surrounding your life?' Sir, I trust that such an act may not mar the history of Texas. Sure I am by my vote it never shall.

"It is related of Napoleon that an officer whom he loved was wounded, and, from the narrowness of the defile in which the contest raged, was in imminent danger of being crushed to death by the feet of contending friends and foes. While the emperor looked on in deep anxiety for his fate, a female, an humble follower of the army, with a babe on one arm, forced her way through the melee to the wounded man, and, supporting him with her other arm, conveyed him to a place of comparative safety near the emperor; but just as she turned away from the object of her daring and benevolent solicitude a bullet struck her dead at the feet of Napoleon. He raised the motherless babe in his arms, and called to an attendant, saying: 'Bear this child to the rear; see that it wants for nothing, for henceforth it is the child of the Empire.' Mr. Speaker, the child of the Alamo is the child of the State; and we cannot treat her with neglect without entailing lasting disgrace upon Texas."

The neglect by Texas of the "Babe of the Alamo" will have to go on record as another instance of the ingratitude of republics.

The so-called "Cart War"

The cart war, as it was called, originated in or about Goliad in consequence of a rivalry between American wagoners and the Mexican cartmen who were engaged in hauling merchandise to the interior towns from the port of Indianola. In transporting goods to San Antonio the Mexicans' tariff of freight was so low as to practically rule the American teamsters entirely out of the competition. The merchants, as a matter of course, patronized the cheapest carrier, other requisites being equal; and, indeed, in point of speed the Mexicans generally were ahead of their rivals.

The consequence of this was that the Americans were left with plenty of spare time on their hands, and very unjustly went to "boycotting" the cart men. Some of these innocent fellows were assassinated on the road as they were laboring to comply with the terms of their contracts by delivering their freight on as good time as it was possible to make, and the wheels of their carts cut down by assassins who could not be detected in the wrong. Often, in addition to the murder of the Mexicans and the destruction of their carts, the lawless *chevaliers de industrie* would rob the carts of their freight and appropriate the valuable cargoes to themselves.

To such an extent did this disgraceful business finally attain that General Twiggs, the United States commander at San Antonio, was compelled to send a guard to protect the government supplies *in transitu*.

The authorities of Goliad County seemed to regard the whole thing with supine indifference, as they made no efforts whatever either to suppress the crimes or to bring the criminals to justice.

The Mexicans made a new road, leaving Goliad some twelve or fifteen miles to the left, and pursued the even tenor of their way. But a higher license than the law countenances cannot be controlled, and once granted, on however circumscribed terms, is sure to usurp new and more extensive privileges. So in this instance; when the supply of Mexicans failed to satisfy the demand the "cart-cutters" discovered an enterprising industry in depredating on the property of the "prominent" citizens who had winked at their lawless robberies. As the wrong bull was being gored this time, the assistance of "Judge Lynch" was invoked, and the blackjacks around La Bahia bore bounteous fruit for the vultures of fate. This summary administration of illegal justice had the desired effect, and peace once more "reigned in Warsaw."

The matter came before the Legislature before its final suppression, and many suggestions were made in quest of some easy solution of the problem. One witty member proposed that the independence of Goliad should be recognized, and that that county should be cut off from the rest of the State. Mr. Baker, in his *Scrap Book*, page 114, errs in stating that State troops were called out to suppress the lawlessness; "Judge Lynch" did it with his little rope.

How a Know-Nothing speech was "nipped"

In the year 1856 General W. R. Scurry and myself were the delegates from Victoria County to the State Democratic nominating convention at Austin. Our Know-Nothing friends had delegated the late Hon. S. A. White and Judge J. W. Allen to represent them at the same time and city in a convention of their own.

The two conventions (on different occasions, of course) met in the Representative Hall. As harmony and union characterized the proceedings of the Democratic body, our labors were soon ended.

Judge White offered divers and sundry resolutions in the Know-Nothing wigwam looking to a modification of their intolerant and proscriptive platform of principles. But his good-intentioned resolutions were voted down as fast as they were put to the house. Whereupon Judge White washed his hands of Know-Nothingism and left the convention in disgust.

Judge Allen—an eloquent speaker, by the way—was announced to address the body upon the conclusion of its labors, and the hall was packed, so eager were the people to hear his elucidations of the new political faith. He was formally presented to the audience by the president of the convention, and commenced: "Fellow-citizens: Four hundred years ago Christopher Columbus, a native of Genoa, discovered America."

The audience were electrified by the rich brogue of a mellow Hibernian in the farther end of the building asking: "*An' who give that bluddy owld furriner permission to disciver America?*"

Judge Allen collapsed, and the cheers, "three times threes" and "a tigers" that greeted the Irishman's witty sally were loud, long, and continuous.

In the election that followed the Democracy was victorious by a handsome majority.

In 1860 Texas, in common with the other Southern States, felt that the election of Abraham Lincoln to the Presidency of the United States by a purely sectional party was a menace to the institution of slavery and to the sovereignty of the States.

Governor Houston failing to respond to the public demand for a constitutional convention, the same was called by the informal action of representative men throughout the State.

An ordinance of secession was passed, and subsequently ratified by the people at the polls in a vote of 38,415 for the measure and 13,841 against it. Measures looking to a confederation of the Southern States were adopted, and Texas became one of the Confederate States of America. Then came the titanic struggle, and Texans were found in the forefront of every engagement from Val Verde, in New Mexico, to the Potomac. The exploits of such leaders and their men as Hood, Granberry, Ector, Ross, Terry, Green, Scurry, Hardeman, and others,[23] have immortalized their prowess and shed an imperishable lustre upon Texan arms. Texas did not suffer so much in the occupation of her territory by the Union soldiers as did her sisters of the east, but she drank sufficiently deep of the bitter cup as it was. Finally, after four

---

[23] Among the troops of Texas was Sibley's Brigade. This command left San Antonio and, after many hardships, reached New Mexico and gained the battles of Val Verde and Glorietta. Meeting with no further opposition from the Union army, they returned to Texas and afterwards joined Taylor's Division in Louisiana, the history of which is well known. My two sons cast their fate with the lost cause. My oldest son, Captain Charles C. Linn, served with distinction through the whole struggle and returned with a reputation creditable to himself and the State. My other son, John J, Linn, Jr., was in Colonel Buchell's regiment, and died while stationed at Brownsville, much regretted by his officers and fellow soldiers. I mention this as a part of my regrets in the lost cause.

years of a contest whose giant proportions have scarcely been paralleled in modern times, came the surrender of Appomattox and the loss of all for which the Southern cause contended.

Then came the hour of the Radical jubilee. Proscriptive reconstruction measures were enacted by Congress, and the Southern States were compelled to assist in their own degradation by the enforcement of laws that challenge in vain a comparison in studied tyranny and oppressive despotism.

The Negroes of Texas conducted themselves during the four years of the war with commendable loyalty to their masters; and, though in many instances they were so situated as to have been able to do the whites much injury, they showed no disposition whatever to do so.

The carpetbaggers who infested the State after the war, each having a "gripsack" to fill, succeeded in leading them (the Negroes) into the Radical party and otherwise demoralized them. But time and the exercise of patience on the part of the whites, and experience on that of the blacks, have wrought many changes even in their political affiliations, and the commendable work is yet progressing.

Never were a people the more loyal dupes of a set of adventurous rascals. They followed in the wake of the "carpet-baggers" and voted them to office with perfect unanimity for years, though remorselessly preyed upon by the greedy cormorants, who plundered them in the name of philanthropists and the cause of benevolence.

The Negroes were taught in the Loyal Leagues that their reward for "loil" services would speedily come in the shape of a mule and forty acres of land. My neighbor, Mr. Brightwell, was informed by a dark-skinned tenant of his that he had selected as his share "de big brown mule and de river cut" of forty acres, or "dereabouts."

Captain Miller was the *oleaginously* loyal agent of the Freedman's Bureau in Victoria. The Negroes had collected several hundred dollars with which to build a church, and, contrary to the advice of many of their old friends, deposited the same with Captain Miller for safekeeping.

Captain Miller left without taking the trouble to hand this amount back to them, and, so far as the proposed new church was concerned, the funds "went where the woodbine twineth!"

But amid so much chaff there was an occasional good grain of wheat.

A Negro stole a horse of Mr. J. R. North, of Concrete, and fled to Major Scott, the provost marshal at Victoria. He complained to this officer of the inhuman treatment of North, stated that he had "beat him with many stripes," starved him, and refused to properly clothe him, etc. Mr. North came in quest of his horse and requested that I should introduce him to Major Scott. I complied, and upon entering the office the Negro in question was present. He did not deny taking the horse, and acknowledged having him in his possession at that time. North challenged the Negro to exhibit to Major Scott the stripes of which he had complained, and promised to pay him ten dollars for each one exhibited that was inflicted by his hands or through his orders. The Negro confessed that Mr. North had never "hit him a lick in his life." He also acknowledged to the questioning of North that he had been well fed and clothed.

Major Scott remanded the horse to the proper owner and dismissed the case.

Among the Negro troops that occupied Victoria were two "ministers ob de gosspill," and who, being strangers and part and parcel of the great army of freedom, etc., drew great multitudes to hear the "expoundin' ob de word." I reproduce for the reader's diversion a specimen style of each:

"Dear brederin, I'm gwine to 'lighten you on de great Day of Jedgment, when de Angel Gabriel, de Son ob God, will come down from de hebbens and put one foot on de sea and de other on de banks of Jordan, with a trumpet in his hand. He will ask, "Father, how loud must I blow?" and God will answer, "As loud, my Son, as seven claps of thunder, so that you will wake up the sleepers under the earth!" Oh! what a stir there will be among de ole dry bones a-flyin' and a-whizzin' through the air! O sinner! how you gwine to keep dem bones from a-hittin' of you, ah?"

It is perhaps worthy of philosophical attention, the fact that the Negro's incentive to spiritual concerns is always the fear of punishment rather than the hope of reward.

The Rev. Jackson Jones discoursed thus:

"I'm gwine ter tell you ob a carcumstance what happened a long time ago. Dare was a ole man by de name of Noah: an de Lord's word came to Noah, saying dat de world was gwine to be 'stroyed by a flood, and for Noah ter make a boat foar hundred yards long and a hundred yards wide. De ole man sot to work on de boat, and de foax dey come ebbery day an' make fun of de ole man. 'Boss,' dey say, 'how's de water gwine to git over dem high mountings ober dar?' and sich-like propagations dey put unto him. De ole man nebber sed nothing; he jist kept pegging away. But de Lord Jesus he was a carpenter, an' he was asistin' Noah wid de boat onbenownst to de foax. Well, 'fo' long de winders ob de hebbens wuz opened, an it dident rain, but jest poured down water, and ebbery thing on de earth was drownded 'cepting Noah and his foax. Who was de fools, Noah or the men what laughed at him?"

The chronology adopted by the Rev. Jackson Jones was certainly original, as the long years that intervened between Noah and the Saviour were wholly ignored.

Those were high old days when General J. J. Reynolds and other satraps lorded it at Austin. A provost marshal was placed in every town of any importance, who assumed the civic functions of sheriff, clerk, tax collector, etc. This last duty seemed to be the most congenial, and the merchants were bled free enough. Each one of these subordinates of the grand satrap was surrounded by minions ready to seize all the crumbs that fell from the official table. Clamorous for office were these foul birds of evil omen, whose rapacity was not exceeded by that of the cormorant. There were not wanting a few of our own citizens who, recreant to every noble sense, were herding with these vultures who came to prey on the carcass of their undone country.

"Where the carcass is, there will the eagles be gathered also," is the declaration of Holy Writ, and in this instance was thoroughly exemplified. These mephitic garbage-mongers of the camp were the officers elected when we were allowed the *form* of election, though it was in fact a mere appointment to office. In many instances illiterate Negroes were elected to the office of clerk, justice of the peace, etc.; and though they knew not "B" from "bull's foot," were much preferable to the white rascals, whose intelligence was but an advantage in the purpose of rascality that had been chalked out.

Another rare specimen of the "fine old Yankee gentleman" was one Colonel Rose, in command of a Pennsylvania regiment raised in the neighborhood of Pittsburgh. After Major Scott and other provost marshals had fattened (presumably in the Victoria pasture) he was turned loose to graze his fill before returning home. Colonel Rose was a veritable czar on a small scale, and altogether a more despicable specimen of humanity than Santa Anna himself. One of our merchants, a German, had a fine stock of groceries, comprising "old Bourbon" whiskey, cigars, etc. He complied with all of the czar's vexatious regulations, paid his license, and, to render himself doubly safe, made his majesty sundry presents of cigars and whiskey. Finally came an edict from Rose, like a thunderbolt from a cloudless sky, ordering the store to be closed and the key turned over to him for alleged violations of his "black-letter" restrictions. Vain were the protestations of the merchant that he had done nothing to merit this severity; the store was closed and the key placed in the pocket of the czar. The merchant made a visit to department headquarters, and after two months succeeded in gaining possession of his store. But the "rats" had smoked most of the cigars, and quantities of the "old Bourbon" had evaporated.

Judge S. A. White, himself an appointee to the district bench, had an altercation with Colonel Rose in regard to some "bench rule" which the colonel refused to regard. After shooting a bullet through the leg of the judge's trousers the czar had the judge incarcerated. The judge granted a writ of habeas corpus from his "bench" in the jail, commanding the sheriff to bring the body of S. A. White before himself, etc.; but the "sacred writ" was also disregarded.

Prominent men of early Texas

The first of these, in many of the qualities of his mind and heart as well as in priority of time, was *Stephen F. Austin*, who in planting his first colony in Texas, then a *terra incognita*, encountered hardships and vexatious trials sufficient to have caused a less resolute man to despair. He made many personal sacrifices of his own comfort and property in the interest of his colonists, and was in return repaid by ingratitude by too many of them. He had the patience of Franklin, and was a man of solid rather than of brilliant parts.

David G. Burnet was an educated gentleman, an accomplished lawyer, and one of the ablest writers in Texas. He was the author of all the principal official documents that were published previous to the declaration of independence. After serving as vice president in the Lamar administration he was not treated with that consideration to which his eminent services to Texas entitled him. He was too modest and retiring by nature, and possessed too much self-respect, to thrust himself forward in the unseemly scramble for office, as was too much the rule at that time. By all means should he have been on the Supreme bench, for he was peculiarly fitted for the administration of justice. He was not an orator, but spoke concisely and to the immediate question in issue. His challenge of General Houston to mortal combat was a mistake, and no doubt he subsequently regretted it.

Thomas J. Rusk was a member of the Nacogdoches bar, a lawyer of high acquirements, a good scholar, and an eloquent speaker. He was a native of South Carolina, and came into notice by taking an active part in the stirring scenes of 1835. In addition to the positions that he filled under the republic he was chosen United States Senator after annexation, and served as such with credit. In consequence of the loss of his wife, which preyed heavily on his mind, General Rusk unfortunately took his own life in the town of Rusk.

Mirabeau B. Lamar was a native of the State of Georgia, a thorough scholar, an eloquent speaker, and sometimes given to "wooing of the tuneful nine." He was of social habits and of a convivial disposition. Being somewhat of an optimist, he was inclined to look on the bright side of affairs and to take things easy. His administration of the government was very unfortunate, the debt incurred during his term aggregating three millions of dollars—a sum representing at that time an amount far greater than now. He was the projector of the quixotic Santa Fé expedition, a semi-military, commercial undertaking, which, after enduring great hardships on the toilsome march, arrived at its destination only to surrender to Governor Armido, of New Mexico. General Lamar retired to private life and married the youngest daughter of the celebrated minister, Mr. Moffit. He was constitutionally an enemy of the Indians and opposed to their being allowed to remain in Texas. He was always highly respected, and his name and fame are indissolubly connected with those of Texas.

General T. J. Chambers occupied a conspicuous place in the early history of Texas, and his many sterling services should rescue his name from oblivion. He expended considerable capital and performed much labor in the interests of Texas under the various aspects and vicissitudes of its cause. He was a judge from 1832 to 1835, was a lawyer of fine abilities, and thoroughly posted in Spanish jurisprudence. He drew odium upon himself by receiving eleven large grants in compensation for his services as judge. His claims were contested, but he defended his title with such ability that he was entirely successful. The city of Austin was located on one of his grants, and Judge Chambers acted in a spirit of liberality to those who purchased of the city authorities. He and President Burnet had quite a newspaper war in 1837-8. He and myself were roommates during the Second Congress, and I found him a clever and accomplished gentleman.

Mrs. Holly. This gifted lady was a sister of S. F. Austin, and the widow of a Unitarian preacher. She was a lady of fine intelligence, cultivated mind, and rare accomplishments. She took great interest in the early affairs of Texas, and through the medium of communications to the press did much material good to the cause. She died before seeing the fruition of her hopes in regard to a free and regenerated Texas. The following description of a Texas prairie is from her pen:

"It is impossible to imagine the beauty of a Texas prairie when in the vernal season; its rich, luxuriant herbage, adorned with many thousand flowers of every size and hue, seems to realize the vision of a terrestrial paradise.

"The delicate, gay, and gaudy are intermingled in delightful profusion; and the fanciful bouquets of fairy nature borrow tenfold charms when associated with the verdant carpet of grass which is modestly spread abroad. One feels that Omnipotence has here consecrated in the bosom of nature, and under heaven's high canopy, a glorious temple in which to receive the praise and adoration of the grateful beholder. And cold indeed must be the soul from which no homage could be here elicited. Even the veriest infidel would be constrained to bow and worship!"

Anson Jones was the last president of Texas, and pronounced the obituary of the republic in the annexed excerpt from his "valedictory address":

"The great measure of annexation, so earnestly desired, is happily consummated. The present occasion, so full of interest to us and to all the people of this country, is an earnest of that consummation; and I am happy to greet you, their chosen representatives, and to tender to you my cordial congratulations. A government is changed, both in its offices and its organization, not by violence and disorder, but by the deliberate and free concert of its citizens; and amid perfect and universal peace and tranquillity the sovereignty of the nation is surrendered and incorporated with that of another.

"The 'Lone Star' of Texas, which ten years ago arose amid clouds over fields of carnage, and but obscurely seen for a while, has culminated, and, following an inscrutable destiny, has passed on and become fixed forever in that glorious constellation which all freemen, and lovers of freedom in the world, must reverence and adore—*the*

American Union. Blending its rays with its sister States, long may it continue to shine, and may generous Heaven smile upon this consummation of the wishes of the two republics, now joined in one!

"May the union be perpetual, and may it be the means of conferring benefits and blessings upon the people of all the States, is my ardent prayer. The first act in the great drama is now performed. *The Republic of Texas is no more!*"

In conclusion but little remains to be said. The first act of the drama announced in the valedictory of Texas' last president, Anson Jones, paved the way for the armies of the great American Republic to become actors in the cast of the pending drama. General Taylor advanced with his men into Texas and encountered the Mexican army at Palo Alto. The Mexicans were driven from the field, but resumed the contest the next day at Resaca de la Palma, and the Americans were again victorious. Taylor pursued the enemy into Mexico, and, after a stubborn contest, took the city of Monterey. On the heights of Buena Vista the American chieftain was attacked by the redoubtable Santa Anna, who led eighteen thousand of the choicest troops of his country. General Taylor was really beaten in this engagement, but he had the remarkable faculty of not knowing when he was whipped, and so turned his reverse into a splendid victory. Santa Anna left the field precipitately and marched to encounter General Scott at Cerro Gordo, where he was defeated and his army dispersed by the triumphant Americans. In all these engagements the Mexicans outnumbered the Americans, and often in the ratio of five to one.

Said a lady correspondent of the *Caelo Nueve*, a periodical of the day: "Five thousand dusty and tired Americans marched into the city of Pueblo—a city of sixty thousand inhabitants—and, after stacking their arms about the public plaza, lay down and went to sleep! Ten thousand Mexican men surrounded them and gazed on the spectacle in mute surprise. This handful of weary men, then, were our conquerors! Could such a thing have happened in any other land beneath the canopy of heaven?"

Of Texas as a member of the American Union it is not necessary to speak, as all of the present generation are conversant with the history of that period.

My own age—eighty-five—should be admitted in evidence of the salubrity of the climate and the efficacy of the health-giving breezes of Texas, especially since fifty-three consecutive years have been passed in Texas. Of the illimitable resources of our State I would say something; but so boundless is the field that I fear to trench upon the subject, knowing too well that I cannot do it justice. Take but one item—livestock—and hear the assurances of gentlemen who have demonstrated the fact that cattle will pay a profit of thirty-three and one-third per centum per annum on the capital invested; and sheep, by good attention, are susceptible of realizing still greater results. As great as is the livestock interest of the western section, the agricultural industry of the east surpasses it in aggregate amount of income. Cotton is the great staple, though it is being forced to divide the honors with wheat and the other cereals, all of which flourish nowhere more luxuriantly than in Texas soil. The planting of sugar cane is being profitably conducted in the southern section, and is susceptible of great development; while all the vegetables known to the latitude find here a congenial clime. Coal abounds in many portions of the State, as do such ores as iron, copper, etc. In Llano County a copper mine is now being developed; while in Cass and Marion counties iron furnaces have been in operation for years.

Texas has all the varied resources, diversity of climate, etc., necessary to an empire; and that she is destined to occupy the position of *primus inter pares* among the sovereignties of the American sisterhood there admits of no doubt.

It is a pleasure to me to speculate upon the future of Texas, and to feast the imagination upon the picture delineating her fully developed proportions—a Texas that shall be the empire State of the proudest republic of earth.

I may never live to witness this proud consummation, and I therefore feel the greater pride in now placing upon durable record my consciousness of her inherent greatness. And now my task draws to a conclusion. Like the years of my own life, the last page is being turned, and all the memories of the past well up in my heart. The infant at whose tempest-tossed cradle we stood forty-seven years ago no longer needs the guardian care of the "Old Guard." As a lusty young giant Texas stands before the world today. Other men now occupy the honored places of "Old Sam," of Austin, Rusk, Burnet, Lamar, and their compatriots—young Texans who have taken up the work where their fathers laid it down. May the succession always fall into worthy hands, and the spirit of patriotism pervading each Texan heart always prompt the lips to exclaim with fond and loyal devotion, "*This is my own, my native land.*"

A list of the governors since annexation

J. P. Henderson, from 1846 to 1847
George T. Wood, from 1847 to 1849
P. H. Bell, from 1849 to 1853
E. M. Pease, from 1853 to 1857
H. R. Runnels, from 1857 to 1859
Sam Houston, from 1859 to 1861
Edward Clark, from March 1 to the end of the year
F. R. Lubbock, from 1861 to 1863
P. Murroh, from 1863 to 1865
F. S. Stockdale, several months in 1865, the governorship being vacated by Governor Murroh
A. J. Hamilton (military appointee), from 1865 to 1866
J. W. Throckmorton, from 1866 to 1867
E. M. Pease (military appointee), from 1867 to 1869
E. J. Davis (fraudulently elected), from 1869 to 1874
Richard Coke, from 1869 to 1876
R. B. Hubbard, from 1876 to 1879
O. M. Roberts, from 1879 to 1883
John Ireland, from 1883

Index

There are challenges to indexing a book of this age and type. Neither Linn's recollections, nor his sources, are perfectly accurate and complete. The original text has been left virtually unchanged, but the index enhances information to some extent, correcting or supplementing incorrect or incomplete names, places, and spellings where noticed, without a comprehensive effort at correction. When the accepted historical spelling of a name or place varies from Linn's, the index place Linn's spelling in parentheses. When Linn provides no first name, the index sometimes provides that name from other accepted historical sources.

Abney, A. H.
    re Long Expedition 57
Adams, E.....................................85
Ad-Interim Government of 1836
    officers and cabinet..............31
Aguirre, _____ (Mexican Capt.)
   188
Alamo, Battle of the................101
    Mexican casualties 141
    survivors 107
Alamo, the 47
    Hymn of 110
    ordered destroyed..............145
Alavez (Alvares), Francita 137
Allen, _____ (Texan Capt.).....191
    at Galveston with prisoners
   198
Allen, John W. 290
Alley, John 82

Almonte, Juan Nepomuceno...75
    at Harrisburg and
        Washington....................184
    at San Jacinto 190
    report on Texas.....................75
Alsbury (Alabery), Horace A.145
Alsbury, Juana G. N. 107
Amador, Juan V. 104
Ampudia, Pedro de
    at Mier 261
Andrade, Juan Jose 140, 145
    encounters Rusk at Goliad 235
Andrews, Richard....................92
Aransas Pass..............................18
Archer, Branch T......................29
Archive War 255
Arenal, _____ (Mexican Lt.)...188
Arredondo, Joaquin de 155
Arrenal, Ignacio 183

Artiaga, _____ 9, 10
Austin, J.
    at Mier 260
Austin, John 7, 12, 56
Austin, Moses 52
Austin, Stephen F. ... 1, 51, 74, 81, 90
    described 296
Austin's Colony 51
Ayers (Ayres), Lewis T. .. 120, 159
Babe of the Alamo 285
Baker, Jacob 5
Baker, John R. 257
Baker, Moseley 27, 85
Barnard, Joseph H. 119
    attends wounded at Coleto, Goliad 130
    dispatched to San Antonio 139
Barragan (Mexican Capt.) 187
Barre, _____ 51
Batres, _____ (Mexican Col.) . 191
Beard, _____ 51
Beard, James 51
Beasley, David H. E.
    at Mier 260
Bell, Josiah H. 52
Bell, Mary 53
Bellow, _____ 51
Benavides (Benevidos, Benevides), Placido 25, 82, 245
Benavides, Ysidore 263
Berry, F.
    at Mier 256
Berry, J.
    at Mier 260
Berry, John Bate
    at Mier 260
Bexar, Siege of 101

Blow, George W. Jr. 249
Bonham, James B. 102
Bowie, James 90
    at the Alamo 102
    prevents wedding 247
Bracken, William 94
Bradburn, John D 3, 7, 108
Bradley, John M.
    and Regulator-Moderator War 266
Bringas, _____ (Mexican Col.) 187
Bryan, Guy M.
    and the Babe of the Alamo 286
    re Austin's Colony 51
Burleson, Edward 84
    at San Jacinto 166
Burnet, David G. 40, 74
    challenges Houston to duel .. 1
    described 296
    letter re Green and Hubbell 252
    rallies troops at Galveston 212
Burns, _____ 57
Caldwell, Pinky
    and Linnville Raid 278
Cameron, Ewen
    at Mier 261
Campbell, Michael
    murder by 249
Canary Islanders 47
Carbajal, Jose M. J. 24, 27
    captured 210
Cardena (schooner) 19
Carrasco Blanco, _____ (Mexican Gen.)
    at Mier 261
Cart War 288

Castaneda (Castonado),
    Francisco de 81
Castrillion (Castrillon), Manuel
    F. 104, 108, 184
Cayuga (steamboat)..................211
Chadwick, Joseph M.
    at Coleto surrender 130
Chambers, Thomas J.
    described 297
Chihuahua, Ciudad 22
Chihuahua, trading in..............20
Childress, George C..................42
Choval, Manuel..........................9
Civil War..................................291
    Reconstruction.....................292
Clark, Edward A. (priest) 48
Coahuila y Texas.......................60
Coleto, Battle of......................125
    aftermath..............................131
    articles of capitulation
        proposed.........................157
    Texan surrender 129
Collingsworth, George M..83, 84
Concepcion, Battle of................90
Conditions, Bexar Dept. 1834..75
Conditions, Brazos Dept. 1834 76
Conditions, Nacogdoches Dept.
    1834 78
Confederacy 291
Congress, First...........................32
Constitution adopted 40
Consultation of 1835....27, 59, 81,
    85, 96
    delegates.................................27
Convention of 1836
    delegates.................................30
Cook, Joe 5

Cos, Martin Perfecto de 18, 27,
    83, 90
    at San Jacinto 167, 189
Council House Fight 242
Cow Boys Gang.......................264
Crockett, David
    at the Alamo 102
Crosby, ____
    and Linnville Raid 277
Daniel, Margaret C. 18
Davis, Jackson 158, 202
Davis, Thomas
    at Mier 260
Declaration of Independence ..34
    author 42
    signers....................................37
Declaration of Principles..........32
Delgado, Pedro
    account of Battle of San
        Jacinto 183
Dexter, P. B. 29
Dexter, Samuel 235
Diaz de Leon, Jose Antonio 43,
    48
Dickinson, Almeron 106
Dickinson, Angelina E.
    Babe of the Alamo..............285
Dickinson, Susanna W. ..107, 112
Dimmitt, Philip 42, 88
Dubuis, Claude Marie (priest) 49
Duels...283
Dunlap, Richard G.
    and Linn's horse 240
Duque, Francisco 105
Dwyer, ____ (Joseph M.?).......95
Ehrenberg, Herman................125
Elizabeth (schooner)
    captured 210

Emmet, Thomas Addis 1
Encinal de Perdido, Battle of..*See*
    Coleto, Battle of
Ewing, William G.
    and Linnville Raid 279
Fannin, James W.
    writes from Goliad 99
Fannin, James W. Jr. 90
    executed 136
    injured at Coleto 127
    ordered to Victoria 97
Farnese, Charles de 268
Fernandez-Castrillion, Manuel
    F......*See* Castrillion, Manuel F.
Filisola (Fillasola), Vicente ... 145, 185
Fisher, Samuel R.
    Linn's arrest as spy 204
Fisher, William S.
    at Mier 256
Flash (steamboat)
    carries Burnet to Galveston
    211
Foster, J. R. 202
Frazer, Hugh M. 122, 160
Gaines, Edmund P.
    letter to Houston 252
Garay (Gary), Francisco 134
Garcia, Don Bruno..................... 3
Garcia, Francisco 17
Garcia, Marcilleno 94
Garey, _____ (customs official). 3
Gaspar, Neel 51
German Texans 284
Goliad
    Campaign of 1836 119
Goliad Guard (newspaper) 119
Goliad Massacre 134

burial of remains 232
list of Texans executed 146
survivors 136
Goliad, skirmishes at 123
Gonzales, Battle of 81, 82
Government
    Ad-Interim of 1836 31
    Confederacy 291
    Consultation of 1835 27
    Convention of 1836 30
    Declaration of Independence
        of 1835 34
    Declaration of Principles of
        1835 32
    list of governors after
        annexation 301
    Provisional of 1835 29
    Secession Ordinance 291
Grant James
    and Matamoros Expedition
    245
Gray, Mabry B. "Mustang"
    ambush near Goliad 264
Green, T. F.
    at Mier 256
Green, Thomas J. 222
    holds Santa Anna captive . 250
Grievances under Mexican rule
    60
Grimes, Jesse 40
Gutierrez (Guttierez) de Lara,
    Jose Bernardo 154
Hanam, _____
    goes native 237
Handy, Robert E. 114
Hannig (Dickinson), Susan J.
    survivor of Alamo 112
Hardin, William

after San Jacinto 199
Harrisburg 41
   sacked and burned 184
Haydon (Hayden), George W.
   (priest) 48
Hays, John
   and Linnville Raid 279
Hean, E.
   at Mier 260
Hewetson (Hewitson), James . 14, 51
Hockley, George W.
   at San Jacinto 167
Holly, Mary A.
   described 297
Holstien, H. 51
Holzinger (Holtzinger), Juan
   Jose 130, 134, 202
Hopson, W.
   at Mier 260
Horton, Albert C. 123
Houston, Sam 86
   after San Jacinto 197
   as President of the Republic
       221
   duel challenge by Burnet .. 283
   first inaugural address 225
   on annexation, 1836 228
   orders Fannin to Victoria 97
   orders Fannin to withdraw
       from Goliad 121
Hubbell, H. A.
   and Santa Anna capture 250
Hudson, H. G. 158, 202
Hunter, William L.
   escapes Goliad 153
Huston, Felix
   duels Johnston 284

orders San Antonio
   evacuation 239
Iberri, _____ (Mexican Col.) ... 185
Ingram, Ira 42, 203
   accused of forgery 207
Irela, _____ 96
Irwine, _____ 51
Jack, P. C. 7
Jack, W. H. 83
Jackson, Andrew
   letter to Houston 253
Jackson, F.
   at Mier 260
Jail, Victoria
   escape 267
Johnson, Francis W. 27, 99, 101
Johnson, Sheriff "Snake" 249
Johnston, _____ (priest) 47
Johnston, Albert Sidney
   duels Huston 284
Jones, Anson
   described 298
Jones, J. E.
   at Mier 259
Karnes, Henry W. 114
   at San Jacinto 168
Kemper, John F.
   killed by natives 274
Kemper, Samuel 154
Kennedy, William 85
Kerr, James 25, 40, 88, 94
   and Navidad Resolutions . 208
Kerr, Peter 210
Kidnapping
   Matilda Lockhart 241
   Putnam family 241
Kimble, H. G. 40
King, Amon B. 99, 121

at Refugio 158
King, William 266
Krantz, _____
    several times killed already
    281
Lafferty, L. D. 57
Lamar, Mirabeau B.
    at San Jacinto 167
    described 297
Latona *See* Letona, Jose Maria de
Lavaca-Navidad Meeting .... *See* Navidad Resolutions
Leman & Perry, Tampico 14
Leon, Fernando de 11, 26, 161, 201
    captured 210
    protects Linn family 202
Leon, Martin de 161
Leon, Patricio de 276
Leon, Silvestre de 11, 161
Letona, Jose Maria de 9
Linn, Charles 4, 15
Linn, Edward 5, 13
Linn, John J.
    consults with Houston 205
    elected alcalde of Victoria ... 96
    elected to Convention of 1836
    97
    evacuates Victoria 201
    failed to attend convention. 40
    interviews Santa Anna 215
    letter re Mexican advance. 218
    letter re San Jacinto 219
    meets with Burnet and Zavala
    206
    supplies corn to Fannin 98
    supplies Texan army 211
    visits San Jacinto battlefield
    213
Linn, Margaret Daniel 18
Linnville
    Comanche raid 277
Lipantitlan 92
    battle of 93
Little, William 51
Liver, _____ de (Mexican priest)
    at Mier 261
Lockhart
    Matilda 241
Lockhart, Andrew 162
Lockhart, Byrd (Bird) 162
Lockhart, Charles 162
Lombardus, Jose 144, 146
Long Expedition 53
Long, James 53, 57
Lord, George
    account of Mier Expedition
    256
Lott, _____ 41
Lovelace, Edward 51
Magee, Augustus W. 154
Maple, _____ 51
Margil de Jesus, Antonio ... 44, 48
Martin, Wyly (Wiley, Wily) ... 27, 85, 87
Martinez, Antonio Maria 52
Matamoros Expedition 1836 . 245
Maverick, Samuel A.
    captured by Woll 267
McHenry, John 4, 11, 53, 57
McKinney, Thomas F.
    visits San Jacinto battlefield
    213
McMullen, John 45
McNeil, Sterling 89

Memorial of 1835 59
Mexia, Jose Antonio 7, 9, 12
Mier Expedition 256
Mier y Teran, Manuel de .... *See* Teran, Manuel de Mier y
Milam, Benjamin R. 84
    death of................................101
Millard, Henry
    at San Jacinto 166
Miller, William P......................133
Mims, Joseph 99
Mina, Francisco Xavier...........155
Mission Valley..........................276
Missionaries................ 44, 274, 276
Missions 48
    de San Jose 44
    La Bahia................................276
    Nuestra Senora de Refugio
       274
    Nuestra Senora del Espiritu
        Santo de Zuniga 276
Moore, John H. 27, 82
Moorman (Morsman), Charles W.
    and Regulator-Moderator War...................................265
Morphis, James M.
    Linn criticizes 246, 268
Morris, John D.........................249
Morris, Robert C.
    and Matamoros Expedition
       245
Muro, Miguel 43
Musquiz (Musquies), Ramon.17, 141, 146
Natives 45
    Apaches.................................277
    Aranamas (Aranames) 275

Comanches..........142, 242, 276
Karankawa (Carankua) 26, 88, 203, 274
Tawakoni (Tawacana) 142
Tonkawa (Toncahua).230, 273
Navarro, Jose Antonio (Angelo)
   141
Navidad Resolutions.............208
Nelson, ____ 5
Newcomb, Thomas.................254
Noyes, ____..................................3
O'Conor, Charles 1
Ocampo, Carlos.....................199
Odin, Jean Marie (John Murry)
    (priest) 49
Old Three Hundred, the 52
Opposition, The (ship)..................4
Padilla, Juan Antonio 40
Pantitlan, La..............................11
Pearson, Thomas K....................99
Perry, Henry 154
Pettus (Pettas), William..........162
Pierce, John 2, 4
Poinsett, Joel R. 56
Politics
    Democratic Convention of 1856 290
    Know-Nothing Convention of 1856 290
Polley, Joseph 51
Population, 1834 80
Porter, J. A..................................13
Portilla (Partilleas), Felipe R. de la 277
Portillo, Jose Nicolas de la
    informs Urrea of order to execute Goliad prisoners
   156

Potter, Reuben M............ 101, 108
Potter, Robert M.
   rallies troops at Galveston 213
Power, James....................... 10, 14
Provisional Government of 1835
   officers and members.......... 29
Quitman, John A.
   leads Mississippi volunteers
   220
Ramirez y Sesma
   Joaquin 183, 230
Reconstruction 292
Red Rovers 130, 135, 237
Reese, C. H.
   at Mier 256
Refugio, Battle of 120, 158
Regulator-Moderator War..... 265
Religious toleration 229
Reynolds, Joseph J. 294
Richardson, Vartland
   and Linnville Raid 278
Robinson, Andrew 52
Robinson, J. W.
   as judge 249
Rodgers, Joseph
   and Linnville Raid 278
Rodriguez, Nicolas............. 93, 95
Rogers (Rodgers), Samuel C. A.
   and Navidad Resolutions . 208
Ross, Reuben 154
Rusk, Thomas J.
   described.............................. 296
Rusk, Thomas Jefferson 160
   at Goliad burial 232
Rutledge, Richard........... 158, 202
Sabriego (Saviriago), Manuel.. 82
San Antonio de Valero, Mission
   de .... *See* Alamo

San Jacinto, Battle of
   aftermath............................. 194
   Houston's farewell to his
      troops............................. 172
   Houston's report 165
   Linn visits battlefield......... 213
   list of killed and wounded 170
   list of Texans engaged....... 173
   list of Texans killed............ 181
   Mexican account 183
   Mexican prisoners freed ... 199
   news reaches San Antonio 143
   spoils..................................... 214
San Patricio, Battle of 99
Santa Anna, Antonio Lopez de 9, 17
   at Harrisburg...................... 184
   at San Jacinto 166, 186
   captured at San Jacinto 194
   enters Bexar 97, 99
   farewell letter to Texas army
   251
   held captive by Green 250
   interviewed by Linn.......... 215
   news of defeat at San Jacinto
   143
Scurry, William R. 290
Seguin, Erasmo 51
Shackleford (Shackelford), Jack
   119
   dispatched to San Antonio 139
Sherman, Sidney..................... 166
Sinnickson, John J. (T. J.)
   at Mier 257, 260
Slavery 89
Smith, Benjamin F. 83
Smith, Erastus "Deaf"............. 114
Smithers, W. 51

Solms-Braunfels, Prince Carl of 284
Somervell (Somerville), Alexander
    Mier Expedition 256
St. Catherine, Chihuahua village
    20
Tarlton (Tarleton), James 97
Tarpley, _____ (lawyer) 254
Teran, Manuel de Mier y 4, 9
Thomas, David
    dies of gunshot 212
Thrall, Homer S.
    Linn criticizes 27, 50
Tinsley (James W.?)
    knife fight with Navarro ... 282
Tomlinson, John 162
Travis, William B. 7, 27
    at the Alamo 102
    last words 112
Trespalacios, Jose Felix 56
Trevino, _____ (Mexican Col.)
    killed at San Jacinto 190
Twohig, John
    captured by Woll 267
Ugalde (Uvalde), Juan de 45
Ugartechea, Domingo de 8, 11, 25, 81
Urbane, _____ 87
Urrea, Jose de 102
    accepts surrender at Coleto
    129
    at Refugio 122, 159
    learns of execution of Goliad
        prisoners 156
    recounts surrender at Coleto
    157

Urreza, _____ (Mexican Capt.)
    187
Vasquez, Antonio
    and Comanches 238
Vasquez, Rafael
    raids San Antonio 1842 255
Veramendi (Beremendis), Juan Martin de 52
Verge, _____ de la (Mexican Gen.)
    at Mier 261
Vickry, _____ (Victoria judge)
    254
Viesca, Jose Maria 17, 96
Villasana, _____ (Mexican Lt. Col.) 10
Wallace, Joseph W. E. 84
Ward, William 99, 121
    at Refugio 158
    troops captured 133
Washington (New Washington)
    41
    sacked and burned 185
Watts, Hugh O.
    and Linnville Raid 279
Watts, Juliet C.
    and Linnville Raid 279
Western, Thomas G. 83
Westover, Ira J. 92
Wharton, John A. 89, 206
Wheeler, Jesse O.
    and Linnville Raid 278
White, Samuel A. 290, 295
Wild Cat (schooner) 18
William Bobbins (ship)
    recaptures *Elizabeth* 211
Williams, Samuel M. 27
Williamson, Robert McAlpin .. 27

Wilson, J. C.
   and the Babe of the Alamo 287
Wilson, Robert 248
Wilson, William 51
Woll, Adrian 230
   after San Jacinto 197
   opinion of Goliad Battle 218
   raids San Antonio 1842 .... 255, 267
   truce meeting with Texans 217
Wright, _____ 2
Yellowstone (steamboat)
   at San Jacinto 197
   escapes to Galveston 212
Yoakum (Yokum), Henderson K. 88, 103
   Alamo account as conjecture 107
   Houston letter fictitious 209
Zambrano (Zembrano), Juan .. 27
Zavala, Lorenzo de 40
Zumwalt (Zumwaldt), Adam
   and Linnville Raid 280

www.ingramcontent.com/pod-product-compliance
Lightning Source LLC
Chambersburg PA
CBHW060414170426
43199CB00013B/2133